Golden
Legacy

Detail from Five Little Firemen.

In memory of
Greta Schreyer Loebl
beautiful spirit
—*L.S.M.*

How Golden Books Won
Children's Hearts, Changed
Publishing Forever, and Became
an American Icon Along the Way

Golden Legacy

BY LEONARD S. MARCUS

A GOLDEN BOOK · NEW YORK

The author's acknowledgments can be found on page 234.
Image, front cover: Ellin Rothstein, age five, 1950, Bronx, New York. Courtesy of Ellin Rothstein.
Illustration, title page: Detail from *The Poky Little Puppy.*
Illustration, page 246: From *Mister Dog.*
Illustration, back cover: From *The Golden Sleepy Book.*
Book design by Roberta Ludlow.

Library of Congress Control Number: 2006939312
ISBN: 978-0-375-82996-3
www.goldenbooks.com
www.randomhouse.com
PRINTED IN CHINA
10 9 8 7 6 5 4 3 2
First Edition

Contents

From The Golden Bunny.

From Scuffy the Tugboat.

Among the books I remember most fondly from my childhood are a series of small, thick, toylike volumes, each filled with the brassy adventures of action heroes like Flash Gordon and Superman. As a boy, I paid no attention, of course, to who had published these "Big Little Books" that brought me so much pleasure. How fascinating to learn now, though, from Leonard S. Marcus' *Golden Legacy,* that my beloved Big Littles were the handiwork of some of the very same creative mavericks who, just a few short years later, sparked the publishing revolution that was Little Golden Books.

Golden Legacy is history at its best—a book brimming with unexpected and thrilling cultural connections.

Who knew, for example, that so many of the same artists who teamed up on the great Hollywood animations of the 1930s came east after World War II to create the classic Golden Books that generations of children have now grown up on?

Who knew that Golden Books played a role in the post–World War II Marshall Plan? And in the exciting early days of children's television? And in the building of Disneyland? And in the post–*Sputnik* renaissance in American science education?

Who knew that those bright, trim twenty-five-cent books were the hard-won realization of an idealistic dream—the quintessentially American dream that good children's books could and should be affordable by all? Or that backing up that dream was some of the best and brightest sales and marketing savvy that the publishing world has ever known? As the author of *Golden Legacy* eloquently shows us, it was a dream eagerly shared by millions of baby boom–generation parents and their children. No wonder that by the 1960s, when my own two children were growing up, Golden Books were already everywhere—as ubiquitous a part of the American home landscape as well-worn stacks of *National Geographic* and *Life*.

So many larger-than-life characters come to vivid light in these pages. There are the great Golden artists and writers—Margaret Wise Brown, Alice and Martin Provensen, Richard Scarry, Feodor Rojankovsky, and others—some already justly famous, others until now largely unsung. But then too there are the art directors, editors, booksellers, and others whose behind-the-scenes roles most of us never stop to think twice about. *Golden Legacy* gives readers a rare, in-the-round view of the book world as I myself have come to know it, of the many hands that have a hand in the creation of a book that lasts.

I have often said about my own career that one of the things I'm proudest of is the fact that children were the first to discover my books. The critics came around eventually—but a bit later! Perhaps for that reason as well as for others, what touches me most deeply of all in the story told in *Golden Legacy* is the absolute determination with which those who created Golden Books set out to make children's books that really are for children.

It is wonderful that Leonard S. Marcus has woven together all the threads of this many-stranded story.

What a grand story it is! A big book about the "Little Books"!

Eric Carle

*"Just think! Every book that's ever been published in the United States
is right here in the Library of Congress."*
"Even 'The Poky Little Puppy'?"

Part One

"The Boys Have Done a Pretty Good Job. . . ."

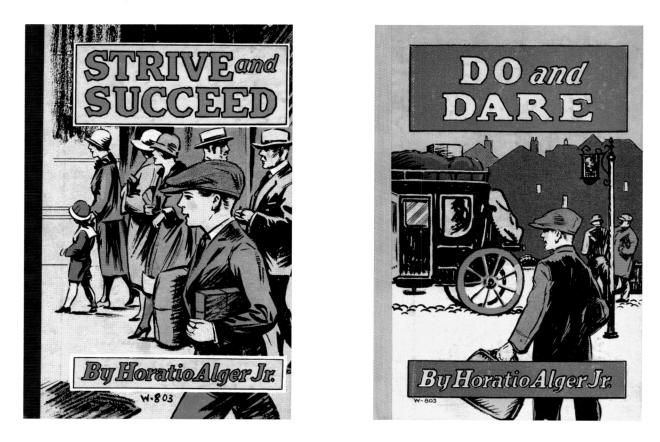

Golden Books began as a tale of two cities, two industries, and two largely compatible visions of the American dream.

The two industries were printing and publishing; the dual visions, those of stylish East Coast urban striving and stolid heartland stick-to-itiveness and common sense. As America's publishing capital, New York was bound to be one of the cities, though it was, as it happened, the second city to enter the story. The first was Racine, Wisconsin, "Belle City of the Lakes," a Midwestern crossroads and agricultural-turned-manufacturing town that by the start of the twentieth century had become a powerful magnet for skilled artisans, upstart entrepreneurs, and, most notably, inventors: men with a knack for creating all manner of new machines, from better threshers and improved automotive tires to the Hamilton Beach blender and some of the world's most advanced printing technology.[1]

Located along Lake Michigan twenty miles south of Milwaukee, Racine had undergone a series of breathtaking transformations over the course of the nineteenth century, its primary economic activity shifting first from wheat to dairy farming, then to shipping and manufacturing. By 1900, the city had established itself both as one of the main ports servicing the thriving Midwestern lumber industry and as an industrial center with scores of manufacturing plants producing farm equipment, trunks, steel-bottomed workers' shoes, motorcars, patent medicines, and, as early as 1888, the elegant horse-drawn omnibuses that clattered up and down New York's Fifth Avenue. As Racine's business and civic leaders vied with Milwaukee's in a classic struggle for regional supremacy, the town's factories and shops swelled with the real-life counterparts of the up-by-their-bootstraps, Horatio Alger self-starters whose inspirational tales crowded the racks of local newsstands.

Pages 1 and 2: Whitman editions of the popular Horatio Alger stories.

Below: From A Name for Kitty, *1948, by Phyllis McGinley, illustrated by Feodor Rojankovsky.*

Top: E. H. Wadewitz, 1910.
Bottom: Roy A. Spencer, 1910.

Facing page: The "Dr. Shoop" Building still stands at State Street and Wisconsin Avenue in Racine, Wisconsin. Undated photograph, Golden Books archives.

One such ambitious young person was Edward H. Wadewitz (1878–1955), a first-generation German American from the northern Wisconsin hinterlands, who as a seventeen-year-old moved to Racine in 1895 to seek his fortune.[2] Starting as a woodworker at a trunk factory owned by his cousins, Wadewitz soon distinguished himself by devising a simple assembly-line operation that greatly increased the shop's efficiency. Intent on continuing his education, he enrolled in night-school classes in accounting at the local YMCA, then gathered up his savings and headed east to further bolster his skills at a small Pennsylvania business school. On graduating from Potts Shorthand College, Wadewitz juggled a variety of odd jobs before returning to his adopted city of Racine, where, in addition to working as a full-time bookkeeper for the Langlois Company, the major ship chandler and supplier to the thriving commercial Great Lakes fleet, he took on after-hours accounting work with a local printer. As Wadewitz soon learned, the West Side Printing Company was having difficulty paying its bills, including those submitted by its bookkeeper. In 1907, as the firm sank deeper into debt, the owner offered him the chance to buy the business outright. Wadewitz, in partnership with his younger brother Al, took the leap that September, not as much because he wished to be a printer as because he wanted to be his own boss. The brothers' youngest sibling, Bill, soon joined the company, as did a respected local printer, Roy A. Spencer.[3] In the months that followed, E.H., as Edward was known, became a familiar sight bicycling around town in a determined quest for business.

True to the Alger prescription, hard work and persistence paid off as an impressive array of Racine's rising manufacturing companies, S. C. Johnson & Son (makers of Johnson's Wax) and the J. I. Case Plow Company, among others, added their names to the client list. By 1910, the company had invested in a costly new lithographic offset press, expanded the range of its services, renamed itself the Western Printing and Lithographing Company, and moved into larger quarters in the basement of the ornate Shoop Building, whose owner, the great Dr. Clarendon I. Shoop—one of America's last old-time purveyors of patent medicines—threw his own considerable printing account their way. By

At right: Western employees, around 1908. Second from left: Johanna Erickson Wiechers. Center: Ernie Boernke. W. R. Wadewitz is on the far right. Golden Books archives. Below: The basement print shop where the business began in 1907. From left: Roy A. Spencer, Catherine Bongarts Rutledge, E. H. Wadewitz, and W. R. Wadewitz. From the Commemorative Issue of The Westerner.

the time the "doctor" retired four years later, Western was big enough to take over the whole of the six-story building.[4]

In early 1916, as the growing business struggled to keep pace with the constant need for new capital, a crisis arose that nearly undid all of E.H. and company's hard-won success. The Hamming-Whitman Publishing Company of Chicago had contracted with Western to print and bind a large quantity of children's books. Western completed the work only to learn that the publisher, on the brink of bankruptcy, could not pay its bills. Ironically, Western had entered into the arrangement in the hope that a book publisher, with its year-round output of new titles, might prove to be an ideal client, providing the steady work needed to keep the presses rolling at maximum efficiency. Now, as Hamming-Whitman's chief creditor, Western could only hope to recoup its loss by assuming ownership of the carloads of books it had in its plant and then selling them off in a market about which it knew nothing. Once again, E.H.'s peculiarly dogged brand of resilience—his ability to triumph in new businesses by internalizing their mechanics, much as he had once, for the fun of it, dismantled and reassembled a typewriter—stood the company in good stead. When Wadewitz met with unexpectedly quick success in finding buyers for the children's books, he became newly intrigued with the publishing business and decided to acquire outright Hamming-Whitman, which he renamed the Whitman Publishing Company and relocated in Racine. He also hired two salesmen, one of whom, Samuel E. Lowe, a social worker by training, was to prove a publishing visionary with a keen grasp of the emerging national market for affordable children's books.

Lowe had come to Racine from New York, where he had served his apprenticeship at the Henry Street Settlement House under its founder, Lillian D. Wald.[5] Hoping to extend the reach of her reformist efforts on behalf of the immigrant poor, Wald had dispatched Lowe and a small number of other protégés to various outposts around the nation. From 1915, as a staff member at Racine's version of Henry Street, the Central Association, Lowe continued his work with school-age boys. Regular contact with these young people inspired him to try his hand at writing stories for them. Whitman's fortuitous arrival in Racine in 1916 spurred dreams of publication. It was as an aspiring author bearing a sheaf of book proposals that Lowe first went to see E.H. *In the Court of King Arthur,* the first of a long list of children's books written or edited by Lowe, appeared under the Whitman imprint in 1918.

But Wadewitz must have been at least as impressed by the young man's business sense as by his writing ability. Lowe went to work right

A day at the Shoop Building print shop.
Below: Western's "fleet," shown parked in front of the Shoop Building around 1915, included the company's two original vehicles: E. H. Wadewitz's bicycle and a delivery cart.
Both photos from the Commemorative Issue of The Westerner.

7

Sam Lowe, probably around 1940. Photo by Malme. Courtesy of Richard Lowe.

away as a Whitman salesman. It was in this capacity—and later as Whitman's president—that he would leave an indelible mark.

The Hamming-Whitman list spanned a spectrum of price categories, starting with a line of coloring books and other cheaply printed novelties that sold for a dime. Recognizing a potentially vast new market for the lower-priced books, Lowe in 1918 made Whitman's first sale to one of the nation's major five-and-ten-cent retail chains, the S. S. Kresge Company. Kresge and such rivals as Woolworth and McCrory's were changing the way American women purchased a wide variety of inexpensive household items. But it was not until Lowe came along that these stores set aside selling space for children's books next to needles, thread, ribbon, biscuit cutters, and apple corers. Lowe, who in later years liked to say that a genius was simply "a man who doesn't know any better," was a most compelling salesman; in one bold stroke, he had set the stage for securing Whitman's long-term financial future.[6]

The sudden upturn in sales that resulted from the Kresge account once again brought Western to the brink of disaster when a clerk misread the initial purchase order and, mistaking "dozens" for "gross," authorized a print run of twelve times the number of books wanted. The unflappable Lowe finessed the situation by persuading Woolworth and the other chains to sell Whitman children's books as well, and to do so year-round rather than just at Christmastime, as was then the pattern with book retailers. It turned out that parents were indeed willing to buy juveniles in April and August as well as in December, provided that the price was low enough and that the books could be found in places parents frequented anyway.[7] These discoveries about the juveniles market would have far-reaching consequences not only for Western but also for the publishing industry as a whole.

By 1918, Western had begun to outgrow the Shoop Building, and for the princely sum of twenty-four thousand dollars, it expanded its headquarters by acquiring "Plant 2"—the name showed the unmistakable no-frills Wadewitz touch—for use as a bindery and warehouse. Good working conditions and a fluid creative culture fed the young company's growth. E.H. won the loyalty of his staff by introducing an innovative profit-sharing arrangement for employees and by rewarding their creativity while downplaying his own role in the company's success. "They did it all," Wadewitz would say of his fellow Westerners. "The boys have done a pretty good job."[8] As more and more relatives of company employees joined the staff, Western became known around Racine and beyond as a "family of families."[9]

One good idea led to another.

After setting up a box department to streamline Western's shipping operation, someone suggested finding a product for the company to make and sell *in* boxes. It was on this basis that Western began manufacturing jigsaw puzzles and games. The company entered the playing card business in 1925, and the stationery business three years later, in both

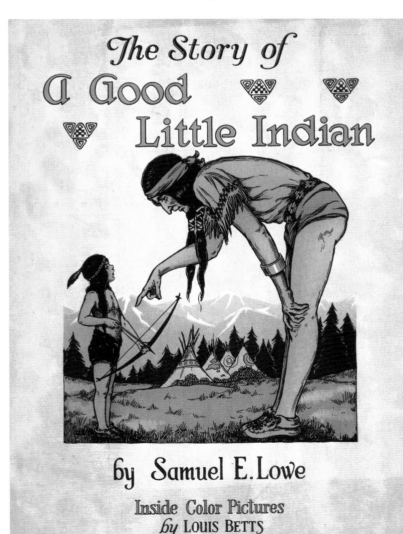

The Story of A Good Little Indian

by Samuel E. Lowe

Inside Color Pictures by LOUIS BETTS

Following pages: A sampling of the Whitman Big Little Books and Better Little Books.

Page 10, top: Dick Tracy Returns, *1939, by Chester Gould, based on the Republic motion picture serial.*
Bottom: Flash Gordon and the Power Men of Mongo, *1940, based on the newspaper strip by Alex Raymond.*

Page 11, top, left to right: G-Man and the Radio Bank Robberies, *1937, by Allen Dale, illustrated by Herbert Anderson;* "Lightning" Jim, U.S. Marshal, Brings Law to the West, *1940, based on the radio series, illustrated by Albert Micale;* Jungle Jim and the Vampire Woman, *1934, by Alex Raymond.*
Middle, left to right: Tiny Tim and the Mechanical Men, *1937, based on the newspaper strip by Stanley Link;* Invisible Scarlet O'Neil Versus the King of the Slums, *1945, based on the newspaper strip by Russell Stamm;* Tom Beatty, Ace of the Service, Scores Again, *1937, by Russell R. Winterbotham, illustrated by Robert R. Weisman.*
Bottom, left to right: Gang Busters in Action, *1938, by Isaac McAnally, based on Phillips H. Lord's Gang Busters;* Don O'Dare Finds War, *1940, by Gaylord DuBois, illustrated by Erwin L. Hess;* International Spy: Doctor Doom Faces Death at Dawn, *1937, by Conrad Vane.*

cases by acquiring specialty-printing concerns located elsewhere in the Midwest. The idea of printing playing cards had come from the buyers at Woolworth, who by then had been doing a brisk business in Whitman books and novelties for nearly a decade.

The manufacture of cards called for the development of a new press capable of achieving an unusually high degree of precision in color alignment, or registration. As E.H. and company marshaled the specialized resources needed to overcome this technical barrier, Western began its emergence as an industry leader. The firm now measured its output in millions, with ten million books and nearly half as many decks of cards manufactured in 1928 alone. Propulsive growth continued even during the Great Depression, as Americans turned for solace and escape to the kinds of low-cost recreational materials that were the company's stock-in-trade. Poignantly, jigsaw puzzles became the focus of a national craze as families struggled to put their own lives back together.[10]

Whitman's other great moneymaker during those years was Big Little Books, a new line of small, square, blocklike novelty books created by Sam Lowe and based on comic strip, radio, and motion picture characters.[11] The series debuted in December 1932 with *The Adventures of Dick Tracy,* followed four months later by *Little Orphan Annie.* By April 1933, more than 600,000 copies of each book had been sold.

The Big Little Books were a triumph of book design and marketing know-how. Their garish, action-laced full-color covers had all the clamorous appeal of movie posters. At ten cents apiece, the fully illustrated volumes, which typically measured just 3-5/8 x 4-1/2 x 1-1/2 inches and ran up to 432 pages, seemed an incomparable value. Not surprisingly, Big Little Books soon spawned imitators (including, notoriously, the Little Big series published by the Akron-based Saalfield Publishing Company). In disdainful response to the Saalfield challenge, Lowe in 1938 renamed Whitman's series Better Little Books.

Lowe's novelty line was not the only new pulp format aimed at capturing young readers' pocket money. In 1935, with the release on newsstands of *New Fun* No. 1, comic books—also priced at ten cents and issued in monthly installments—entered the fray as purveyors of up-tempo

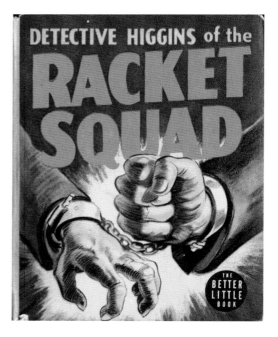

Detective Higgins of the Racket Squad, *1938,*
by Millard Thacksen, illustrated by Herbert Anderson.

tales of superheroics, survival ordeals, and crime-stopping derring-do.[12] The market proved more than ample to sustain both forms of unfussy, mildly sensational entertainment. For children, choosing one was like choosing between two favorite kinds of candy. In one respect, however, Big Little Books had it all over the magazine-style competition: youngsters compelled to hide their forbidden stashes of subliterary fare from disapproving parents doubtless found the highly compact Big Littles easier to keep under wraps.

To publish the Big Little series, Lowe first had to secure the rights to use the popular characters whose proven mass appeal was the key to the success of his plan. Undaunted by his lack of experience, he blithely dummied up two Big Little samples, boarded a train bound for New York, and presented his handiwork at a meeting with executives of the powerful *Chicago Tribune–New York News* syndicate. The wee volumes Lowe had cobbled together were impossible to resist: once seen, they *had* to be held in hand. Once held, they were more likely than not going to be purchased. The precedent-setting agreement that Lowe reached with the syndicate called for the licensor to receive a negotiated percentage of the wholesale price of each character-based book or product sold. By the spring of 1933, with sales of well over half a million copies of each of the first two Big Littles, Lowe felt ready to make his next major foray into the brave new world of character licensing. Armed with the new line's impressive first-round sales figures, he approached the most attractive potential licensing partner of all. "We wonder," Lowe wrote Walt Disney on April 19, "if it is possible to get the right to 'Mickey Mouse' in a book of this kind, which is different than anything already published."[13]

Just five years earlier, Disney had introduced Mickey Mouse to audiences as the hero of one of the first synchronized sound cartoons ever made, *Steamboat Willie.* Popular response to the short film—and to the many sequels the Walt Disney Studio had followed up with, featuring the same saucy, irreverent mouse—had been nothing short of rapturous. By 1933, the Mickey Mouse franchise was already supporting a robust merchandising operation spurred by the formation of hundreds of local theater-sponsored Mickey Mouse Clubs in the United States, Canada, and Great Britain. Walt

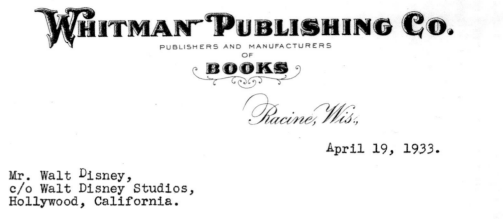

WHITMAN PUBLISHING CO.

PUBLISHERS AND MANUFACTURERS
OF
BOOKS

Racine, Wis.,

April 19, 1933.

Mr. Walt Disney,
c/o Walt Disney Studios,
Hollywood, California.

Dear Sir:

      With this letter we are sending you a sample
of our "Orphan Annie" and "Dick Tracy" books, both of which
we publish and sell to Woolworth and similar stores.

      "Dick Tracy" came out about two or three weeks
before Christmas and we have printed over six hundred thousand
of these books. "Orphan Annie" has been out about five weeks
and we have printed over six hundred thousand. In the case
of "Dick Tracy" we are already publishing a second book and
we are planning to do the same with "Orphan Annie." You will
notice that in the make-up of these books we work a picture
on the right-hand side and the story on the left-hand side,
using the material for the story from the balloons that go
with the comic strips.

      We wonder if it is possible to get the right
to "Mickey Mouse" in a book of this kind, which is different
than anything already published.

      We would be glad to pay one-half (1/2¢) cent
royalty per book for the use of "Mickey Mouse" and would be
satisfied to put down a substantial payment to apply against
first royalties on such a book.

      The writer is fully aware of the fact that
"Mickey Mouse" is used in various kinds of books, but this
"Big Little Book" is unique in itself, and we are intending
to follow up the books already published with other titles
that will have appeal to the children.

Very truly yours,

WHITMAN PUBLISHING CO.

S. E. LOWE.

SEL/EFG.

The first Mickey Mouse Big Little Book. Courtesy of the Wellesley College Library.

Disney had learned a hard lesson in licensing in 1926 when, after signing away the rights to an earlier popular cartoon creation, Oswald the Lucky Rabbit, he watched his distributor, Universal Pictures, reap profits from merchandising ventures from which he and his own struggling company would otherwise have benefited.[14]

Roy O. Disney, Walt's brother and business manager, responded positively to Lowe's proposal, and the first Big Little Mickey Mouse book, based on preexisting comic-strip material, was soon being readied for the printer.[15] In early June, however, relations between the two companies abruptly turned frosty after the animation studio learned that Whitman not only had designed but also had gone so far as to print the cover of the book without first obtaining Disney's approval. Lowe's customary lightning efficiency had run afoul of the animator's unbending insistence on artistic control over all work bearing his name. A stiff letter of rebuke from Roy contained the bad news that Disney had decided not to proceed with additional Big Little Books, at least for the time being.[16] Prudent Roy took care, however, to leave the door ajar for a resumption of business relations; within a month, the bad feelings had been repaired, thanks in no small part to word from Lowe that Whitman expected *Mickey Mouse* to reach the 600,000 mark in sales in short order. Noting that demand for the novelty books tended to flatten out at that level, Lowe pressed his eagerness to have a new Mickey Mouse title to place on store counters as soon as possible. As he put the matter to Kay Kamen, the studio's newly hired New York–based licensing agent, "We have found it extremely advisable to keep changing these books."[17]

Before the year was out, Disney and Whitman not only were back on cordial terms but had greatly expanded their original plans to encompass a variety of new projects, including "Three Little Pigs" playing cards and a "Lullaby Land" book of paper dolls, as well as the second and third volumes in what was to become a lengthy roster of Mickey Mouse Big Little Books.[18] That year, Lowe also negotiated agreements for a special edition of *Mickey Mouse* to be distributed by Procter & Gamble as a premium to its customers.[19] It was all part of the impressive Sam Lowe whirlwind that eventually prompted Disney, who in the early days had

1938.

1935.

casually granted licenses to an array of publishing houses including David McKay and Blue Ribbon Books, to sign an exclusive licensing agreement with Western covering all Disney characters in all book formats. The arrangement lasted, largely unchanged, into the 1980s, resulting in important financial consequences for both companies.[20]

For all the success Lowe brought Whitman's way, Western remained first and foremost a printing concern. By 1934, as the company reached the five-million-dollar mark in annual sales, the search for new customers pointed inexorably to New York, the chief center of American publishing as well as the headquarters of numerous other potential corporate clients.[21] Whitman's growth and prosperity had long since confirmed E. H. Wadewitz's early hunch that book publishers could become the printing company's bread and butter. With that idea in mind, Western in 1934 ventured beyond the Midwest to open a large printing plant in Poughkeepsie, New York, eighty miles north of midtown Manhattan.[22]

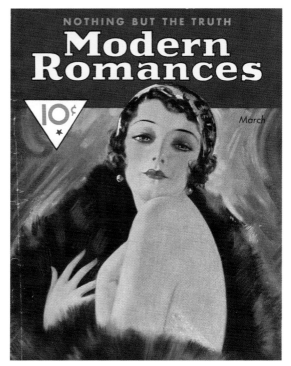

March 1933.

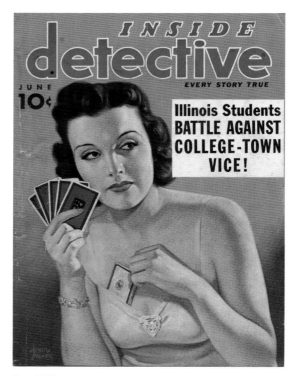

June 1939.

Lowe, for one, did not think that the new "Pokip" plant's success should have to depend solely on a combination of traditional salesmanship and proximity to the city. Applying his knack for innovative reformatting to the company itself, Lowe in 1935 set up a small Western subsidiary in Manhattan for the purpose of producing original books to be offered, ready-made, to publishers.[23] Western would furnish the manuscript, illustrations, and design, as well as the printing and binding, but the book would appear under the client-publisher's name, as would any book the publisher originated. Here was a most unorthodox printing-industry business plan: the assumption, in advance, of the publisher's editorial and design roles, in the expectation of generating presswork. The new office was given a vaguely medieval-sounding name—the Artists and Writers Guild—meant to highlight the collaborative workshop aspect of the enterprise. (Lowe or one of his colleagues took the name from that of a Midwestern printing company that Western owned; the original Guild was best known for a Prohibition-era playing card pack featuring kings and queens in irreverent drunken poses.)[24] Building on Whitman's backlog of licensed-character experience, the Guild soon secured the Dell Publishing Company as its first major client.

Founded in 1921 by a dashing recent college graduate named George T. Delacorte, Jr., Dell first skyrocketed to profitability on the popularity of such racy, mass-appeal pulp magazines as *Modern Screen, Modern Romances,* and *Inside Detective.*[25] Having established a presence on America's newsstands, Delacorte tried as early as 1929 to extend his reach into the juveniles market with *The Funnies,* a weekly tabloid-style compilation of newspaper strips. Although this first foray into the comics trade failed, the young print mogul remained determined, and in February 1936, his patience was rewarded when the first issue of Dell's *Popular Comics,* a monthly compilation in the comics magazine format that other publishers had by then made standard, proved a major success. Within two years, Western was engaged in printing Dell Comic books by the millions. Dell also sublicensed from Western various Disney and other characters whose publication rights the printer controlled. As Western continued tenaciously to pursue its two-pronged strategy,

At left: George T. Delacorte. From the May 1949 issue of
The Westerner.

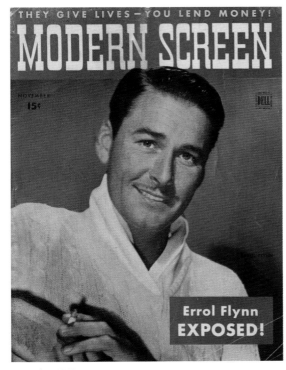

November 1943.

simultaneously acquiring more character licenses and more client-publishers, the company increasingly found itself in the extraordinary position of profiting regardless of whether a consumer purchased a Whitman publication or one published by a Whitman competitor.

Over the next few years, the Artists and Writers Guild created children's books for Grosset and Dunlap, Random House, Simon and Schuster, and Harper and Brothers, among other New York firms. Of the four publishers on this partial client roster, Harper stands out as the one seemingly least in need of such services, being much older and more upmarket than the others. That Artists and Writers did indeed have something definite to offer venerable Harper and Brothers—"established in 1817," with a juveniles backlist that included books by Mark Twain, Howard Pyle, and Peter Newell—suggests that Western's New York out-post had quickly achieved a reputation for high-quality work as well as for commercial nimbleness.

Among the small group hired to staff the New York office was Georges Duplaix, an urbane European polymath—"every American's idea of a Frenchman," as his son Michel would later remark—who had come to New York from Paris with a knowledge of literature, art, and color printing technology, and with numerous contacts in the publishing and illustration worlds.[26] After training in France and the United States for a medical career, Duplaix had thought better of becoming a doctor and shifted into the business side of the profession, where he'd made a fortune by selling medical equipment. Then the Great Depression ruined his business and with it his plans for early retirement and a cultured life of leisure. Forced to start over, Duplaix turned to writing and illustrating children's books as a source of income, for a time leading a frenetic seminomadic existence, with his wife and two small children in tow, as he created books for publishers on both sides of the Atlantic while also scouting fresh business opportunities on two continents. No wonder he thought to call one of the stories he wrote at this time *The Merry Shipwreck*.

A soft-spoken but fiercely competitive man, Duplaix engineered the transfer of a fellow staffer to another Western division just in time to secure for himself the top spot as director of the Artists and Writers Guild.[27] In most respects, the job suited him perfectly. He was soon happily absorbed in translating French picture books for American publication by Guild client-publishers, writing (and in some cases also illustrating) picture books for Whitman and other houses, and even arranging to introduce to the American market examples of France's fabled *Albums du Père Castor* under the Artists and Writers Guild's own imprint. He also experimented with refinements to the Benday color printing process, a screen method traditionally associated with comic-book production, making the process more suitable for use with illustrated books, at a great savings to Western.[28]

One type of work Duplaix had no taste for was the day-to-day management of an office. He was the first to admit as much, and underscored the point by keeping an easel set up near his office window. Visitors might arrive for a business meeting to find the spry, intense,

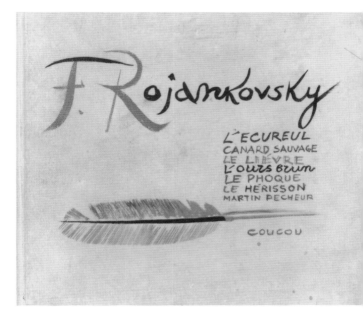

goateed pipe-smoker dreamily wielding a palette and brush while those around him typed or answered the telephone.

Duplaix compensated for this shortcoming with his canny choice of surrogates. In the fall of 1936, he set the Guild on a firm course by hiring Lucille Ogle as the Artists and Writers Guild's second-in-command.[29]

Born in Cleveland, Ohio, in 1904, Ogle was a talented amateur concert pianist who had considered pursuing a career in music before deciding, while still in her early twenties, and after a brief stint as a schoolteacher, to accept the position of editor in chief at the Harter School Supply Company, a Cleveland publisher of children's books for the school market.[30] A Harter picture book offered the young reader useful knowledge leavened with touches of gaiety. Titles published during Ogle's years there included *The Alphabet That Was Good to Eat* (by Louise Price Bell, illustrated by Dorothy Whidden, 1932) and *The Daily Dozen: A Good Health Picture Book with Jolly Rhyme* (by Mildred Plew Merryman, 1933).

Facing page, top: Georges Duplaix (left) with colleague H. M. Benstead in an undated photograph. Golden Books archives.
Bottom: Duplaix as sketched by Feodor Rojankovsky for the jacket of Animal Stories.

This page: Examples of Rojankovsky's work for the Père Castor series of books. Courtesy of Tatiana R. Koly.

The children depicted in the books were uniformly well dressed, rosy cheeked, and adorable. It goes without saying that they were white.

Eager to advance herself professionally, Ogle enrolled in Western Reserve University (later Case Western Reserve), from which she graduated in 1936 with a bachelor's degree in education. Later that year, she moved to New York City, where she worked on the Artists and Writers Guild staff while earning a master's degree in merchandising from New York University. Whether Ogle went to New York to take a job that had already been offered to her, or moved originally only to pursue her education, or did so with both plans in mind, is unclear. A woman of extraordinary energy and focus, she seems in any case to have immediately hit her stride, thereby epitomizing the segment of the city's populace who, as E. B. White later wrote, had come there "in quest of something" and who gave New York its "passion." Such "settlers," White went on to suggest,

Lucille Ogle and Walt Disney in an undated photograph.
Courtesy of Special Collections and University Archives,
University of Oregon Libraries.

accounted for New York's "high-strung disposition, its poetical deportment, its dedication to the arts, and its incomparable achievements."[31]

High-strung indeed. A short, stocky woman with a booming stage voice, a helmet of prematurely white hair, and a gregarious, welcoming manner, Ogle had learned early how to hold her own in a man's profession.[32] Decisive in business matters and firm in her editorial judgments, she was as quick to fly into a rage as she was to laugh, swore easily, and, when necessary, could put up a fearsome front at a meeting. She once hurled a heavy tape dispenser across her office to punctuate her impatience with a junior editor.[33]

Ogle got along splendidly with artists, who regarded her as a peer. Her keen understanding of design and especially of color eventually earned her a coveted place on the board of the American Institute of Graphic Arts. Ogle discovered that around the office, color could even be used as a tool for reinforcing her authority. To maximize the impact of her best feature—her piercing aquamarine eyes—during business meetings, Ogle often dressed for work in royal blue. When the Guild moved to elegant new offices in Rockefeller Center, she installed a rug of vibrant blue in her corner office to further heighten the effect.[34] Decades later, Ogle's penetrating gaze was the first thing that nearly everyone recalled of their encounters with her.

As tough as she made herself out to be, those who came to know Ogle regarded her as a warmhearted, generous woman and a natural teacher with a great store of worldly wisdom at her disposal. Once, when the author Margaret Wise Brown showed her a large diamond-encrusted pin she had just inherited, and remarked on the difficulty of safeguarding such a treasure, Ogle advised the author simply to wear the showpiece whenever and wherever she wished: "No one," the editor reasoned, "will ever believe it is real."[35] Having struggled since childhood with dyslexia, Ogle was also known for the colorful malapropisms with which she sometimes rendered her sage advice. "Let's face it, Frank," she once told a Disney official who she thought was going overboard in his efforts to exploit one of the studio's licensed properties. "You can't milk an apple twice." On another occasion, counseling calm to an irate colleague, she said, "That's just washing your hands to spite your face."[36]

Ogle, who never married, often visited her far-flung artists and authors at home, attended their weddings and holiday celebrations, guided them through rough patches in their private lives, sent them beautifully wrapped, memorable gifts, and loaned or simply gave them money. It was as though when not caught up in "making grown men cry," as one junior editor, who grew quite fond of Ogle, recalled, she became everybody's favorite aunt.[37] And it was this warm and committed approach to her working relationships that allowed her to speak her mind with candor, as when she instructed a newly hired staff member, "You've got a lot to learn, but around here you can learn it. Stick by me, and if any of these goddamn people give you any problems, just remember that they don't know half as much as they think they know. But also remember: they're all a lot smarter than you are. So just keep learning!"[38]

On other occasions, she relied upon charm, as when she wrote a letter to Ruth Adler, a longtime author whose manuscript needed further revision, reminding her that however motivated a piece of writing might be by good intentions, it still needed an appealing "twist" to make children care for it.

"Have you heard the story," Ogle slyly inquired, "about a mother mouse who tried to impress her mouselet with the virtues of education and learning? She was constantly teaching, and every question her baby asked was answered fully. The day came when they went out on the baby's first food-foraging expedition. The mother was proud, for her little pupil found some seeds and tasty morsels all by herself. They then proceeded together, and at a turn in the road, came face to face with an ENORMOUS cat. Without hesitating for a moment, the mother looked steadily at kitty, and loudly said, 'BOW-WOW-WOW!' The cat's fur rose, and she streaked away. Mama mouse turned to her offspring and said, 'See how it pays to have a second language?'

"The moral in my telling this story is this: George [sic] Duplaix and many authors of juvenile books use a good, funny story as the base for their plots. They change the characters and situations and embroider a bit—but they work with the view of *delighting* the children."[39]

O Mamy our cat
is boiling!!
(Copyright by T. Rojan......)

13 Jan
1951
615 NCR
913
FLA

Dear Lucille
Thank you for nice chex. that
was welkomed and apreciated

Tatiana R. Koly Remembers Her Father, Feodor Rojankovsky

Q: Tell me about *The Kitten's Surprise*.

A: Well, it was published when I was just three years old, so I don't remember my father illustrating it. Nina, the author, was my mother, but I don't remember her writing it, either. And I don't know whether it's a real story or if it is fictional.

What I do know is that the girl on the cover is me as a child and that a lot of the toys that are pictured were mine then: the monkey, the red horse, and the little tiger cub. And the jumper the little girl is wearing was an actual piece of clothing of mine, which my daughter wore too. I still have it! The carriage that the poor cat is tortured in was my doll carriage. We always had cats at home and I'm sure that like all children, I must have tried at some point to make a doll or a child out of a kitten.

Q: Would your father have you pose for him?

A: No. But there are lots of drawings of me in his sketchbooks.

Q: Did you watch him work?

A: Oh, yes. In our first Bronxville [New York] house, where we lived when I was ages five to eleven, he transformed the garage into an incredible studio. I would go there just for the atmosphere. He would stand at his table when he drew.

Q: People say he had great energy.

A: He was a firecracker—very quick and agile. He played the balalaika and loved to dance and give parties. He was fifty-eight when I was born and even when I was in my teens he would start jumping up on tables, imitating a monkey!

Normally, my father was a very cheerful individual. He would talk about World War I, which was such a horrendous experience. But as my mother said, the way the stories came out made it sound almost "like a joyride." If he wasn't pleased with something, however—whether it was the story he was illustrating, or his artwork, or the restrictions under which he had been placed—he would get into a very bad humor. My mother referred to these moods as "the throes of creation." He often worked with watercolor, and I remember watching as he washed something out and started again, then washed it out again—starting over and over.

Q: Did he do much research?

A: Whenever we traveled he always had a sketchbook with him. We often went to the zoo. He also clipped reams and reams of animal photos from magazines. And he kept a lot of my childhood drawings, as well as fans' drawings, and had books on the subject of children's art. He said that what he especially loved about children's art was the naïve, uninhibited, brilliant use of color.

Q: How did he organize his day?

A: He was very disciplined when he was on a project. He would get up early and begin work. Later in the day he would take a break and go for a walk or work in the garden. Evenings, he read. He was an avid, avid reader.

My father also loved woodworking. He made lots of furniture, most of it very modern in design. My mother called these projects his "furniture sketches." They were always very beautiful but not always practical. You'd have to be careful about sitting on some of his chairs!

Feodor Rojankovsky with his daughter, Tatiana, in 1956, in his Bronxville, New York, studio. Photo by Robert Browning Baker. Courtesy of Tatiana R. Koly.

25

Part Two

Entrepreneurs and Émigré Artists

From Scuffy the Tugboat, *1946,*
by Gertrude Crampton, illustrated by Tibor Gergely.

$\mathcal{T}$he most consequential publishing relationship forged by the Artists and Writers Guild in its first years started rather tentatively, in 1937, with the production for Simon and Schuster of a lavish, higher-priced book for older children called *A Child's Story of the World: From the Earliest Days to Our Own Time,* by Donald Culross Peattie, with illustrations by Naomi Averill.[1]

In 1937, Simon and Schuster was a midsized thirteen-year-old New York house with a reputation for marketing brashness and editorial daring, and with no experience whatsoever in the juveniles field. The two founding partners, Max Schuster and Richard Simon, had met when the latter, a recent Columbia graduate who had taken a sales job with the Aeolian Company, called on Schuster one afternoon to try to sell him a piano. Simon's prospect was a graduate of Columbia Journalism School and was working as a magazine editor. The conversation soon turned from pianos to books, and a close friendship was born. Not long

Both images from Daddies, *1953, by Janet Frank, illustrated by Tibor Gergely.*

afterward, Simon became a publisher's sales representative. In the months that followed, the friends began discussing a possible future for themselves in publishing. Both men were cultured, ambitious American-born German Jews who, much like their contemporaries Bennett Cerf and Alfred A. Knopf, had been quick to realize that the future was barred to them as Jews at the clubby, old-guard New York firms. Going into business for themselves was their only option. Both were still in their early twenties when, in 1924, they pooled their resources and set up shop in a one-room midtown office without a single author committed to working with them.

As it turned out, the first book to which Simon and Schuster put their names needed no author in the usual sense and hardly qualified as a book from the standpoint of their publishing betters. *The Cross Word Puzzle Book* was the first American compilation of its kind. As an incentive to browsers, each copy came with a free pencil. The new publishers need not have worried about the public's response: *The Cross Word Puzzle Book*

sparked a national craze and was later credited with having popularized in the United States what until then had been a British pastime. Much to the partners' astonishment, a project concocted as a stopgap had mushroomed into the kind of lopsided success that could easily spell financial ruin for a small firm unprepared for an unforeseen surge in business. That the novice publishers not only survived their first bestseller but also were able to channel the profits into building a list varied enough to accommodate Will Durant's *The Story of Philosophy* and Dale Carnegie's *How to Win Friends and Influence People* spoke admirably for their business acumen and their feel for American popular taste and cultural aspirations, whatever the Maxwell Perkinses and Alfred A. Knopfs of New York's publishing firmament might murmur to the contrary.[2]

The maverick Simon and Schuster tweaked their old-guard rivals by declaring at every public opportunity that publishing was "fun." To underscore the point, they made an amusing show of the Ping-Pong table they kept in their office.[3] Hugely energetic young men, they recognized kindred spirits in Duplaix and Ogle. By 1938, the foursome, joined by the publisher's sales manager Albert R. Leventhal and treasurer Leon Shimkin, were engaged in ongoing conversations about long-term projects that the Guild and "Essandess" might undertake together. "We will gladly do some juvenile books with you," Simon told Duplaix one day, "but we will not do anything anybody else is doing. We want something absolutely different."[4] With small children at home, Simon and Leventhal (who shared a taste for elegant suits and fine dining) and Shimkin (a brilliant numbers man and more of a nail-biter) had all grown deeply curious about the market for juveniles. Leventhal would later recall, as a turning point in his interest, an evening at home when his three-year-old daughter had unceremoniously tossed a picture book into her bath, reducing the slim volume to a soggy ruin. This experience, he later wrote, as much as any, had shown him that, given the wear and tear to which children naturally subjected all their belongings, lower-priced books might be greatly appreciated by parents.[5]

Born in New York City and trained as a journalist at the University of Michigan, Albert Rice Leventhal worked as a police reporter, rewrite

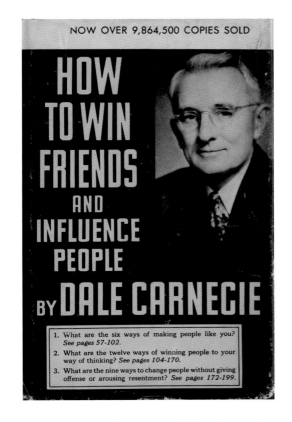

NOW OVER 9,864,500 COPIES SOLD

HOW TO WIN FRIENDS AND INFLUENCE PEOPLE
BY DALE CARNEGIE

1. What are the six ways of making people like you? See pages 57-102.
2. What are the twelve ways of winning people to your way of thinking? See pages 104-170.
3. What are the nine ways to change people without giving offense or arousing resentment? See pages 172-199.

Facing page, top: Max Schuster (left) and Richard Simon (right) at a 1931 party they gave for Robert L. Ripley (center), creator of "Believe It or Not." Wide World Photo. From the March 1951 issue of The Westerner.
Bottom: From Daddies.

Albert R. Leventhal as vice president and director of sales for Simon & Schuster. From the March 1951 issue of The Westerner.

Facing page: A 1942 Pocket Book.

man, and Sunday editor at the *Brooklyn Times Union* before landing a job as Simon and Schuster's promotion manager.[6] Leventhal scheduled his interview with the publisher for the afternoon of the Vanderbilt Cup Bridge Tournament, in which he planned to compete that evening. His bridge partner (and devoted boyhood friend), Jack Goodman, already worked at Essandess and was standing by to share a cab uptown.[7]

Max Schuster, the more formal of the two publishers, began the interview. Then Dick Simon breezed by to size up the candidate. When Simon, who, like Schuster, was a bridge enthusiast, learned of Leventhal's after-hours plans, his interest was piqued, and he asked the applicant, "May we join you guys?" After Goodman and his partner scored an easy victory in the duplicate competition, Simon turned to Leventhal and told him he was hired.

Leventhal proved to be a publishing natural. He had wide-ranging curiosity, a keen grasp of the market, a ready command of the language of persuasion, and a gift for inspiring and mentoring those around him.[8] Colleagues were put at ease by his straightforward and eminently reasonable manner. They admired him for his generosity of spirit and enjoyed his quick sense of fun. Once, in response to a hostile question about his devotion to the mass market, Leventhal blithely skewered a highbrow interviewer with the cryptic rejoinder, "As we say in publishing: Rumpelstiltskin!"[9] No day at the office was complete without a convivial round of late-afternoon drinks at Rockefeller Center's Mayan Room or another of Leventhal's favorite watering holes.

By 1938, with the worst of the Depression over for most Americans, there was a growing sense among publishers that the market for children's books was ripe for expansion. Bolstering publishers' expectations, the American Library Association that year presented the first Caldecott Medal for distinguished work by an American children's book artist. The new award lent added prestige to the picture book as an art form just as a growing number of American illustrators were turning to the genre as an outlet for their talents and an influx of European émigré artists was further enriching the scene. A possibility-laden time clearly lay just ahead. As the Essandess and Guild group considered their place in this promising future, their weekend discussions at Georges Duplaix's Sands Point, Long Island, home began to focus on the creation of a new line of picture books higher in quality than those Whitman was known for, yet priced well below the picture books then currently sold in stores.[10] Underlying this idea was the populist conviction, far from universally shared by publishers, that the known book-buying market represented only a fraction of the market's potential, and that a large unserved portion of the public—consisting of Americans who, though less educated and less prosperous than traditional book buyers, were eager to better themselves and their children—could be reached only if good books were manufactured and sold far more cheaply than in the past. Simon had already summed up this publishing philosophy in the five words engraved on the plaque he kept on his desk: "Give the reader a break!"[11]

Richard Simon and Max Schuster were ideal partners in the venture, having given considerable thought to the question of how best to reach untapped markets for books. On the adult side of their publishing business, they were already engaged in just such a mass-market experiment. Only recently, Leon Shimkin, the company treasurer later to become known as the third S of the Simon and Schuster operation, had guided Essandess into a joint venture with Robert de Graff, a publisher-entrepreneur who had made it his mission to overcome the book industry's long-standing resistance to paperbacks.[12] De Graff was eager to trump publishing snobbery and supply the nation with a broad array of worthwhile paperbacks at a mere twenty-five cents a copy—a revolutionary plan for expanding the possibilities of book ownership. De Graff's scheme depended on a variety of cost-cutting measures and an ingenious approach to distribution: Pocket Books, as the new line was named, would be primarily sold not at bookstores but rather from specially designed wire racks strategically placed in drugstores, train stations, and other heavily trafficked nontraditional locales. The key to accomplishing this lay in the forging of new alliances with the nation's independent news wholesalers, with their armies of cigar-chomping men with trucks who delivered magazines and newspapers to the country's retailers.[13] By harnessing this powerful distribution channel, Pocket Books

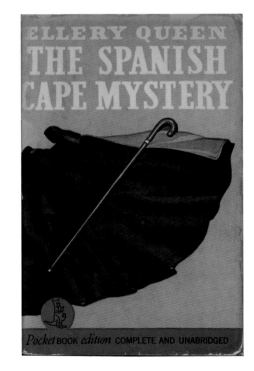

rapidly thrust itself into the very mainstream of American life. Racks of Pocket Books soon seemed to be everywhere.

In the late 1930s, the average price of a hardbound children's picture book—the kind of elaborately illustrated, often oversized story-hour book, such as Jean de Brunhoff's *The Story of Babar* or Virginia Lee Burton's *Mike Mulligan and His Steam Shovel,* that libraries purchased for their collections each year and that a parent or a grandparent might buy for a child as a special gift—was between $1.50 and $2.00. The most elegant of these books approached the quality of fine press editions and were meant to offer children an aesthetically uplifting experience: their first exposure to the twin realms of timeless literature and art. Such handsome books, which seemed to demand gentle treatment by well-scrubbed little hands, made suitable holiday gifts and appeared destined for awards-committee recognition. There was no disputing the idealistic impulse behind this tendency in children's publishing, yet it was fair to ask whether such books met the real needs of small children and their

At left: The current edition of The Story of Babar.
At right: The 1954 Little Golden Book edition of Madeline.

parents. As a first experiment, Lucille Ogle was assigned the daunting task of preparing samples for a line of less high-toned yet still somewhat comparable picture books, to be sold in stores for fifty cents. The chosen target price indicated a swing toward caution. Other fifty-cent picture books, notably those in Grosset and Dunlap's Story Parade series, were already on the market and proving their worth.[14] Had not Richard Simon insisted that the group come up with something unprecedented? Finally, someone—by various accounts it was Duplaix or Leventhal— proposed raising the stakes by publishing a line of high-quality picture books priced at a quarter. To do so would put the books within the price range of merchandise stocked in vast quantities by Woolworth, Kresge, McCrory's, and the other national chains. (The aim would be to out-Whitman Whitman.) At that price, the independent news wholesalers, who had helped make a resounding success of Pocket Books from the time of their launch in May 1939, might be enlisted once again. As had been the case with Pocket Books, making the new scheme work would require risking dauntingly large print runs—50,000 copies of a book instead of the standard 5,000 to 10,000—to be matched, of course, by correspondingly large sales. Once again, Ogle was given the job of creating sample books.

Simon and Schuster, meanwhile, was considering its options, hiring away Viking production managers Tom and Margaret Bevans with a view to setting up a full-fledged children's book department of its own.[15] Not by chance, one of the first books the Bevanses worked on in their new posts was by Ludwig Bemelmans, an artist who until then had been exclusively associated with Viking. May Massee, Viking's legendary junior-books editor, had been shown the manuscript first but had thought the mischievous tale, called *Madeline,* "too sophisticated" for young children. (Massee regretted the decision later, published each of the Madeline sequels, and eventually acquired the rights to the original book.)[16]

Another early Simon and Schuster juvenile was an unconventional square "tactile" book for preschoolers that called for bits of real cloth, sandpaper, and other embellishments to be affixed to its pages, the better for youngsters to have the kind of firsthand sensory experiences

Top: Dorothy Kunhardt with her husband, Phil, and their youngest child, Edith, 1937.

Facing page: Dorothy Kunhardt's daughter Nancy in 1928, holding the toy rabbit that would inspire Pat the Bunny (current edition, below), to be created ten years later for Edith. Both photos courtesy of Edith Kunhardt Davis.

then being touted by progressive educators. Not surprisingly, given the novelty book's many special manufacturing requirements, Harcourt Brace, the first publisher to be shown Dorothy Kunhardt's prototype for *Pat the Bunny*, turned the project down, albeit reluctantly.[17] True to their devil-may-care reputation, Simon and Schuster, however, opted to rise to the occasion. With some effort, the Bevanses found the eleven suppliers needed for the book's special effects and managed to get *Pat the Bunny* into stores in time for the 1940 holiday season. When it came time to advertise Kunhardt's fanciful creation, the witty young men and women at Essandess had a field day preparing a widely circulated ad in which they favorably compared the new book for preschoolers with two current adult best-sellers: "*Oliver Wiswell* (an historical novel of the American Revolution by Kenneth Roberts) is a wonderful book—but it won't squeak if you press it. *For Whom the Bell Tolls* (Ernest Hemingway's latest) is magnificent—but it hasn't any bunny in it."[18] In the five weeks before Christmas 1940, *Pat the Bunny* became the year's bestselling children's book.

Judy can pat the bunny.

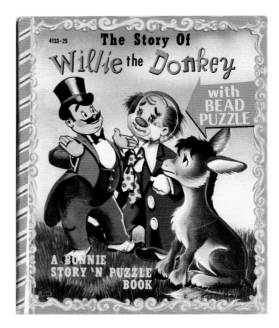

A 1950 Bonnie Book.

Facing page, top: Tibor Gergely, at work on the poster for the 1949 New York Herald Tribune Children's Spring Book Festival. *Courtesy of Greta Schreyer Loebl.*
Bottom: Gergely's 1928 drawing of Josephine Baker, drawn for the Viennese newspaper Der Tag *and signed by Baker. Courtesy of Linda Schreyer.*

Following pages: From Scuffy the Tugboat.

In 1940, Sam Lowe, who by then had been president of Whitman for more than twenty years and was a major Western stockholder, resigned to start his own publishing house, the Samuel Lowe Company, in Kenosha, Wisconsin, ten miles from Racine. (Bonnie Books, Abbott Publishing, and England's John Martin's House all became Lowe imprints.) Whether his decision was sudden or a long time in coming is not altogether clear, but there is no doubt that the parting was bitter. In an article published a few years after Lowe's death in 1950, the *Kenosha Evening News* reported that he had "severed his connections with another large publishing firm" to "gain greater liberty for his ideas and methods of producing high quality and low cost books for children."[19] Evidently, the relentless innovator had concluded that Western had become too big to act constructively on his ideas and that, as a publisher with essentially a printer's mentality, it set its editorial ambitions too rigidly in terms of what its presses were capable of producing.[20] As Lowe told the *New York Times* not long after making his new start, "If you have partners you must spend a lot of your time convincing them, persuading them, thinking up answers to objections."[21]

Was Lowe also disappointed not to have been included in the discussions that culminated in the launch of Little Golden Books? Once on his own, he methodically set about reprising his earlier triumphs, inaugurating his list with a ten-cent *Three Little Kittens* that in its first six months sold one and a half million copies in five-and-dime stores. The *Times* had sought him out after the *Publishers' Weekly,* a book industry trade journal, reported that the top-selling novel of 1940 was not, as everyone supposed, *Oliver Wiswell* or *For Whom the Bell Tolls.* It was a maudlin antebellum-era page-turner by Mary Jane Holmes called *Lena Rivers,* an 1897 publication that Lowe had reissued and sold by the million (also for a dime) through the chain stores. Pointedly opening a New York office in the same building as Western, at 200 Fifth Avenue, as well as establishing a third office in London, Lowe spent much of the last ten years of his life shuttling between cities and continents. With Bonnie Books, the line of twenty-five-cent picture books he introduced in 1946, Lowe even made a direct run at Little Golden Books.[22] But the momentum belonged to the older, larger, better-financed firm, and though he met with considerable success as a supplier to the chain stores, Lowe in the larger scheme of things remained one of Western's shadow competitors, and by no means the greatest among them when all was said and done.

Hardly a day passed at Western's New York offices without a telephone call from some lonely author or painter wishing to know how one went about joining the Guild. With a practiced air of sympathy, the receptionist would respond by saying that she was sorry but it was not that kind of guild.[23] Duplaix and his staff were, however, always on the alert for talented freelancers. Ogle, for example, arranged a meeting with Lucy Sprague Mitchell, the founder of New York's Bank Street School, and attended sessions of Mitchell's Writers Laboratory, an advanced workshop in children's writing that convened weekly over a bottle of sherry at the school's tumbledown Greenwich Village headquarters.[24] Among the regulars at the gatherings, where manuscripts were read and critiqued, were Margaret Wise Brown, Edith Thacher Hurd, Louise Woodcock, Jessie Stanton, Irma Simonton Black, and (a few years later than the others) Ruth Krauss, all of whom Ogle eventually published.

During the late 1930s, as the European political situation worsened, a great many artists, writers, and intellectuals under threat from Hitler fled their homelands and took up life in exile in New York City. Among the new arrivals in the spring of 1939 was an accomplished Hungarian-born Jewish artist named Tibor Gergely. Gergely and his wife disembarked with "a few suitcases and about two dozen rolled canvases and some of his drawings—all that was left of his former life."[25]

Making the rounds with his portfolio, the artist soon met Georges Duplaix, who was happy to secure his services for the Guild. Ogle did her part by helping arrange a part-time teaching job for Gergely at New York University.[26] With the publication of *Topsy Turvy Circus* (1940) and *The Merry Shipwreck* (1941), both written by Duplaix himself and packaged by the Guild for Harper and Brothers, American readers were introduced to the lighter side of a keenly observant self-

taught artist who had made his reputation in Europe between the wars as a stage designer, political caricaturist, and painter of brooding expressionist landscapes, still lifes, and portraits.

A physically slight, soft-spoken man with a wild gaze and an explosive grin that called to mind Harpo Marx, Gergely had come of age in Budapest during the 1910s as the youngest member of a brilliant group of progressive intellectuals known as the Sunday Circle. Other Circle members included the Marxist critic Georg Lukács, the film theoretician Béla Balázs, composers Béla Bartók and Zoltán Kodály, and the painter

Anna Lesznai, whom Gergely later married. In 1921, after a reactionary government came to power in Hungary, members of the group fled Budapest for neighboring Vienna, where Gergely won renown as a newspaper cartoonist and the cofounder of the avant-garde puppet theater Gong. A decade later, he returned with Anna Lesznai to Hungary, where, as one chronicler of his career has remarked, he "displayed [through his varied work] an intense curiosity toward people and their environment . . . and . . . a sharp eye for . . . what lies under the surface . . . Armed with a sketchbook and pencil, he roamed the countryside and recorded village

life. The various scenes, faces, activities or celebrations evoke a way of life now gone. Even more poignant, his presentation of the types of diverse commercial activities of the pre-Holocaust Jewish communities of the countryside is a testament to a people destroyed."[27]

The manic mischief of Gergely's illustration work for the Guild masked—or perhaps, by its sheer intensity, obliquely expressed—the bittersweet quality of the artist's life in exile. In Hungary, Anna Lesznai had been the most revered painter and decorative artist of her generation. In New York, however, she met with little interest in her work and was reduced to giving private painting lessons in their apartment. Gergely never attempted to show the paintings he'd brought from Hungary, but left them neatly bundled in a closet, as though consigned permanently to the past; friends rediscovered the paintings only after Gergely's death in 1978.[28]

Notwithstanding these disappointments of his new life, Gergely rejoiced in experimenting with full-color book illustration, a luxury made possible by the Guild's access to Western's powerful web presses. He basked in the glow of this newfound freedom, even as he drew fresh inspiration from the brashness and dynamism of the fast-paced skyscraper city he now called home. Starting with *The Merry Shipwreck,* Gergely made a point of incorporating affectionate tributes to New York into illustrations that brimmed with warmth and respect for the ordinary working people whom he never tired of sketching, and with whom he identified.

This page, top: The Happy Man and His Dump Truck, *1950, by Miryam, illustrated by Tibor Gergely.*
Bottom: The Great Big Fire Engine Book, *1950, illustrated by Tibor Gergely.*

Facing page, top: The 1942 Harper & Brothers edition of The Merry Shipwreck, *which was later issued as a Little Golden Book.*
Bottom: From The Happy Man and His Dump Truck.

Following pages: From The Great Big Fire Engine Book.

The
MERRY SHIPWRECK

by
GEORGES DUPLAIX
Pictures by
TIBOR GERGELY

Feodor Rojankovsky, in a self-portrait for the jacket of Animal Stories.

Facing page: Examples of Rojankovsky's European commercial artwork.
Top left: Cover artwork for the May 3, 1930, issue of Le Rire.
Top right: Orient Line Cruises brochure, 1930s.
Bottom: Pilgrims, *R. Wegner, publisher, Lvov, Poland, probably late 1920s. Courtesy of Tatiana Koly.*

Meanwhile, Georges Duplaix kept a close watch on events in Europe. He did so for both personal and professional reasons. When, in the summer of 1941, he put up the money needed to bring the Russian émigré illustrator Feodor Rojankovsky from Nazi-occupied Paris to New York, he was not only coming to the aid of a friend. He was also seizing an important opportunity for the Guild.

The two men had met in France between the wars, about the same time that the peripatetic Sam Lowe, on a trip to Europe, acquired American rights to a new series of French picture books for which Rojankovsky was one of the principal illustrators.[29] In 1935, the year in which Duplaix assumed the directorship of the Guild, Artists and Writers released one of Rojankovsky's first American publications, a picture book from the Père Castor series. In Duplaix's nimble English-language translation, *Les Petits et les Grands* (Flammarion, 1933) became *Wild Animals and Their Little Ones.*[30] In 1941, in a gesture intended to cement the artist's loyalty to the Guild, Duplaix sent Rojankovsky a substantial sum to cover the cost of his transatlantic passage; along with the money came the assurance of steady work once he arrived on American shores.

Feodor Stepanovich Rojankovsky had been born in 1891 in Mitava, Latvia.[31] By the time he came to the United States, forced uprootings had long since become a routine part of his life. Throughout Rojankovsky's childhood, his father, a secondary school headmaster, had been transferred from one far-flung imperial outpost to another; a curious consequence of all this bureaucratic reshuffling was that each of the headmaster's five children entered the world with a different nationality.

Rojankovsky was still a boy when he discovered his lifelong passions for painting and the study of nature. Not long after he began his formal training at the Moscow Fine Arts Academy, however, his studies were cut short. With the outbreak of World War I, he was drafted into the White Russian army. After the war, he enjoyed a brief apprenticeship as a children's book illustrator, only to be called up for military service once again during the early days of the Russian Revolution. During his second tour of duty, Rojankovsky contracted typhus and spent the balance of that confused and turbulent time being nursed back to health in

a Polish prisoner of war camp. Upon his release in 1920, by then so accustomed to adapting to new circumstances, he decided to remain in Poland and, resuming his fledgling art career, widened the scope of his activities to include work not only as an illustrator but also as a stage designer and an art director of a fashion magazine.

In 1927, Rojankovsky moved to Paris, the world capital of art, and quickly firmed up his reputation as a Fauve-inspired illustrator and designer of extraordinary verve. Renewing his interest in children's book illustration, he produced memorable work for the aesthetically rarified Domino Press, owned by American expatriate Esther Averill, as well as for the new Père Castor series of modestly priced picture books published by Flammarion under the supervision of French educator Paul Faucher.[32]

Faucher had come of age professionally after World War I as a bookseller with reformist ideals and ambitions. Horrified by the war and inspired by encounters with leading European proponents of the "new education" (most notably the Czech pedagogical theorist Frantisek Bakule, whom he had met in 1927 at the Congress for New Education

held in Locarno), Faucher created *Les Albums du Père Castor* (*The Picture Books of Father Beaver*) in 1931 as an expression of faith in the power of imaginatively conceived children's books as instruments of antiauthoritarian social and political change. From the start, the Père Castor series placed a premium on graphically dynamic, colorful illustration in books aimed at stimulating independent thinking in pre-readers. Rojankovsky soon emerged as one of the series' major contributors; as the famed Ballets Russes designer Alexander Benois wrote of his fellow Russian artist-in-exile, "Rojankovsky, from the educational point of view, deserved the palm for encouraging children to observe nature in all phases of its creation."[33] For Georges Duplaix, the success of the Père Castor experiment sparked visions not just of American editions of the French books but also of an equivalent homegrown American series. To Duplaix, Little Golden Books were the realization of that vision.[34]

In August 1941, Rojankovsky made his way out of the occupied French capital and across the Pyrenees to the Spanish port city of Seville. He planned to sail to New York aboard the Spanish freighter SS *Navemar*. On arriving in Seville, however, and learning that the *Navemar*'s departure had been delayed, Rojankovsky apparently put off purchasing his ticket and set about exploring the city. According to one account of what happened next, the artist impulsively squandered a portion of his travel money on a Japanese folding screen he saw in a shop window on one of his walks around town. When on August 6 the *Navemar* was at last ready to set sail, Rojankovsky, now short of funds, had to talk his way aboard ship.[35]

Originally fitted out for just fifteen passengers, the Spanish freighter, before setting off on what would prove to be its final ocean crossing, jammed an estimated eleven hundred refugees into its hold. The majority of them were European Jews fleeing the Nazi slaughter.[36] Ever the quick study, Rojankovsky, it seems, managed not only to take his place on the ship but also, by offering to paint the captain's portrait, to secure comparatively comfortable quarters in one of the lifeboats. Six weeks later, on a summery mid-September afternoon in Brooklyn Harbor, Georges Duplaix finally greeted his colorful friend at the pier. "Rojan" looked dapper in a dark suit as he stepped down the gangway,

his arms wrapped incongruously around his precious cargo, with little else to his name. Not long afterward, Duplaix assigned him the illustrations for *The Tall Book of Mother Goose* (Harper, 1942), the first in what would become an immensely popular series of children's books designed by Duplaix himself in a novel, Baedeker-like format.[37]

In 1940, building on the success of its New York outpost, Western opened a small Guild office in downtown Beverly Hills, a short drive from the movie and animation studios whose licensed character business had become such a mainstay of the company's activities.[38] In addition to its work with Disney, Western was producing books, comics, games, and puzzles based on Looney Tunes and Merrie Melodies characters or inspired by the cowboy film star Gene Autry. From the outset, the Western Front, as the new office was nicknamed, had enough going on to provide steady employment for six freelance artists and two writers. E.H., by then more a corporate father figure than a day-to-day decision-maker, drove to the coast with his wife to preside at the ribbon cutting and to have his picture taken with Western's growing roster of celebrity clients.

Meanwhile, advance work for the launch of Little Golden Books continued. To test the waters for the new venture, Albert Leventhal, the project's point man at Essandess, started by canvassing the traditional end of the market, giving booksellers with whom the publisher did regular business a first look at the sample volumes prepared by Ogle. On the whole, the reaction was deeply discouraging.[39] At stores all around the country, more than half of the merchants with whom Leventhal met expressed variations of two concerns: customers, they believed, would assume that books selling for twenty-five cents were of inferior quality, and books sold at twenty-five cents would provide too small a profit for retailers no matter how many copies they sold. Leventhal must have anticipated some of what he heard, but he seems to have been shaken by the ferocity of the resistance. In the partnership arrangement negotiated with the printing company, Simon and Schuster had agreed to purchase outright (at 35 percent of the retail price) 50,000 copies of each of the first twelve books that Western manufactured. Although bookstores had never been counted on as the primary outlet for the books, Leventhal had hoped to sell a considerable portion of the inventory through that traditional channel.[40] As the prospects for doing so seemed to evaporate, Richard Simon and Max Schuster briefly considered backing out of the deal and writing the experience off as a dead loss.

Then, however, book buyers for some of the nation's major department stores—Chicago's Marshall Field's, New York's Macy's, and the Philadelphia branch of Gimbels—began to show real interest. By mid-September, the response from those merchants had proven strong enough to warrant giving the final go-ahead for the Poughkeepsie plant to start its giant rotary presses rolling.

Ironically, the first hint of what the public's true response to the books would be came from a small independent bookseller in New Britain, Connecticut, to whom a large advance shipment of Little Golden Books was rushed for a prepublication sneak preview. To everyone's astonishment, 864 of the books were sold in the first two and a half days.[41] Rather than pick and choose from among the dozen titles on display, many customers simply bought one copy of each.

Facing page: From Rojankovsky's The Three Bears, *1948.*

This page: Rojankovsky's 1959 Book Week poster, inspired by sketches he'd made several years before of his daughter, Tatiana. Copyright © 1959 by the Children's Book Council. Courtesy of Tatiana Koly.

"The North Wind Doth Blow"—an illustration by Miss Elliott for *Mother Goose*
This is one of the 172 pages in color from the first 12 Little Golden Books

That month, a lavish four-page full-color insert in the *Publishers' Weekly* heralded the October 1 launch of "a new series of 25¢ books for children."[42] The announcement, from Simon and Schuster's oracular "Inner Sanctum," featured full-color art from *The Poky Little Puppy* and Miss Elliott's *Mother Goose* and gave details of the Little Golden Books' "hows, whys and wherefores," boldly declaring that the high quality of the books would in every respect—art, text, printing, paper—set them worlds apart from all other books in their price category. A partial roster of the series' illustrators was submitted as evidence, followed—in a bid to cinch the quality side of the argument—by the assurance that the entire series was being published under the supervision of "Dr. Mary Reed of Teachers College, Columbia University." The educator's imprimatur, emblazoned on the copyright page of every Little Golden Book until the time of Reed's death in 1960, would soon become as well known a guarantor of excellence as the *Good Housekeeping* Seal of Approval. Having planted the fine notion that an authority associated with one of American education's leading institutions was watching over the proceedings, the publisher got down to the business of reeling off a raft of genuinely impressive advance sales figures. The buyer at Marshall Field's had not only liked the Little Golden Books that Albert Leventhal had shown her, she had ordered fifty gross of them, as had New York's Womrath bookstore chain. FAO Schwarz, the Manhattan toy emporium, had gone in for eighteen gross. St. Louis's Stix, Baer and Fuller department store had taken twenty gross. Confronted with this litany of "breath taking" facts, even booksellers who normally shunned children's books except at Christmastime (and the majority of them still kept to this pattern) at least had to take notice. Feigning befuddlement, the cunning oracle of the Inner Sanctum confided, "Never having had any experience along these lines in the past we are still not quite used to that word 'gross.'" Back in Racine, E.H. and the few others at Western old enough to recall the mix-up with gross and dozens that had once nearly bankrupted them must have prayed that Simon and Schuster were kidding.

One last frank piece of advice to booksellers was about all that remained to be offered: "In case our salesman does not call on you, may we suggest that you mail in your order now. . . . From the standpoint of advertising and promotion *Little Golden Books* are going to be given the works by Essandess."

To encourage retail customers to make multiple purchases, booksellers were given cardboard slipcase boxes gaily printed to resemble suitcases and sized to hold either four or six books each.[43] Special floor racks designed to house only Little Golden Books were distributed free of charge to any store that wanted them. In this way, the line became a fixture in about half of the eight hundred stores nationwide that originally stocked them.[44] As two further incentives to booksellers, a sliding discount, pegged to the quantity of books ordered, was offered and a guarantee was given that Simon and Schuster would (at least for the time being) refuse orders from chain stores (such as Woolworth) in cities where the book trade had "cooperated with the project from the first."[45]

The first printing of 600,000 books sold out so rapidly that Simon and Schuster canceled a planned first wave of advertisements for fear of frustrating its bookseller friends by stoking greater demand for the books than the company could satisfy. Even so, within five months, a third printing had nearly been exhausted, for a total of 1.5 million copies sold, and Simon and Schuster claimed to have back orders for an additional two million books.

Overwhelmed by the public's response, the publisher felt compelled that spring to apologize to booksellers both for continuing shortfalls in its inventory and for the decision to postpone the release of the next four Little Golden Books from February to May 1943. Each new book, Essandess promised, would be issued in a generous first printing of 150,000. Another set of four books would follow by summer. "Our Keeping-Its-Fingers-Crossed Department is also working hard . . . [to] enable us to supply our regular accounts with all—well, nearly all—of the first twelve Little Golden Books they are going to need during the forthcoming fall and Christmas season."[46] War or no war, a publishing phenomenon of historic proportions was clearly under way.

Facing page: From the four-page Publishers' Weekly *ad insert.*

The first twelve Little Golden Books.

Illustrated by Masha.

Illustrated by Gustaf Tenggren.

Leah Gale.
Illustrated by Vivienne Blake.

Selected by Phyllis Fraser.
Illustrated by Miss Elliott.

Illustrated by Rachel Taft Dixon.

Illustrated by Rudolf Freund.

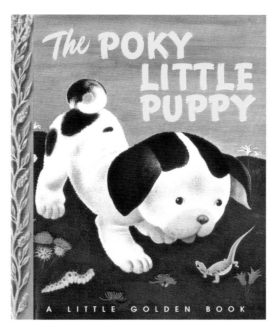

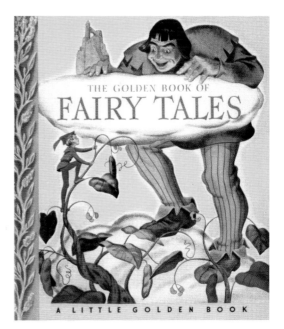

Arranged by Leah Gale.
Illustrated by Corinne Malvern.

Janette Sebring Lowrey.
Illustrated by Gustaf Tenggren.

Illustrated by Winfield Hoskins.

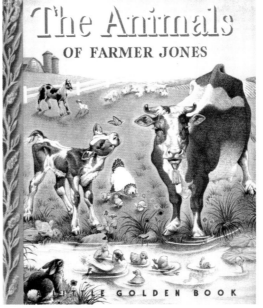

Illustrated by Bob Smith.

Illustrated by Rudolf Freund.

Selected by Phyllis Fraser.
Illustrated by Roberta Paflin.

Steven Guarnaccia Remembers Feodor Rojankovsky's *The Three Bears*

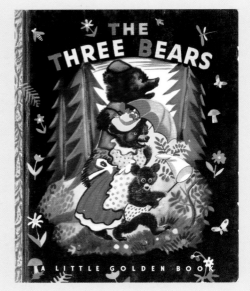

The original cover.

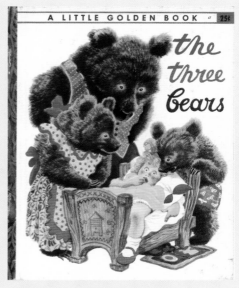

The 1948 revised, and better-known, cover.

Q: What are your first memories of Golden Books?
A: I grew up with Golden Books and remember going to the grocery store, where the books were displayed on spinning racks and you could bring one home for twenty-nine cents. Tenggren was the artist I gravitated toward. What I liked about Tenggren was that his painting, while extremely stylized, was also fully rounded, dimensional. He created a believable world but with characters who looked like they were carved out of wood: they seemed like toys.

Q: When did you discover Rojankovsky?
A: Not until I began collecting Golden Books as an adult. Rojankovsky was the more realistic of the two artists, although not always in obvious ways. Everything in the first illustrations of *The Three Bears,* for instance, is highly exaggerated, almost torturously engorged: the knobbiness of the furniture, the way every bit of wood grain is lovingly and maybe a little too intensely put down. The chairs look as if they could come alive at any moment. Then the bear family goes off on a walk. This to me is the first great image in the book. Suddenly, as in a Persian miniature, everything is flattened out. The first thing you notice is the beautifully detailed yet abstract, graphic patterning of the forest foliage. But then you notice how wonderfully bourgeois the bear family is: the father bear with his fez and vest and walking stick, the mother with her parasol, the little bear boy chasing butterflies. It's all so Nabokovian, so middle-class! They live in the woods, but you begin to suspect that this is just their country house; that these are city bears going native. And Rojankovsky makes a point of showing you that Goldilocks herself comes from a much more ordinary home.

Goldilocks looks almost elfin. Rojankovsky's child characters all have that same apple-dumpling quality about them. Yet they are never generic. They are all particular children who you as a child could believe really existed and whom you could possibly know.

And then there is Papa Bear. He has some of the facial expressions of a human. Yet when you look into those beady little eyes of his, it's a bit terrifying: you know then that he's all animal. And when Papa sits down to eat his porridge, Rojankovsky has you wonder: Where's the vest? Where's the hat? He's just a bear now, and an angry bear at that. The gloves are off! I think that's wild.

Part Three

"Books and Bread"

𝒲hatever else might have accounted for the spectacular success of the first Little Golden Books, praise from the library world had little to do with it. In the 1940s, many of the field's most respected critics were librarians, and public libraries constituted the lion's share of the market for children's books published by older houses such as Scribner, Houghton Mifflin, and Harper. For the books those publishers specialized in, favorable notices from a few key librarian-critics all but assured a respectable sale of perhaps five to ten thousand copies over a period of years. At influential professional journals such as the *Horn Book Magazine* and the American Library Association's *Booklist,* where these critics passed down their judgments, the review process proceeded at a slow, even stately pace. After all, for reviewers trained to think of a good children's book as a "timeless" work of literature and art, what was the hurry? In stark defiance of this well-established pattern, Little Golden Books

Left: From The Little Red Hen. *Right: From* Three Little Kittens.

From The Poky Little Puppy.

were designed as impulse-buy items that parents would purchase not because an authority had praised them but because the books were affordable, visually appealing, and ready at hand. The librarian-critics, who prided themselves on being cultural gatekeepers and moral guardians of the nation's youth, suddenly realized, much to their dismay, that in the case of Little Golden Books, they had been factored out of the equation. No wonder their anger was palpable.

The librarians' strong dislike for the new books had a long and complex background. From the late nineteenth century, when children's library service first emerged as a specialized profession, leading figures within the group had objected to a wide range of ten-cent formula series fiction that youngsters of the day could purchase at newsstands with their own money. Labeled subliterary and often also sensationalistic by the librarians, the scorned works included the Horatio Alger books; the Tom Swift, Rover Boys, and Hardy Boys series; and assorted other adventure stories and potboilers, many of them the work of one feverishly industrious publisher-entrepreneur, Edward Stratemeyer, and his workshop of write-to-order scribblers. Such was the librarians' disdain for these vexingly popular books—and for the comic books that from the 1930s aimed at satisfying the same childhood and adolescent cravings—that they came to regard all juvenile fiction published in series form with the same deep suspicion. They held adamantly to this view even when, as in the case of Laura Ingalls Wilder's Little House books, the writing had unassailable literary merit. Little Golden Books suffered the misfortune of being dismissed out of hand as representing the projection of mass-production methods and values into the picture book realm.

One might have thought that the endorsement of a Teachers College faculty member would ameliorate matters. In all likelihood, it had the opposite effect. Librarians and progressive educators had clashed bitterly during the 1920s, when the latter group, led by the Bank Street School's founder, Lucy Sprague Mitchell, cited their own empirical research as they challenged the standards by which librarians evaluated children's books.[1] Arguing that young children were naturally curious about everyday modern life (airplanes, telephones, cities) and apt to be confused by the "timeless" fairy tales librarians favored, Mitchell, in her widely debated, bestselling *Here and Now Story Book* (1921), went on to propose prototypes for a new kind of child-centered children's literature. The New York Public Library's Anne Carroll Moore and her colleagues at the *Horn Book Magazine* dismissed Mitchell's efforts as an ill-conceived attempt at conjuring literature in the laboratory. To these critics, Mitchell and her fellow educators—like Mary Reed—were no less the enemy than Stratemeyer himself. By the early 1940s, the library world's antipathy toward progressive education had begun to moderate, but it had not done so to the extent that librarians were willing even to consider purchasing Little Golden Books.

With parents as the primary market, Ogle and her staff made certain that everything about the visual design of the books encouraged their purchase. The alluring name chosen for the line made for a good beginning. "Little Golden Books," first proposed by Simon and Schuster's production manager, Tom Bevans, always had prominent placement on the front cover. And in a striking departure from publishing practice, the names of the author and the illustrator did not appear on the cover at all.[2] The focus remained on the book itself as part of a larger entity. It was as though each volume in the line was a piece of a puzzle that children moved closer to completing every time they went shopping with their parents. The series number assigned to each book made it easy for youngsters to keep track of the titles they did or did not yet own. The name plaque printed on the inside front cover, bearing the legend "This book belongs to," reinforced the child's pride in ownership.

Further strengthening the line's brand identity were the cozy, uniform size and look of the books and the preference for titles—*Bedtime Stories, Mother Goose, The Alphabet from A to Z*—that managed to sound both generic and classic. Taken together, the original twelve books composed a complete first library for preschoolers—and all for the price of two traditional picture books. What parent would not welcome such a bargain?

Although the modest selling price had always been assumed to be a key ingredient of the line's chances for success, the Golden creators were determined to counter the suspicion that the books were "cheap"

Top: The original Little Golden Book interior front cover.
Bottom: A later version.

Ursula Nordstrom, 1946. Photo by Erich Hartmann, Magnum Photos.
Below: Detail from The Poky Little Puppy.

Facing page: Janette Sebring Lowrey, 1950. The San Antonio Light *Collection, UT Institute of Texan Cultures at San Antonio, No. L-4019-b. Courtesy of John and Dela White.*

in the pejorative sense. In a clear bid for upmarket respectability, the first thirty-five titles, including most of those released through 1947, were published with a traditional dust jacket over a four-color heavy-board binding. (The last book bearing a dust jacket was *The Happy Family,* by Nicole, illustrated by Gertrude Elliott.)[3] Each jacket featured a burnished gold-colored strip along the spine, decorated with a wheat pattern—the first of several versions of the line's trademark golden design.[4] The books were "side-stapled" using a Swedish method that was less costly than more traditional binding alternatives; a dark blue tape along the spine concealed the staples. When, as a cost-cutting measure during the postwar recession, the dust jackets were finally eliminated, the now iconic gold foil strip replaced the blue tape along the spine.

Most of the first twelve Little Golden Books offered standard renditions of classic material in the public domain: nursery rhymes, folktales, children's prayers, and the like. The notable exception was *The Poky Little Puppy,* an original story written by an up-and-coming San Antonio author named Janette Sebring Lowrey.[5] (Lowrey also wrote, without attribution, Little Golden Book No. 10, *Baby's Book,* illustrated by Bob Smith, for this first list.)[6] Just how the manuscript for what would become the bestselling picture book of all time found its way to the Guild is not entirely certain. In all likelihood, the person most responsible was, curiously enough, Ursula Nordstrom, the dynamic young editorial director of Harper and Brothers.[7] At the time that Ogle was putting together her first list, Harper had published two of Lowrey's first three children's books— *Silver Dollar* (1940) and *Rings on Her Fingers* (1941). Nordstrom, who had taken an instant liking to the tartly witty Texan, had decided that Lowrey's principal gift lay in the genre of realistic fiction for older girls. Harper published Laura Ingalls Wilder's Little House books; Nordstrom might well have had the idea that Lowrey would one day write a comparable series with a Texas background. In the meantime, she was eager to help and encourage the author in any way she could. And because she was also fond of Ogle, a fellow publishing maverick with whom she occasionally did business, it would have been a small thing for her to tell Lowrey about a chance to earn some extra money by tossing off an amusing picture

Gustaf Tenggren, 1951, on his 55th birthday, with his new puppy, Wulf.

Facing page, top: A 1943 Tenggren magazine cover.
Facing page, bottom: Tenggren's illustration from "A Story of New York and Nova Scotia," by Maurice Clark, from an unidentified publication.
All images courtesy of the Kerlan Collection, University of Minnesota Libraries.

book text for a colleague, especially a manuscript that would have little to do with her real work as a novelist. Lowrey received a seventy-five-dollar flat fee as the author of *The Poky Little Puppy.*[8]

Early Golden advertising touted the visual side of the books, the contributions of "America's top-flight juvenile artists" to the line.[9] That claim, though certainly exaggerated—where, one had the right to ask, were the Little Golden Books illustrated by Marjorie Flack, Robert Lawson, Virginia Lee Burton, and Robert McCloskey?—was nonetheless an accurate reflection of Ogle and company's view that while text mattered, the books would stand or fall on the strength of their graphics.

The star of the first group of Golden artists was Gustaf Tenggren, the illustrator of *Bedtime Stories* (No. 2) and *The Poky Little Puppy* (No. 8). Born in Vastergotland, Sweden, in 1896, to a family of decorative artists, Tenggren began his formal art education at the age of twelve, received rigorous classical training in life drawing, landscape, and still life, and won early acclaim as a draftsman of exceptional power. Tenggren's first published illustrations appeared in the 1917 Swedish holiday annual *Bland Tomtar Och Troll* (Among Elves and Trolls). Three years later, he was eager to conquer new worlds. Following his father's and sisters' examples, he immigrated to the United States and settled in Cleveland, where an unexpectedly cool response to his flamboyant, fantasy-laced art propelled him into an intensive two-year period of introspection and cultural readjustment. As Tenggren retooled his illustration style and mulled over his future, he earned a living by making fashion sketches for a local department store and contributing deliberately toned-down drawings to the aptly named *Plain Dealer.*[10]

In 1922, Tenggren at last felt ready to take on New York, and opened a studio there, where he churned out reams of smart advertising graphics, the art for nearly two dozen children's books, and romantic illustrations for *Good Housekeeping, Redbook, Ladies' Home Journal,* and other magazines. Tall and athletically built, and possessing a rugged, leading-man profile, Tenggren played the artist's role to the hilt, dressing in a "camel hair coat with a sash and suede shoes," smoking and drinking heavily, and making no secret of the high regard in which he held his

Gustaf Tenggren, in a self-portrait for the jacket of
Tenggren's Story Book, *1944.*
Below: Detail from Tenggren's The Shy Little Kitten, *1946,*
by Cathleen Schurr.

Facing page, top: Tenggren's studies for The Shy Little Kitten.
Courtesy of the Kerlan Collection, University of Minnesota
Libraries.
Bottom: From The Shy Little Kitten.

Following pages, a sampling of Tenggren's many styles.
Top left: From Pirates, Ships, and Sailors, *1950, by Kathryn*
and Byron Jackson.
Bottom: From The Lion's Paw, *1959, by Jane Werner Watson.*
Facing page: From Tenggren's Golden Tales from
the Arabian Nights, *1957, retold by Margaret Soifer*
and Irwin Shapiro.

own talent.[11] By the mid-1930s, his work had come to Walt Disney's attention. In April 1936, Disney hired Tenggren for his story department, just as the Burbank, California, studio was gearing up to make the world's first feature-length animated film, *Snow White.*[12]

In this way, Tenggren, at forty, joined the select corps of (mostly much younger) Disney artists whose job was to create speculative concept paintings and drawings for the inspiration and guidance of the studio's frontline animators. He worked in this capacity on *The Old Mill, Pinocchio, Fantasia,* and *Bambi,* in addition to *Snow White,* before returning to New York in 1939, having grown disenchanted with Disney's unwillingness to share credit with his artists, and with the studio's insistence on retaining ownership of the artwork produced there. An indiscreet affair with an underaged summer intern most likely moved up the timetable for his departure.[13] But other factors also played their parts. Faced with widespread dissention within the ranks of his mushrooming staff, Disney stubbornly resisted all attempts at unionization; Tenggren was hardly the only artist to make his exit when he did.[14]

Once back in New York, the accomplished and supremely confident artist had no trouble restarting his solo illustration career. Given his recent association with Disney, the Guild must have seemed an obvious place to start. But even if there had been no long-standing Disney-Western relationship, Tenggren might well have signed on to work with Duplaix and Ogle, whose office was generating a seemingly endless supply of interesting projects. As it happened, Tenggren's sojourn in Burbank had given him the ideal preparation for a thriving new career as a Golden illustrator. For a European artist intent on Americanizing his style, there was no better school than the Disney Studio. Tenggren's Poky Little Puppy had far less to do with the guileful elves and trolls of Swedish folklore than with the uniformly endearing Disney Seven Dwarfs, in whose creation Tenggren himself was deeply involved. As the Golden list expanded to encompass a variety of formats intended for children in every age group, Tenggren would have many chances to exercise the full range of his remarkable powers.

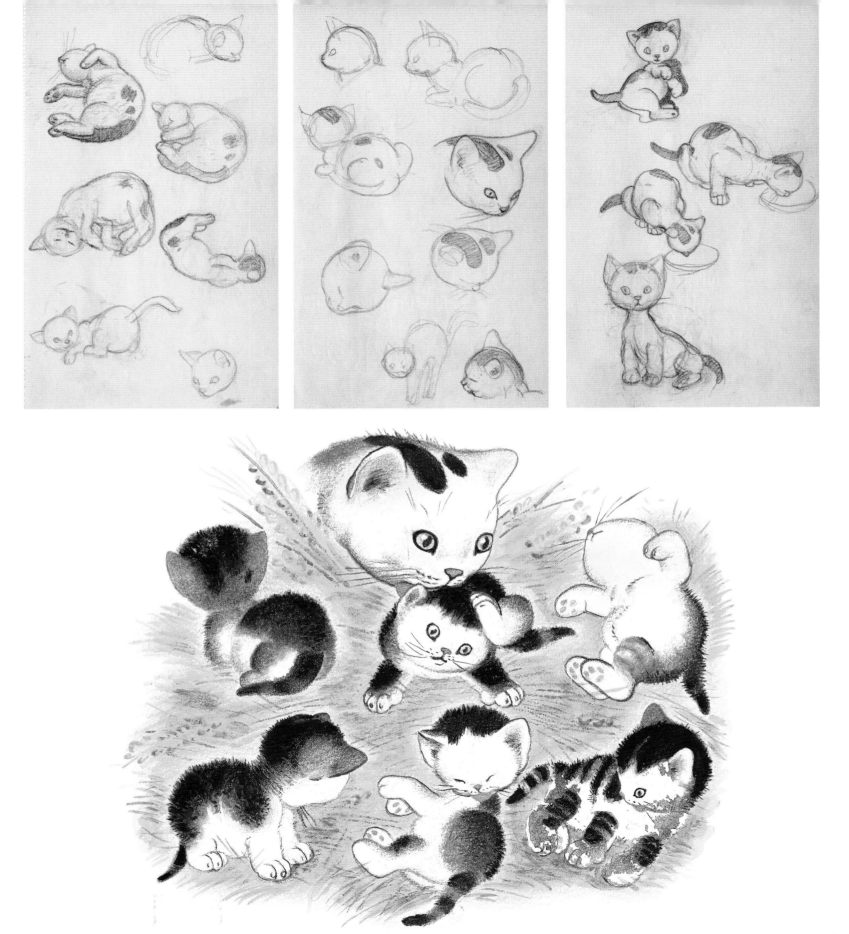

Most of the art featured in the first dozen Little Golden Books was notable for its cozy, old-fashioned, déjà vu quality. In *Nursery Songs,* the rosy-cheeked boys and girls depicted by Corinne Malvern look much like those seen running and jumping across the pages of the new Dick and Jane primers with which young schoolchildren around the country were becoming acquainted.[15] (During the 1940s and the 1950s, Malvern herself would be called upon to illustrate primers aimed at competing with the widely adopted Scott Foresman series.) Both the illustrator and her sister Gladys Malvern, who was a writer, had been child actresses before giving up the touring stage performer's patchy itinerant life for the only slightly more regular routine of pen-and-brush freelancers. Corinne worked as a fashion illustrator in Los Angeles before settling in New York. Not surprisingly, the children who frolic and play in her Golden illustrations are smartly dressed. More surprising, Malvern gave their soignée mothers the look of women with places to go and things to do quite apart from raising their children.

The honor of illustrating Little Golden Book No. 1, *Three Little Kittens,* went to Marie Simchow Stern, or Masha, a promising newcomer with an affinity for lighthearted fantasy and, as it later emerged, for illustration in the Christian inspirational vein.[16] Stern seems to have met Lucille Ogle and Harper's Ursula Nordstrom at about the same time; perhaps an introduction had been made between editor friends. Nordstrom was responsible for Masha's only other appearance in print that year, as the illustrator of *Tap-a-Tan!,* a novel by Janette Lowrey.

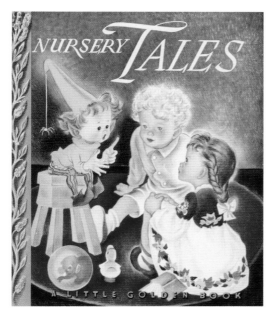

Facing page, top: Corinne Malvern in an undated photograph.
Middle: Malvern's How Big, *1949.*
Bottom: Malvern's The Night Before Christmas, *1949,*
by Clement C. Moore.
Bottom right: Detail from Malvern's Nurse Nancy, *1952,*
by Kathryn Jackson.

This page, top: Masha's Nursery Tales, *1943.*
Bottom: Masha in an undated photograph.
At left: From Masha's Three Little Kittens.

A Guild discovery, Gertrude Elliott was a pen-and-ink artist of considerable subtlety and refinement. The illustrator, it seemed, had longed since childhood to be known to the world as Miss Elliott.[17] Starting with *Mother Goose*—Little Golden Book No. 4 (selected by Phyllis Fraser)—she adopted the honorific as her professional name. In the artist's private life, she was Gertrude Elliott Espenscheid, and she lived with her husband and daughter on an old New Jersey farm. Elliott gave readers charming glimpses of her idyllic home surroundings on the end-papers of *The Golden Dictionary* (written by Ellen Wales Walpole, 1944). An antique, toylike impression adroitly balanced the coiled-spring verve of Elliott's precise line work. The quaintness was what one noticed; but it was the underlying energy of her drawings that made the experience of encountering them memorable.

Unlike most of his new Golden colleagues, Rudolf Freund was primarily a scientific illustrator.[18] Freund had worked as a preparator at the

American Museum of Natural History, where, as he later recalled, "through association with the leading scientists and museum men of our time, my artistic meanderings were finally brought to an end and natural history became my sole interest."[19] He later illustrated for *National Geographic* and *Life*. As the illustrator of *The Animals of Farmer Jones* and *The Little Red Hen*, Freund may have felt that he was simply embarking on a sort of busman's holiday. Yet as he came from a museum famous for its vigorous education program, the thought of illustrating a children's book must not have been all that foreign to him. In turn, the Guild's association with Freund anticipated one of its most ambitious plans: to publish a home library of illustrated non-fiction for grade-schoolers who had outgrown their Little Golden Books.

The aura of comfort and security that surrounded the twelve little books assumed new meaning in wartime. In speeches, interviews, and her syndicated column, "My Day," Eleanor Roosevelt urged parents to read aloud to their children as a way of bolstering family morale and maintaining an atmosphere of normality on the home front.[20] The advent of Little Golden Books gave parents an ample, affordable supply of calming, cheerful stories and pictures with which to put the First Lady's advice into action. Even aside from serendipitous prompting from the White House, home front conditions worked to the books' advantage. As a memo from Simon and Schuster to the trade had predicted, the strict wartime rationing of metals, rubber, and other materials used in the manufacture of toys increased demand for children's books both as gifts and as sources of everyday home recreation. The prevailing thrift mentality further burnished the appeal of the low-priced Little Goldens.

All but the very youngest Americans had some awareness that their nation was at war, and the first Little Golden Books acknowledged as much. The back flap of every dust jacket carried a patriotic appeal, delivered by the story's own characters, for the purchase of War Savings Stamps. The advertisement accompanying *The Poky Little Puppy,* for example, bore this message:

> The poky little puppy sat near the bottom of the hill, looking hard at something on the ground in front of him.

BUY U.S. WAR SAVINGS STAMPS AND BONDS

THE LITTLE RED HEN

This year the Little Red Hen has a Victory Garden. She has extra food to sell to the duck, the goose, the cat, and the pig, who will not grow their own.

With the pennies she saves, she buys War Stamps every week. Soon she will have enough stamps to buy a War Bond. If you buy War Stamps every week, you will soon be able to buy a Bond too.

BUY U.S. WAR SAVINGS STAMPS AND BONDS

Facing page, bottom left: The Happy Family, *1947, by Nicole, illustrated by Gertrude Elliott. Right: From Elliott's* Two Little Gardeners, *1951, by Margaret Wise Brown and Edith Thacher Hurd.*

This page: From the back flap of The Little Red Hen.

"What is he looking at?" the four little puppies asked one another. And down they went to see.

There was a War Savings Stamp lying in the grass.

And the poky little puppy hurried home faster than he had ever run before, to paste the stamp in his War Stamp Book. All the five little puppies buy War Stamps every week.

So should you.

Besides boosting demand, wartime conditions worked in Golden Books' favor in other ways. Under the rules of the mandatory rationing of paper instituted by the federal government in 1943, a printer's or publisher's annual allotment was calculated as a percentage of the quantity of paper that the company had used the previous year. On this basis, Western's vast commercial printing operation entitled it to a substantial paper supply—a much larger quantity than granted to any of the major trade publishers. Launching Little Golden Books in 1942 must in itself have significantly raised Western's allotment for the following year. In any case, without Western's access to paper, the Golden venture could not have proceeded. The rationing system also required publishers to withhold every tenth book ordered from retailers.[21] Simon and Schuster was said to have refused thousands of new Little Golden accounts as a result of this stipulation alone.

Other publishers, in an effort to stretch their paper allotments to the limit, resorted to printing books in smaller trim sizes and with fewer illustrations and narrower margins. In dramatic contrast, Simon and Schuster in 1944 introduced the first Giant Golden Books, a new format calculated, as the name implied, to stand out all the more conspicuously beside the competition on bookstore shelves. One wonders if the oversized books might have stirred a patriotic backlash had they not offered the consumer such a good value. Leading the list of Giants were *Tenggren's Story Book; Animal Stories,* retold by Georges Duplaix and illustrated by Feodor Rojankovsky; *The Golden Dictionary,* prepared by Ellen Wales Walpole and illustrated by Miss Elliott; *The Golden Almanac,* written by Dorothy A. Bennett, with illustrations by Masha; and two Disney-inspired titles.

Introducing a series of lavishly illustrated oversized books just then had to have been a high-stakes gamble. Yet the decision to do so was made with an essentially conservative long-term strategy in mind. Priced higher than Little Golden Books (although, at $1.00 to $1.50, still well below the average retail price of books of comparable size and scope), the Giants represented another attempt to win support for the Golden line from Simon and Schuster's core bookseller customers.

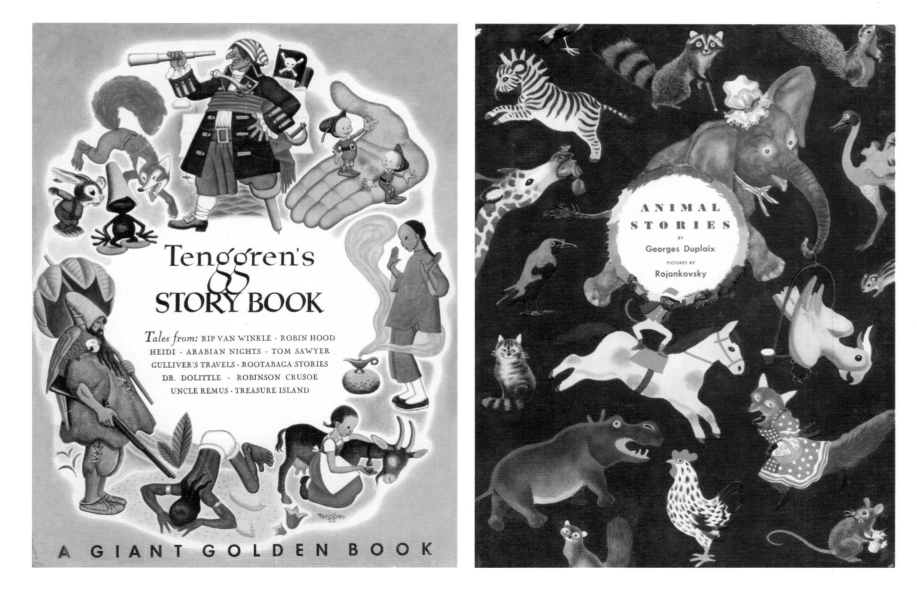

As one of the nation's largest printers, Western diverted much of its staff and equipment to war-related work. The company's contributions to the war effort were many: it produced, under contract with the government, 50 million military maps, 10 million packs of playing cards, and 12 million books for recreational reading by members of the armed services.[22] Airplane spotter charts, handbooks for navy fliers, pocket Bibles, and inspirational material on the "Rights We Defend" and the American "Way of Life" rolled off the presses in huge numbers. In addition, Whitman published *The Victory March,* a Disney children's book encouraging youngsters to collect War Savings Stamps, as well as dozens of other fiction and nonfiction books for schoolchildren, including some in the Better Little format, about all aspects of the war.

As hundreds of Western's male employees entered the armed services, women were given the chance to take over their jobs in the pressroom and bindery as well as on the publishing side of the business. By the spring of 1942, two Artists and Writers editors, Jerome Wyckoff and his assistant, George Wolfson, had received their induction notices. To fill in for them, a versatile young Whitman staff member named Jane Werner was dispatched from the Whitman office in Racine, where she had already proved her worth as both an editor and a writer. Werner later recalled her arrival at New York's Grand Central Terminal from Chicago on the overnight all-coach Pacemaker (a budget-minded far cry from the luxurious 20th Century Limited). During her tour of the Guild's drab offices on lower Fifth Avenue in a large commercial building occupied primarily by toy manufacturers' showrooms, Werner was surprised to find that the desk assigned to her did not come with a typewriter. When she mentioned this to Wolfson, he advised the newcomer to keep the fact to herself; otherwise, as he predicted in what proved to be one of the major understatements about her career, "They'll expect you to use it."[23] In all, over the next thirty-five years, Werner—writing under her own name and a variety of others, first as a staff member and from 1955 as a freelancer—supplied the text for more than a hundred Little Golden Books as well as more than four dozen Big, Giant, and Deluxe Golden editions spanning an encyclopedic range of subject matter, styles, and genres.

Notwithstanding Western's comparatively advantageous situation, the war began to take its toll. The total number of Little Golden titles published in 1943 was seven instead of the twelve (in three groups of four) that had originally been planned. To make way for the first Giants, it was decided that no new Little Goldens would be added to the list in 1944. (An exception was made for the not quite identically formatted first two Walt Disney's Little Library books, based on Disney licensed characters. These were *Through the Picture Frame,* written by Robert Edmunds, illustrated by the Walt Disney Studio, and based on *Ole Lukoie,* by Hans Christian Andersen; and *The Cold-Blooded Penguin,* written by Robert Edmunds, illustrated by the Walt Disney Studio, and based on the feature film *The Three Caballeros.*)

Western used what additional paper it had on hand to go back to press with the proven earlier Little Golden titles, all of which were effectively out of stock by late 1943.[24] In a further adjustment to circumstances, some of these reprints were prepared in truncated, twenty-eight-page editions (down from the original forty-two-page format), in some cases also with slightly reduced trim sizes. (Little Golden Books were later reduced to twenty-four pages, which remains standard today.) Thus began, in wartime, Golden's long and tangled history of repackaging its backlist titles, a practice greatly facilitated, from a business standpoint, by the flat-fee basis upon which the artists and writers typically worked, an arrangement that left the publisher free to reuse and alter their work at will.

In 1944, as the Golden partners continued to adapt to wartime conditions, they made the first major adjustments to their internal organization. In that year, Simon and Schuster created a new division, the Sandpiper Press, to work in tandem with the Artists and Writers Guild on all Golden projects.[25] Georges Duplaix left Western to head the new office (or was it rather that Sandpiper had been established in part to make a place for him at Simon and Schuster?).[26] The precise nature of the relationship that these two creative hothouses were to have with each other seems to have been left purposefully vague. Years later, Jane Werner [Watson] recalled having suspected, along with Lucille Ogle, that when Duplaix left the Guild, he "assumed A & W would gradually fade away,

Facing page, top: This paperback "Armed Services Edition" printed by Western would have fit neatly in a serviceman's back pocket.
Middle: Jerome Wyckoff as a senior editor at Artists and Writers Guild, Inc. From the February 1950 issue of The Westerner.
Bottom: George Wolfson as vice president of Artists and Writers Press, Inc. From the April 1966 issue of The Westerner.

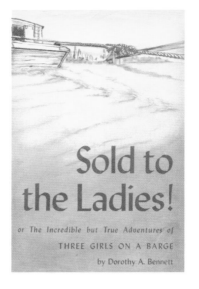

Below: The Golden Encyclopedia, 1946,
by Dorothy A. Bennett, illustrated by Cornelius DeWitt.

Facing page, top, left to right: Dorothy Bennett, Walt Disney, and
Jane Werner, around 1953. Courtesy of Special Collections and
University Archives, University of Oregon Libraries.
Bottom: The Golden Almanac, 1944, by Dorothy A. Bennett,
illustrated by Masha.

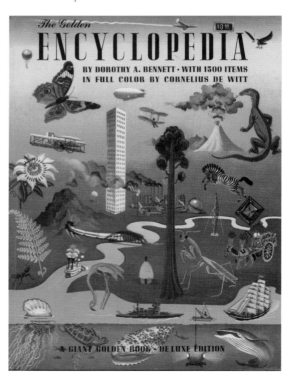

leaving the entire responsibility for creative production of the Golden Book line with Sandpiper Press." This did not happen, however, and according to Watson, a "degree of tacit and usually friendly competition [arose] between the two offices."[27]

Although most Little Golden Books still originated with the Guild, Sandpiper now contributed books to the line as well and cultivated its own group of authors and artists. From time to time, a Sandpiper staffer was called upon to write a book based on an idea floating around the office. To do so was considered a part of the job, as had long been the case at the Guild. When a Sandpiper secretary who completed one such assignment at home mustered the courage to ask Georges Duplaix whether she was not entitled to additional pay for her efforts, Duplaix, in his best Gallic manner, put a swift end to the conversation by decreeing that in his mind there was "no difference between the night and the day" and that he expected all Sandpiper employees to think likewise.[28]

In its first years, Sandpiper had its offices at 200 Fifth Avenue, the same building that the Guild was in, an arrangement that encouraged a relaxed give-and-take between the two staffs. Later, when the Guild's offices were in Rockefeller Center, and Sandpiper, after an interlude there, moved farther uptown to its own "ivory tower" above an elegant Madison Avenue jewelry shop, meetings became less frequent and more ritualized, and a "trunk line" was installed to maintain ready telephone communication. If a cultural divide defined the rivalry between the two groups, it came down to the Sandpiper staffers' belief that they hewed to a higher set of editorial standards, and to the Guild staffers' counter-conviction that they had the better understanding of how to make books succeed in the real world. Guild jokes vented frustration with Sandpiper perfectionism. A typical Sandpiper gibe was the remark that Ogle never accepted a book for publication without first consulting her doorman.[29]

Once established at Sandpiper, Duplaix made it known that he intended to spend as much of his time as possible painting at his villa in the south of France. Accordingly, he hired a second-in-command who he hoped would prove every bit as capable as Ogle. Dorothy A. Bennett came

to her new assignment with solid experience as an editor at the University of Minnesota Press and, more recently, as assistant curator in the education department of New York's American Museum of Natural History. Bennett, like Ogle, was widely traveled and widely read, and they shared a keen interest in science that in Bennett's case centered on astronomy and archeology. Her breezy memoir, *Sold to the Ladies!,* in which she recalled the Depression-era adventure of restoring by hand, and then inhabiting, a dilapidated barge moored in the Long Island Sound, attested to her steely resolve as much as it did to her spirit of enterprise and love of craftsmanship.[30] Bennett herself was less breezy than brisk, a hard-driving perfectionist who did not suffer fools gladly. But she easily won the respect of colleagues by sheer dint of her capacity for mastering the complexities of long-term, research-driven projects. Evidence of this talent emerged almost immediately in the form of *The Golden Almanac,* a Big Golden Book that Bennett both authored and shepherded into print during her first year on the job, to be followed two years later by the still more remarkable one-volume *Golden Encyclopedia.* Bennett's arrival did

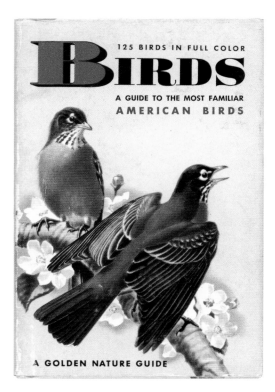

125 BIRDS IN FULL COLOR

BIRDS

A GUIDE TO THE MOST FAMILIAR
AMERICAN BIRDS

A GOLDEN NATURE GUIDE

Birds, revised 1956 edition.

Facing page, top: Lucy Sprague Mitchell, around 1951. Photo by Blackstone Studios. Courtesy of Bank Street College Archives, Bank Street College of Education.
Bottom: Mitchell's The New House in the Forest, *1946, illustrated by Eloise Wilkin.*

much to pave the way for Golden to press ahead with plans to publish its projected library of nonfiction books for school-age children. Illustrated reference books for adults would soon be in the offing as well, notably the Golden Guide series, which would start in 1949 with *Birds,* by Herbert S. Zim and Ira Gabrielson, illustrated by James Gordon Irving.[31]

Bennett's unwillingness to compromise her editorial standards was, by all accounts, a bit hard on colleagues' nerves, especially when it came time to cut corners or costs for the sake of keeping a project on schedule or within budget. A complex woman, she could be simultaneously generous and churlish, as when, responding to a poorly written unsolicited manuscript, she sent the hapless writer a dictionary by return mail, along with a rejection letter.[32] Still, it was hard to fault someone so clearly driven by selfless, high-minded motives. Taking the idealist's view, Bennett never tired of quoting an early slogan used to promote the Golden line: "Books and Bread."[33] It was simply obvious to her that, as one of life's necessities, the best possible children's books ought to be affordable to everyone.

Lucille Ogle's closest friends in publishing were Ursula Nordstrom and Louise Bonino, both of whose houses—Harper and Random House—were Artists and Writers clients. Perhaps what really drew the women together, however, was their shared sense of being outsiders within an already marginalized sector of publishing. Random's president, Bennett Cerf, made no secret of his disdain for "baby books," his admiration for *Babar* and Dr. Seuss notwithstanding; as a result, Bonino's department had drifted toward commercialism and failed to build the cachet of those at Viking, Houghton Mifflin, and Scribner. The department headed by Nordstrom rested on far more solid historical ground. But Nordstrom herself reveled in publishing books that poked holes in the library world's stuffy assumptions. With Little Golden Books, Ogle had given the librarians far worse to cluck their tongues at.

Looking back from retirement, Ogle recalled the ferocity of the librarians' resistance. "They did very, very nasty programs about [Golden Books]," she told a reporter, "and wrote critical articles about them, too.

They rejected the fact that you could make a good book cheap—basically, that's the real reason behind it. They all did."[34] Faced with this situation, Ogle remained stubbornly determined to win greater respectability for the line. Securing the endorsement of "Mary Reed, PhD" had been the first of many attempts to accomplish this goal by associating Golden with the work and reputations of a wide array of trusted authorities. Ogle's second such venture came in late 1943, when she and Georges Duplaix approached Lucy Sprague Mitchell, founder and chair of New York's Bank Street School, with the possibility of tapping the school's famed Writers Laboratory for manuscripts to be published in a special series of Little Golden Books.[35]

For the past three decades, Mitchell had worked tirelessly toward a systematic understanding of the stages of language development during the first seven years of life. And, in a bold attempt to pursue the real-world implications of her findings, she had created prototypes for a new, child-centered "here and now" literature for preschoolers, starting with *Here and Now Story Book* (1921), followed by a sequel coauthored by her students. Mitchell's conclusion that the very young were better served by playful stories about everyday experiences than by "timeless" fantasies about castles and kings put her directly at odds with the nation's most influential librarian-critics. For better or for worse, by the time Mitchell and Ogle met, the contempt of Anne Carroll Moore was something that Golden Books and Bank Street already shared.

A pragmatic visionary, Mitchell welcomed Ogle's proposal as a chance not only to generate much-needed income for the school but also to reach the largest possible audience with child-tested "here and now" stories. On the strength of a preliminary agreement that any such Little Golden Book would highlight the school's name, and that a full-fledged Bank Street series might follow, Mitchell and her colleagues went back to their typewriters. The first manuscripts to be accepted under the arrangement were Mitchell's own *The New House in the Forest* and a three-way collaboration coauthored by her, Bank Street nursery school director Jessie Stanton, and Irma Simonton Black, a music teacher and psychological researcher at the school and for years a Writers Laboratory regular.

The latter story, published as *The Taxi That Hurried,* with illustrations by Tibor Gergely, gave a slapstick account of a modern-day traffic jam. In their portrayal of the mother as a frazzled and demanding backseat driver, the authors offered young children a notably unvarnished appraisal of grown-up behavior. To do so might simply have seemed "progressive" to the coauthors, but mainstream America was not prepared for such candor; as historian Barbara Bader later reported, "there were complaints."[36] Publication of the first Bank Street books was originally planned for the 1944 Golden list. In December 1943, however, the prospect of continuing paper shortages forced an indefinite postponement.[37] The first two titles in a series that would eventually run to ten would finally see the light of day during the first full postwar year of 1946.

Unpublished artwork for The Taxi That Hurried, *1946, illustrated by Tibor Gergely.*

Meanwhile, as Mitchell and her colleagues braced themselves for a long wait, they explored other avenues for putting their ideas before the public. The syndicator of the Superman comics approached Mitchell about creating a comics series based on the two *Here and Now* storybooks. Also being considered was a children's series to be created by Bank Street under the sponsorship of various labor unions.[38] Neither possibility came to fruition, but the common premise—that reaching children with books might no longer require working within the library-sanctioned publishing system—now seemed less far-fetched than it had in decades.

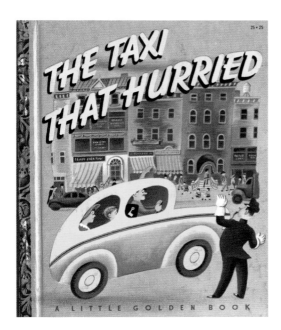

Given the library world's antipathy toward Little Golden Books, Ogle and her colleagues had no illusions about the prospects for any of their books' winning the American Library Association's Caldecott Medal. The best that Ogle could therefore hope to do was raid the henhouse by adding an occasional distinguished illustrator to the Golden list through the judicious use of money. In the summer of 1945, Ogle launched a behind-the-scenes campaign to enlist the services of the current medalist, Elizabeth Orton Jones.[39] As members of the American Library Association gathered in New York for their annual convention, Ogle scrambled to put her plan into action.

Jones had won the great prize for her ink and watercolor illustrations for *Prayer for a Child,* a picture book written by the celebrated author Rachel Field and published by Macmillan. It is easy to see why Ogle would have wished to work with her, even apart from the illustrator's newly elevated status. Jones, who had studied at the Chicago Art Institute School and in Paris, drew in a firmly delineated, nostalgic style that showed a striking affinity with the work of Eloise Wilkin, an artist whose illustrations Ogle had admired since her days at Harter.[40]

Before the festivities, Jones, an unassuming Midwesterner, took up temporary residence in the Waldorf-Astoria, the hotel in whose grand ballroom she would receive the medal and deliver an acceptance speech before an audience composed of hundreds of the field's luminaries. On her first morning in New York, while she was still settling into her luxurious quarters, she found a note tucked into a side compartment of her

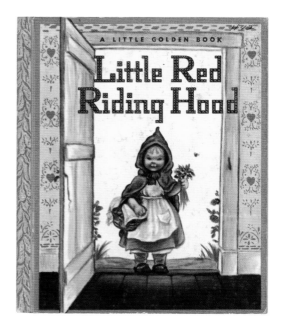

silver breakfast tray. It was a message from Lucille Ogle, an editor then unknown to her, praising her work and urging Jones to consider illustrating a Little Golden Book. Each morning thereafter, another note from Ogle appeared on the tray, expressing more or less the same sentiments. Before the convention adjourned, the two women met, and Jones, both charmed by the editor's attentions and happy about the substantial sum Ogle offered her, agreed to illustrate a story of Jones' choosing. Her *Little Red Riding Hood* appeared in the spring of 1948. Ogle's pride in having published the book remained keen even after members of the Woman's Christian Temperance Union flooded her office with letters expressing their outrage at Jones' final illustration, in which, at a celebratory meal shared by the young heroine, her grandmother, and the woodsman, Little Red raises a glass containing what appears to be a few drops of wine.[41]

At the time of Ogle's sporting pursuit of Elizabeth Orton Jones, Eloise Wilkin herself had only recently become a Golden Books illustrator. Ogle had written to Wilkin (via standard ground mail) in 1944 after admiring a book the artist had just illustrated for Oxford University Press, and had invited her to New York to talk about illustrating Golden Books.[42] Several years had passed since the two women had last been in touch, when Wilkin, as a relative newcomer to the field, had met the editor from Harter. They'd first worked together when, not long after Ogle's move to New York, Wilkin had illustrated a rather pedestrian book, *Work and Play the Healthy Way,* written by Ogle and published under the Guild imprint.[43] Hearing from Ogle again after all those years had taken Wilkin by surprise. She responded "nonchalantly," as she later recalled, to the editor's overture, noting that since she now had a husband and four children to take care of, it would not be easy for her to take the long trip to the city from her home in the Finger Lakes region of upstate New York. Undeterred, Ogle telephoned the artist long-distance, an extravagant gesture at the time, with the news that she had not just one book project in mind for her but three. Duly impressed by the extent of Ogle's interest and pleasantly reminded of the editor's abundant warmth, Wilkin agreed to a meeting at Simon and Schuster's luxurious Rockefeller Center offices. A friend she mentioned

all this to beforehand cautioned her "not to be awed" by the publisher's headquarters, which (unlike the Guild's far more Spartan downtown shop) boasted a terrace garden and spectacular wraparound Manhattan views.[44] There was little chance of this, of course, not only because Wilkin had spent the first four years of her freelance career living in the city, which she had come to know quite well, but also because, as the clear-eyed, plain-talking self-described rebel of her family, Wilkin had never been fooled by the glittery surface appeal of either people or places. It was for this very reason that the artist, while still a student at the Rochester Athenaeum and Mechanics Institute (now the Rochester Institute of Technology), had realized that she would never succeed as a fashion illustrator. As she later recalled with amusement, a freelance fashion sketch of hers for a Rochester department store had prompted the buyer to "complain . . . bitterly of my dowdy women with oversized feet."[45] She was simply incapable of flattering others, and of being flattered.

Ogle's overture could not, however, have come at a better time. Starting in the 1930s, Wilkin had illustrated books for a number of publishers, including a picture book written by her older sister, Esther, called *Mrs. Peregrine and the Yak* (Holt, 1938), which received a flurry of good publicity. But then motherhood had taken over her life, leaving her with much less time to pursue her career than she might have wished. As she wryly commented of this period, "I found myself growing less and less interested in PAINTS and more and more interested in POTS AND PANS."[46] By 1944, Wilkin felt ready to reimmerse herself in her artwork.

The meeting with Ogle went exceedingly well. Their old acquaintance quickly blossomed into full-blown friendship. On subsequent visits, Wilkin would come to town as her editor's houseguest; Ogle in turn would become a favorite visitor at the artist's home. Before the year was out, the Guild signed Wilkin to a multibook contract and put her on a demanding schedule that committed her to illustrating as many as four books a year.[47]

Wilkin made her Golden debut in 1946 as the illustrator of one of the long-postponed Bank Street Little Golden Books, Lucy Sprague Mitchell's *The New House in the Forest*. Thereafter, hardly a year passed

Facing page, top left: From Busy Timmy, *1948, by Kathryn and Byron Jackson, illustrated by Eloise Wilkin. The Poky Little Puppy adorns Timmy's bucket.*
Top right: Eloise Wilkin, 1953.
Bottom: Eloise Wilkin, left, and her sister, Esther, at work on Mrs. Peregrine and the Yak, *1938. Both photos courtesy of and copyright by Deborah Wilkin Springett.*

This page: From Wilkin's Baby Listens, *1960, by Esther Wilkin.*

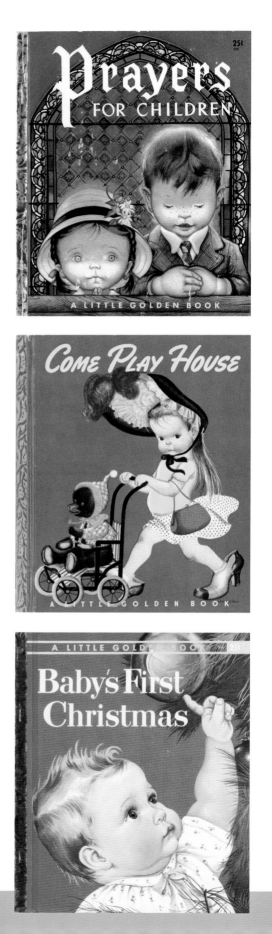

without two or more new Wilkin books on the Golden list. In nearly all of them, the artist depicted her own children or their friends, the family dog, and the rustic stone cottages of her region.

A fastidious researcher, she often consulted the pages of the 1901 *Sears, Roebuck Catalogue* in search of the right period wallpaper design or wicker chair with which to complete the harmonious interior settings that are a hallmark of her work. At the same time, Wilkin enjoyed a certain reputation for absentmindedness. When her artwork for *Come Play House* (1948), written by Edith Osswald, arrived at the Guild office, someone noticed that Wilkin had, as she later recalled, drawn "a picture of a little boy sucking a lollipop with the underside of his tongue. The drawing came back with a note to the effect that they had conducted a survey in the office. They sent out for lollipops for everyone, including the elevator boy. They tried in vain all afternoon to lick lollipops with the underside of their tongues, and came to the conclusion that I would have to change the drawing."[48]

Although Ogle would always remain Wilkin's closest friend in publishing, the artist came to know Georges Duplaix well enough to learn a valuable lesson in book design from him. According to Wilkin's daughter and biographer, Deborah Wilkin Springett, Duplaix urged the artist always to "make her cover illustrations large and uncluttered in order to create an immediate impact on the buying public. Eloise knew that her fans found her rendering of children's faces especially appealing. Many of her best-selling books had covers that were a reflection of this knowledge."[49] Ole Risom, Western's art director from 1952 to 1972, pinpointed another, related strength when he observed, "[Wilkin] managed to illustrate children just as people imagined their own children should look or did look like."[50] Sackloads of fan letters testified to this aspect of her illustrations' appeal. One mother who had purchased a copy of *The Wonders of the Seasons* (written by Bertha Morris Parker, 1966) for her family's home library wrote, "And what has made it even more enjoyable is the fact that we all agree the little girl on the cover is a perfect likeness to our baby."[51]

This page, top: Wilkin's Prayers for Children, *1952.*
Bottom: Wilkin's Baby's First Christmas, *1959, by Esther Wilkin.*

Facing page: From Wilkin's Baby Dear, *1962, by Esther Wilkin.*

Following pages: From Wilkin's My Little Golden Book About God, *1956, by Jane Werner Watson.*

Avi Remembers *The Poky Little Puppy*

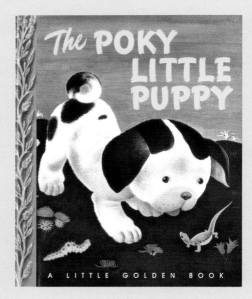

Q: In your 2003 Newbery Medal acceptance speech, you recalled *The Poky Little Puppy* as one of the first books you knew as a child.

A: I adored that book. The funny thing about it is that for years I had a distinct memory of what it was about and identified closely with the story's hero. But when I picked up a copy a couple of years ago I found it was very different from the book I remembered, that I had supplied a story that was very much my own.

In the book it's the puppy's curiosity that makes him "poky." He's curious about simple, basic things. It's so elemental. And the sense of return is also such a powerful thing: you venture forward, but there's always home to come back to. There are echoes of "Peter Rabbit."

But for me as a child, my sense of identification with the character was simply based on the fact that I was late all the time. I was the one who was always "behind," who was always having to be called up, as it were.

Q: You seem to be describing not just a slowpoke but also an outsider.

A: I certainly would have identified with that element of the character. I think most kids would. I have a twin sister, and there was always some level of sibling rivalry between her and me, and between the two of us and our brother, who is two years older. There were always shifting allegiances.

Q: Did you have a dog?

A: Not a dog of my own but a family dog. My father was a psychiatrist, and the story he told was that a grateful patient had presented him with a cocker spaniel puppy—but that it had grown up into an Irish setter! The dog grew so big that we eventually had to give him away. I always thought it was a brilliant piece of revenge by that patient.

Q: How did books come into your house?

A: My mother was interested in children's books. At one time she had even aspired to writing them. She bought us books and took us to the library and read to us every night. In the early years, my brother, my sister, and I were all in one room, dormitory-style, so I think she must have read *The Poky Little Puppy* to us together.

Q: Would you have known the author's or illustrator's name then?

A: No, but younger children don't generally. I knew a book by the way it looked. I knew *The Poky Little Puppy* by the golden trim along the edge.

NO DESSERTS EVER
UNLESS PUPPIES NEVER
DIG HOLES UNDER THIS
FENCE AGAIN
!

Books for Baby Boomers

During the immediate postwar years, Golden Books experienced explosive growth as a dramatic rise in the birthrate—a trend first registered in 1942—created a rapidly expanding market for children's books. The impressive postlaunch statistics of the early 1940s were about to be dwarfed. In 1946, when Albert Leventhal told Western executives that he would need a supply of one million Little Golden Books to sell for the following year, the people in Racine responded with skepticism, expressing doubt both that Western was capable of printing that many books and that Leventhal was capable of selling them. As it turned out, not one million but five million books were printed and sold in 1947.[1]

The Saggy Baggy Elephant, by Kathryn and Byron Jackson, illustrated by Gustaf Tenggren, and *Noises and Mr. Flibberty-Jib,* by Gertrude Crampton, illustrated by Eloise Wilkin, both joined the Golden list that year, as did *The Golden Egg Book,* by Margaret Wise Brown, illustrated

Facing page: From Animal Friends, *1953, by Jane Werner, illustrated by Garth Williams.*

by Leonard Weisgard. For the next decade and a half, no Golden season lacked for titles destined to last.

In cities, suburbs, and small towns all across America, youngsters pored over the pages of *When I Grow Up* (by Kay and Harry Mace, illustrated by Corinne Malvern, 1950), wondering whether to become cowboys or ringmasters or mechanics in later life. Those with newborn siblings at home had *The New Baby* (written by Ruth and Harold Shane, illustrated by Eloise Wilkin, 1948) and *Linda and Her Little Sister* (written by Esther Wilkin, illustrated by Eloise Wilkin, 1954) to help them get a bit more comfortable with the idea. Those preparing to make the great leap from stay-at-home to kindergartner had *Jerry at School* (written by Kathryn and Byron Jackson, illustrated by Corinne Malvern, 1950) to help demystify the experience. For children about to embark on their first long-distance train trip, there was *All Aboard!* (written by Marion Conger, illustrated by Corinne Malvern, 1952). For youngsters who loved their pets (as well as for those whose parents would not allow them to have any), there were *Laddie and the Little Rabbit* (written and photographed by Bill Gottlieb, 1952) and any number of other choices.[2] More than a few books took their places on the racks purely for the fun they held in store: *The Lively Little Rabbit* (written by Ariane, illustrated by Gustaf Tenggren, 1943); *The Seven Sneezes* (by Olga Cabral, illustrated by Tibor Gergely, 1948); and Gertrude Crampton's *Noises and Mr. Flibberty-Jib,* in which Eloise Wilkin revealed a waggish side to her gift that one might hardly have suspected of the painter of angelic children and their serenely calm and collected mothers.

Youngsters encountered few unconventional role models in the books. Fathers went to work while mothers stayed at home, did the cooking and shopping, and looked after the children. If *Bobby and His Airplanes* (written by Helen Palmer, illustrated by Tibor Gergely, 1949) typified the Little Goldens addressed primarily to boys, then *Susie's New Stove* (written by Jane Werner as Annie North Bedford, illustrated by Corinne Malvern, 1950) exemplified those aimed at their sisters. Most readers doubtless accepted the picture of the world presented in the books as an idealized but essentially accurate reflection of their own.

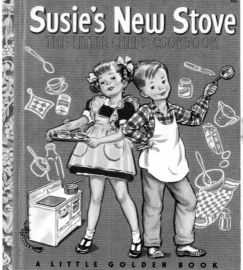

From Susie's New Stove.

When, in *The Lonely Crowd,* sociologist David Riesman cited *Tootle* as an emblematic fable of mid-twentieth-century Americans' growing preference for conformist, or "other-directed," styles of decision-making and group behavior, he touched on a theme that countless first-generation Golden readers would live out for themselves in the years to come, whether as go-getting "organization men" and suburban Republican cloth-coat "homemakers" or (for those who chose to reject the story's lesson about the rewards of staying on track) as alienated, Jack Kerouac–inflected rebels and partisans of the 1960s counterculture.[3]

Little Golden Books' focus on early childhood's most widely shared experiences was highlighted by the manner in which the books were ultimately displayed to shoppers. During the 1940s (and periodically afterward), retailers were required to order preselected assortments of the books rather than purchase individual titles, as was customary in the book trade.[4] The titles for each assortment were chosen as representative of one or another of the line's preestablished thematic or subject "slots." In stores,

each book in the assortment had its slot in the specially designed Little Golden sales rack. A given assortment might consist of a dog book, a circus book, a baby book, and so on. Oblivious to the hidden machinery of the strategy, the writers for the Bank Street series were taken aback one day when they received a raft of rejection letters in response to their latest submissions. The new stories, it was explained, were too similar to others of which the publisher already had an ample supply. The writers agreed to consult with Ogle about future story ideas.[5] In this way, the Bank Street collaboration inched forward.

With the war's end, hundreds of Western employees returned from military service to their old jobs. The company had always enjoyed a well-deserved reputation for taking care of its employees. Now, aware of the need to retrain many of the veterans, the management in Racine established the Western Technical Institute as an in-house apprenticeship and reorientation program. A sign of the company's overall health was Western's ability to expand even during this choppy transitional period. It absorbed related businesses such as the Wolff Printing Company, of St. Louis, which printed billboard graphics and point-of-purchase displays used by retailers. And as the publishing operations in New York and Beverly Hills continued to prosper, the Institute added a weeklong Orientation in Graphic Arts course aimed at introducing editors and other publishing personnel to the basic processes entailed in the manufacture of a book.[6] In 1947, in a powerful reaffirmation of E.H.'s life-long commitment to his employees, Western extended its profit-sharing program to include not only executives and middle managers but all its salaried and hourly-wage workers.[7]

For some of Western's women employees, however, the transition from war to peacetime proved to be problematic. Among the veterans who returned to the Guild's New York offices in 1945 were the two editors Jane Werner had been sent east to substitute for. With Werner's services apparently no longer needed in New York, Western reassigned her to Beverly Hills, where she thrived, however stoically, as a writer and overseer of scores of licensed character projects. Perhaps in part to maintain her

Facing page, bottom: Unpublished artwork for Tibor Gergely's Tootle, *1945, by Gertrude Crampton.*

This page: Jane Werner in an undated photograph. Courtesy of Bette Bardeen.

Above: The Golden Bible, *1946.*

Facing page, top: The Jacksons as sketched by Gustaf Tenggren for the jacket of their collaboration, Farm Stories, *1946.*

sense of balance as she adjusted to her new role, Werner, writing under the pseudonym Elsa Jane Werner, undertook one of the most intellectually demanding (and gratifying) projects of her career, the text of *The Golden Bible: Stories from the Old Testament,* for which Feodor Rojankovsky created impressive illustrations. Within two years, Ogle concluded that the Guild, with its burgeoning list, needed Werner in New York more than ever, and arranged for her return. As for the shelfful of licensed character books that she churned out on assignment, Werner, whatever her thoughts about them as literature, found that she had a knack for writing in that vein and continued to do so from her New York office. As she later recalled, "I felt particular private satisfaction when, in the [1952] *New York Times* Christmas round-up of books for children the reviewer said she never had thought she would find herself recommending a Disney book, but that she had liked *Donald Duck and Santa Claus* by Annie North Bedford."[8]

As a senior Guild editor, Werner worked with Byron and Kathryn Jackson, the Golden list's only writing team and the coauthors of some of the line's most popular titles, starting with *The Saggy Baggy Elephant*

(illustrated by Gustaf Tenggren, 1947). The Jacksons had both begun their professional lives as visual artists. They'd met when Byron, whom Werner found "rather quiet and serious," was a college art instructor and Kathryn—"tall, slender, and glamorous"—was a student in his class. Werner never learned the secret of the couple's writing procedure but came to believe that Byron most likely provided "much of the substantial information in the background of the stories" and Kathryn contributed the "poetic imagination and a touch of the fey." Whatever their arrangement, they kept any number of Golden artists well supplied with manuscripts. In 1951 alone, the Jacksons added five new books to the line: *Christopher and the Columbus* (illustrated by Tibor Gergely), *A Day at the Beach* (illustrated by Corinne Malvern), *Here Comes the Parade* (illustrated by Richard Scarry), and *Pantaloon* (illustrated by Leonard Weisgard), as well as a *Wizard of Oz*–inspired book written under the joint pseudonym Peter Archer. The following year, they published several more, including Kathryn's classic *Tawny Scrawny Lion,* illustrated by Gustaf Tenggren. As Watson later observed, theirs was a "monumental" contribution that over the years "filled a Golden Book shelf of their own."[9]

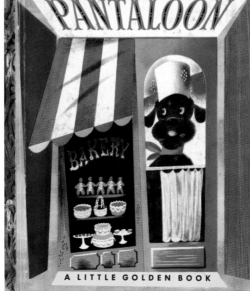

Tempering somewhat the jubilation following the end of combat in August 1945 was the realization that the home-front shortages that Americans had patiently endured were going to remain a fact of their lives awhile longer. In early 1947, Simon and Schuster was still offering earnest apologies to booksellers for failing to fulfill as many orders, and failing to issue as many new Golden titles, as the publisher had pledged to do. More than fifty new titles *were* nearing completion, readers of that year's spring catalog learned, but "because of manufacturing uncertainties, we did not feel it wise to list them [all] in this catalogue of the year's 'definite' publications."[10]

Leading the roster of "definites" for 1947 was the title that marked the auspicious debut on the Golden list of Margaret Wise Brown, a writer (then best known for Harper's *The Runaway Bunny* and *Little Fur Family*) to whom *Life* magazine had recently devoted a celebrity profile.[11] This was *The Golden Egg Book,* a Big Golden Book illustrated by Leonard Weisgard. It featured the artist's winsome bunnies and lavishly detailed wildflower borders, and a characteristic Brown fable about curiosity's leading to a deeper, more satisfying connection to life. The prolific author, who enjoyed exploring the opposite sides of a question, had already written many "here and now"–style picture books about contemporary city sights and sounds, and decided in this instance to offer urban children a heady encounter with wild nature's everyday wonders. To bring this off, she invited Weisgard, her most frequent collaborator, to her primitive summer cottage on the island of Vinalhaven,

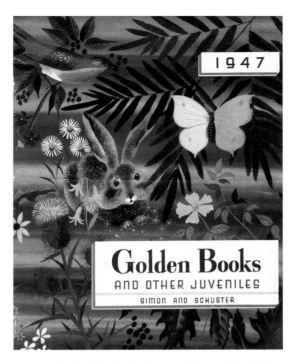

off the coast of Maine. When Weisgard's hay fever got the better of him, she simply put the artist to work indoors, stationing him by a window to which she returned, periodically, with armloads of fresh-picked flowers for him to paint from behind the glass.[12]

Further fueling anticipation of the spectacular book as its spring publication date neared was the news that Weisgard had won the 1947 Caldecott Medal for *The Little Island,* another picture book written by Brown (as Golden MacDonald, published by Doubleday). What was more, he had *also* won a Caldecott Honor that year for *Rain Drop Splash,* written by Alvin Tresselt. Released in time for Easter, *The Golden Egg Book* was a great and immediate success. Satisfied that her latest publishing relationship was off to a solid start, Brown flew to Ireland in August for a rest before the fall publication by Harper of three new picture books, including one intriguingly titled *Goodnight Moon.*[13]

Facing page: From The Golden Bunny, *1953, by Margaret Wise Brown, illustrated by Leonard Weisgard.*

This page, top left: Leonard Weisgard at work on a UNICEF card, around 1954.
Top right: The cover of the 1947 Golden Books catalog featured Weisgard's artwork for the endpapers of The Golden Egg Book.
Below: The Golden Christmas Tree, *1988, by Jan Wahl, was one of Weisgard's final projects for Golden Books.*

Following pages, left: Detail of Weisgard's endpapers for Pussy Willow, *1951, by Margaret Wise Brown.*
Right: Detail of Weisgard's cover artwork for The Golden Bunny.

Margaret Wise Brown's swift emergence as Golden's lead author dramatically extended the impact of Lucy Sprague Mitchell's ideas. Other Little Golden Books, from *Scuffy the Tugboat,* by Gertrude Crampton, illustrated by Tibor Gergely (1946), to *Let's Go Shopping with Peter and Penny,* by Lenora Combes (1948), also bore the unmistakable imprint of Mitchell's "here and now" brand of realism for preschoolers. Not even these contributions marked the limit of Mitchell's influence. By the spring of 1945, while the official Bank Street series remained in limbo, another of Mitchell's one-time protégées, Edith Thacher Hurd, had decided, in the progressive spirit of cooperative enterprise, that it might be fun to write a few Little Golden Books in collaboration with her old friend Brownie.[14] Brown and Hurd rendezvoused in San Francisco, where Hurd was completing her wartime military intelligence service, and devised a plan for a handful of "little civics books," which would chronicle the activities of the working people—postmen, milkmen, coal miners, and others—who made modern daily life function effectively. With a book about firefighters at the top of their list, Hurd arranged for an interview with the men at her local station house while Brown, who preferred to sleep late and keep to a leisurely schedule dictated by her mood, found some excuse for not going along. Brown's contribution to the project was far from negligible, however, as she could always be counted on to call out just the right phrase from her bath as her diligent collaborator, huddled over a typewriter in the next room, pecked away at the keyboard. If Hurd did the legwork, she also brought to bear her own considerable skill as a story-teller. As a good-luck gesture, the collaborators named the head of the household whose family is saved from the fire Hurricane Jones, Brown's affectionate nickname for Edith's husband, illustrator Clement Hurd, who remained on active duty in the Pacific.

Centered as the story was on the unsung heroism of ordinary working people, the dynamism of powerful machines, and the helter-skelter drama of modern-day city life, *Five Little Firemen* proved the perfect vehicle for illustrator Tibor Gergely. Some of the most robust work of his career found its way onto the book's pages.

Facing page, top left: The original cover of Scuffy the Tugboat. *Top right: Margaret Wise Brown with Crispin's Crispian, in an undated photograph by Consuelo Kanaga. Margaret Wise Brown. Copy print from original safety negative, 2½ x 2½ inches. The Brooklyn Museum 82.65.1833. Gift of Wallace Putnum from the Estate of Consuelo Kanaga. Middle: Tibor Gergely's 1955 revised cover of* Scuffy the Tugboat.

This page, top: Gergely's Seven Little Postmen, *1952, by Margaret Wise Brown and Edith Thacher Hurd. At left: From* Seven Little Postmen. *Bottom right:* Five Little Firemen, *1948.*

In 1947, Simon and Schuster opened a major new channel for the sale of Golden Books by introducing the twenty-five-cent books to supermarkets. The unconventional plan hinged on a series of new alliances forged with the nation's food brokers, a network of distributors whose existence, until then, had not been seen as relevant to publishers.[15] The Jewel Tea and Food Fair chains were the first to carry the Golden line. Within a year, Little Golden Books could be purchased in more than 1,200 supermarkets nationwide.

In 1948, the publisher circulated an elaborate four-page advertising piece, with illustrations by an unknown artist named Richard Scarry,

Facing page: From Five Little Firemen.

This page: From the whimsical ad aimed at supermarket chains, illustrated by Richard Scarry.

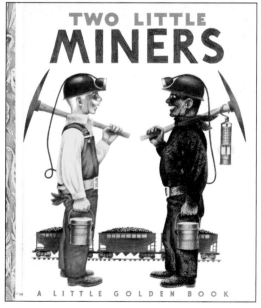

recounting in tongue-in-cheek fairy-tale fashion the details of the company's latest sales masterstroke.[16] The logic of the ad, which was aimed at persuading laggard food merchants to make a place in their stores for Golden's highly profitable display racks, was unassailable: "Turnover? As fast as in canned goods. Just put them out and *s-w-i-s-h!*—they're gone!" Not only were the racks free, the advertisement pointed out, but stocking the books entailed no financial risk whatsoever. "*Guaranteed sale* means . . . they're 100 percent returnable." Simon and Schuster had been the first publisher to allow its retail customers to return unsold copies of a book for a full refund—a practice that had rattled the industry when it was introduced in the 1920s. The arrangement worked so well as an incentive that other publishers felt compelled to offer comparable terms of sale; eventually, a return policy became the industry standard.[17]

Jane Werner Watson recalled the day late in the summer of 1948 when Lucille Ogle summoned her to her office to meet Richard Scarry, the "tall, meticulously groomed, solemn young man" who had stopped by to show his portfolio. "Round-faced and wide-eyed," Scarry had come to them "fresh from a Boston art school and the army, and very much the proper Bostonian of half a hundred years ago."[18] His father, it later emerged, owned a Boston department store that he very much wished to pass down to the younger Scarry. When the latter chose not to abandon art for commerce, the elder Scarry grimly forecast a life of poverty and spaghetti dinners for his son.[19]

For Scarry, as it turned out, fame and fortune were what lay in store, though not for several years to come. In the meantime, the Guild presented him with the prospect of steady employment and a comfortable living. In December 1948, Scarry signed a one-year exclusive services contract that obliged him to create the artwork for two Little Golden Books and two Golden Story Books (the latter being part of a series, which ran from 1949 to 1951, of 128-page story collections). In return for this substantial amount of work, Scarry was to receive $4,800, payable in $400 monthly installments. The contract, which was renewable for up to five years, seemed generous enough, even if the agreement did not provide for royalty payments based on future sales.[20] Grateful to have landed as well as he had, the newly married artist completed a total of six books—two more than were required of him—in 1949. *Two Little Miners,* by Margaret Wise Brown and Edith Thacher Hurd—the latest installment in the coauthors' "little civics" series—appeared first in store racks, even though it was the second book, after *The Boss of the Barnyard and Other Stories* (a Golden Story Book written by Joan Hubbard), that Scarry had illustrated. The artist who had begun his association with Golden Books by depicting the Golden rack system of supermarket sales now found his own work subject to the vagaries of that system's mysterious laws of assortment.

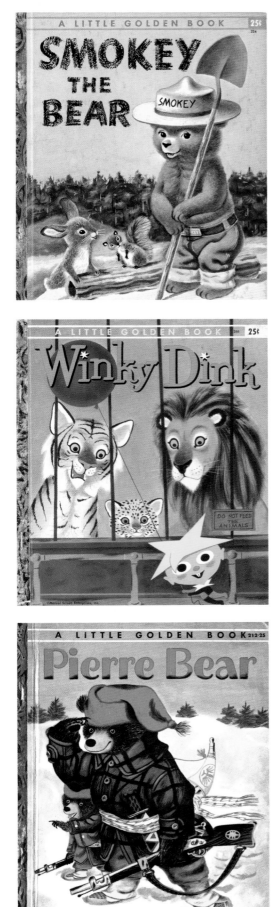

Top: The spring 1949 Golden Books catalog heralded the success of the "canary-colored, unbreakable" Little Golden Records. Bottom: A 1959 Little Golden Book and Record.

As the Golden partners extended their reach into new sales channels, they also experimented with new media. In the fall of 1948, Little Golden Records debuted with a list of twelve 78-rpm records selling for twenty-five cents apiece. Each durable bright yellow disk came in a decorative board sleeve approximately the size of a Little Golden Book. A story text was printed on the inside sleeve. The idea had come from the suggestion cards that Simon and Schuster had inserted in some of the first Little Golden Books. Parents who were fond of the books had expressed their frustration with not having enough time to reread the stories aloud as often as their children wished. Records, reasoned Arthur Shimkin, Leon's nephew and the person put in charge of the project, could do the reading for them, leaving the mother of the house free to bake or sew or attend to baby. Shimkin hired Mitchell Miller, the bandleader later known for the popular television program *Sing Along with Mitch,* to conduct his orchestra on recordings that featured musical settings composed by Alec Wilder, Ruth Cleary Patterson, Miller himself, and others. In the venture's first few years, an extraordinary roster of performers lent their talents to the enterprise, including Jimmy Durante, Hoagy Carmichael, Bing Crosby, Roy Rogers and Dale Evans, Burgess Meredith, Danny Kaye, Art Carney, and *The Milton Berle Show*'s "Men of Texaco" quartet.[21]

About that time, a second wave of artists in exile came to work for the Guild, greatly increasing the depth of the Golden talent pool. Far from being escapees from a war zone, however, as Rojankovsky and Gergely had been, these illustrators had fled to New York from Southern California, where, during the years immediately before World War II, they had worked in the burgeoning animation industry, nearly all of them for Disney. Members of the group included Aurelius Battaglia, John Parr (J. P.) Miller, Alice and Martin Provensen, and Mary Blair. Only Alice Provensen had no connection to Disney, having practiced her craft at the rival Walter Lantz Studio, creator of the Woody Woodpecker cartoons. Alice met her husband, a former member of the elite Disney Character Model Department, during the war years while both were engaged in making U.S. Navy training films. Toward the end of 1945,

when the couple moved to New York, their old friend Gustaf Tenggren introduced them to Ogle and her staff. J. P. Miller, who served in the navy, met Georges Duplaix in New York during the war and was perhaps responsible for bringing his friend Battaglia, a freelancer for *Vanity Fair,* to the Guild. Blair's path to becoming a Golden artist was a bit more complicated, and followed the others' by a few years.

Although their individual stories varied, it is fair to say that most of the former animation artists left California in search of greater creative control and recognition than they were likely to be granted by Disney. Like many another émigré group, they kept up their friendships once in New York. J. P. Miller, a slightly built, gregarious native of the city, made it easy for them to do so by opening his studio in the evening as an informal salon, where the regulars enjoyed rubbing shoulders and clinking glasses with the seemingly endless parade of celebrity artists and writers

Left to right: J. P. Miller, Richard Scarry, and Martin Provensen in an undated photograph. Courtesy of George Miller.

of Miller's acquaintance. Richard Scarry and his wife, Patsy, who was an advertising copywriter, happily fell in with this sociable crowd, becoming regulars at Miller's midtown soirées before moving to Connecticut, where on weekends the party continued. Good fellowship seems largely to have trumped professional jealousy within the fiercely talented group. Scarry, for one, was generous in praising Miller's lightly held mastery of the elements of illustration: draftsmanship, composition, characterization, and color. In turn, Miller—the unsung creator of Disney's immortal Dopey, Gepetto, and Dumbo and ever the puckish prankster when he was not sidetracked by periodic bouts of depression—had his own ways of showing his friendship. Once, after having lent Jack, as J. P.'s friends called him, their Connecticut house for the weekend, the Scarrys returned home to find a cow—or rather, a very lifelike painted wooden cutout of a cow—lolling on their lawn, compliments of the artist. It was perhaps a playful nod to Miller's greater accomplishments when Scarry, in the cover drawing for his first solo effort as both author and illustrator—*The Great Big Car and Truck Book* (1951)—depicted himself and Patsy blithely tooling along in their little MG beside a far more substantial vehicle driven by "Jack the Sign Painter."[22]

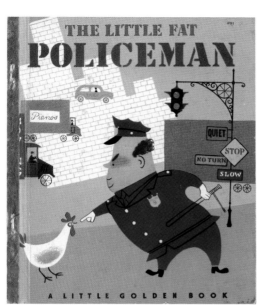

At left: Officer Renny Hoogerhuis of the Racine Police Force poses with The Little Fat Policeman *for the May 1955 issue of* The Westerner. *The 1950 book, by Margaret Wise Brown and Edith Thacher Hurd and illustrated by the Provensens, was included in the orientation kit given to every rookie cop on the New York police force in 1955.*

Miller, the Provensens (who, like the Jacksons, worked for Golden in mysterious, seamless collaboration), and their colleagues all painted and drew in highly individualized styles that nonetheless reflected some of the major tendencies in postwar graphic art and design. Deftly straddling the line between traditional representation and modernist abstraction, each of these inventive artists strove for an airy lightness and brightness of being-on-the-page that belonged to the new streamlined age of glass-box skyscrapers, ribbon highways, and casual middle-class suburban living. Festive colors applied in bold, surprising combinations made simply opening one of their books a challenging as well as playful visual adventure.

In the banner Golden year of 1948, the Provensens debuted on the Little Golden Book list as the illustrators of Jane Werner's *Mr. Noah and His Family* (the couple had already made a great impression the previous year with their artwork for another Guild project, *The Fireside Book of Folk Songs,* edited by Margaret Bradford Boni); Battaglia made his first appearance with *Pat-a-Cake;* and Miller had the first two publications of his career with *Little Peewee Or, Now Open the Box,* written by *Pat the Bunny* author Dorothy Kunhardt, and *Tommy's Wonderful Rides,* by Helen Palmer. Before the year was out, memorable new work by nearly all the earlier major artists had also been added to the line: Rojankovsky's exuberant broad-brush watercolors for Phyllis McGinley's *A Name for Kitty* and its companion, *Our Puppy,* by Jane Werner as Elsa Ruth Nast, and his sprightly but nonetheless haunting *The Three Bears;* Eloise Wilkin's *The New Baby,* by Ruth and Harold Shane, and *Busy Timmy,* by the Jacksons; Gertrude Elliott's *The Little Golden Book of Words,* by Selma Lola Chambers; Gustaf Tenggren's *Little Black Sambo* (a reillustration of the Helen Bannerman text that would become an object of controversy decades later); and Tibor Gergely's uproarious comic art for *Five Little Firemen* and *The Seven Sneezes.* And Elizabeth Orton Jones was not the only illustrious artist to publish a Little Golden Book that year. Garth Williams illustrated Margaret Wise Brown's *The Golden Sleepy Book* and Dorothy Kunhardt's *Tiny Animal Stories.*

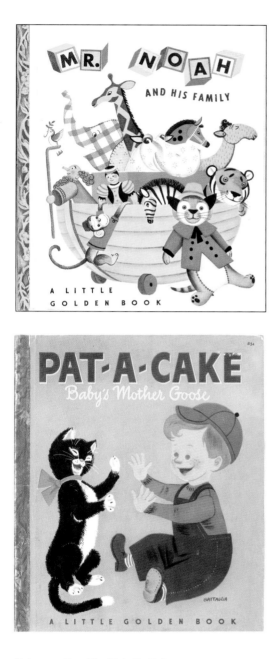

Facing page: From The Little Fat Policeman.

This page, at left: From The Color Kittens.

The addition of Williams to the list just then was a particular cause for alarm at the traditional trade houses. Although the London-trained artist had made his American debut only three years earlier as the illustrator of E. B. White's *Stuart Little,* Williams' adroitly witty black-and-white line drawings for the longtime Harper author's latest bestseller had received more than the usual passing nod of praise. Knowing that White was unlikely to produce another juvenile manuscript anytime soon, Nordstrom hastened to involve Williams in the work of the prolific Margaret Wise Brown, trusting that once the author and artist met, creative sparks would fly, with Harper thereby standing a chance of monopolizing Williams' services. The plan seemed to be working as Williams followed up his initial Harper triumph with full-color illustrations for Brown's *Little Fur Family,* an extravagantly produced novelty book that *Life* magazine singled out for attention.

Although Nordstrom was a controversial enough figure to have her detractors in the library world, she was regarded as an industry standard-bearer. Almost any illustrator would have considered it a high honor to appear on her list. Thus, when news of Williams' defection spread through publishing circles, it was taken as a sign that the Golden operation, with its leviathan print runs and aura of money, did indeed pose a serious threat to the old order. If Golden could lure Williams, department directors had to ask, what artist's loyalty might still be taken for granted?

Impulsive, restless, and often in need of money, Williams was not the sort to be bound by old-fashioned loyalties. He might well have gone to the Artists and Writers Guild on his own. Years later, he recalled that it was in the Guild offices that he and Brown met, shortly after he had agreed to illustrate her *Little Fur Family* for Harper.[23] The mercurial author and artist enjoyed working together. They shared a taste for mischief, had compatible ideas about children and books, and could sympathize with each other's tumultuous private lives. Because both spent money lavishly, they also welcomed the chance to present Nordstrom with an additional reason to keep the two of them happy. In late October 1946, as they awaited publication of *Little Fur Family,* Brown telegrammed Nordstrom, threatening—rather fantastically, considering

Garth Williams in an undated photograph. Courtesy of HarperCollins Children's Books.

Following pages, left: Williams' cover artwork for Home for a Bunny, *1956, by Margaret Wise Brown.*
Right: Williams' cover artwork for The Giant Golden Book of Elves and Fairies, *1951, edited by Jane Werner.*

HOME FOR A BUNNY

ELVES AND FAIRIES

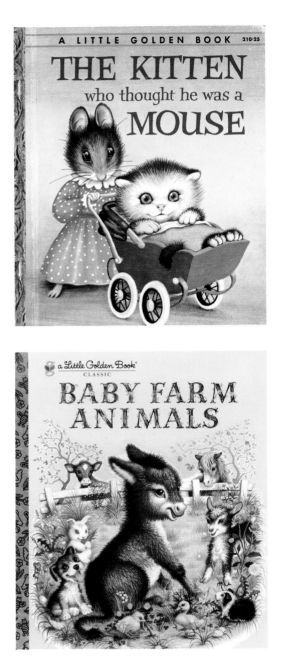

that a contract was already in force—that if Harper did not agree to commit to what she deemed a sufficiently large first printing of the book, she and Williams would pull the project and offer it to Simon and Schuster.[24] Nothing came of the threat, of course, any more than *The Golden Sleepy Book*'s publication heralded the end of either Brown's or Williams' Harper association. But publishing with Golden did open new creative opportunities for both collaborators, and it also put each of them in a stronger bargaining position as a freelancer.

All in all, the 1948 list represented a spectacular achievement. That June, Lucille Ogle's contribution was recognized with her elevation to the rank of corporate vice president. Ogle was the first woman at Western to attain this high executive status. In a congratulatory letter, Roy O. Disney dourly joked that he hoped his old friend's promotion came with benefits more tangible than a flattering title.[25] All indications are that it did. Elegantly appointed apartments, smart clothes, elaborate vacation travel, and a seemingly endless array of carefully chosen gifts for friends and colleagues—a costly paint set for an artist she knew needed one, one hundred silver dollars beautifully wrapped for a young bride and groom—were some of the outer trappings of success that Ogle seems to have enjoyed thoroughly. In later years, Ogle would savor the satisfaction of having become a wealthy woman in an arena of professional life in which women in particular were expected to consider the creative opportunities afforded them as their own rewards.

Guild editor Jerome Wyckoff never forgot the day Margaret Wise Brown, after a meeting at the author's fanciful Upper East Side writing studio, Cobble Court, gave him a ride to the subway in her massive Chrysler Town and Country convertible.[26] A glamorous forty-year-old with a wild mane of ash-blond hair, Brown had purchased the showy car with the hefty advance she'd received for *The Golden Egg Book*. Brown later told a friend that she had spent the money all at once just to prove to herself that the check was real.[27] The starstruck editor slid into the richly upholstered leather passenger seat as the author's snappish Kerry blue terrier, Crispin's Crispian, bounded into position behind them.

Moments later, a truck pulled up alongside the Chrysler at a stop sign, and the driver, leaning out his cab window for an eyeful of the attractive woman at the wheel, purred leeringly. Whereupon Brown, who was practiced at this sort of thing, coolly turned to the dog and said in a stage whisper, "Look, Crispian. A cat driving a truck!" before driving on.

For Brown, unlike her more prosaic Bank Street friends, the boundary between fact and fancy always remained a bit porous. As the writer, who once claimed to have "translated" a story from "the Owl," confided to an interviewer, "Crispian has a book of his own."[28] This was *Mister Dog, or the Dog Who Belonged to Himself*. As depicted by Garth Williams, the rambunctious Kerry blue's "doghouse" was an approximation of the improbable wood-frame cottage, tucked into an interior

Facing page, top: The Kitten Who Thought He Was a Mouse, *1951, by Miriam Norton, illustrated by Garth Williams.* *Bottom: Williams'* Baby Farm Animals, *1953 (current edition).*

This page: From Williams' The Friendly Book, *1954, by Margaret Wise Brown.*

courtyard along Manhattan's York Avenue, that Brown had taken over years earlier as a writing studio and a retreat from the cares of a complex, storm-tossed life. When, in 1952, *Mister Dog* became one of the first Little Golden Books to be published in France, the author, a lifelong Francophile, made a point of visiting the publisher's office in Paris, with Crispian at her side, before continuing southward to a friend's vacation hideaway in Èze, on the French Riviera. Brown had taken away several copies of *Monsieur Chien* to give to the children of Èze and was enjoying her break from work and New York busyness when an acute pain caused by an ovarian cyst prompted an emergency trip to a nearby hospital.

Two weeks later, when word reached New York that the unpredictable forty-two-year-old author had died of an embolism after routine surgery for the removal of the cyst, the stunning news was greeted with varying shades of disbelief. Lucille Ogle, who had spent weeks at a time with Brown at her remote Maine cottage, was deeply saddened but also surprised to learn from the obituaries that Brown had had a brother, whom the author, in all their conversations, had never once thought to mention.[29] To Jane Werner, who had idolized Brown, it seemed a bad ending to a fairy tale. For her, Brown in life had occupied a remote, goddesslike plane, and had "personif[ied] the antithesis of my rather humdrum existence. Her casual blonde beauty certainly outshone my bespectacled brunette plainness beyond any thought of rivalry. Her spark of fanciful genius flashed out brilliantly from time to time and the resultant manuscripts (on one occasion at least scribbled in dazzling spirals rather than in conventional lines) were received with humble gratitude."[30] Werner's own experience of doggedly typing away at her desk, fielding with admirable aplomb whatever assignment was thrown at her, whether it concerned Old Testament figures or Bugs Bunny, was far and away the more typical scenario for the creation of Golden manuscripts. "And all my work," she recalled, a bit ruefully, in her unpublished memoir, "was so casually accepted, that no one even bothered to enter the value of my manuscripts into the joint bookkeeping system as a credit to our office."

The Artists and Writers Guild had two standard contracts for nonstaff authors and illustrators. One contract provided for the outright purchase of all rights to the freelancer's contribution to a book, and the other granted a modest royalty payment based on sales. The latter contract was held in reserve for marquee figures, such as Gustaf Tenggren and Margaret Wise Brown, whose association with the Golden list brought prestige as well as profit to the line. Those lucky enough to belong to that group could choose to draw funds against future earnings, an arrangement that helped tide over some authors but in other cases had the adverse effect of putting the author ever deeper in the company's debt. Perhaps with that prospect in mind, those invited to choose between

Facing page and this page: Images from Mister Dog, *1952, by Margaret Wise Brown, illustrated by Garth Williams.*

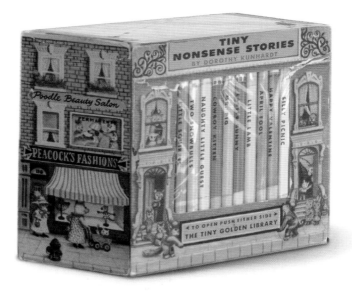

Dorothy Kunhardt's Tiny Nonsense Stories, *illustrated by Garth Williams, followed* Tiny Animal Stories *in 1949. The two sets of books were boxed together in 1968.*

contracts sometimes preferred to accept one-time payment of a sum that exceeded the amount of the royalty-arrangement advance by just enough to make it a tempting option. This took place before most artists and writers had agents to represent their business interests, and before many in publishing realized that children's books could be more than a marginally profitable enterprise. Golden's historic success played a major part in altering the perception that they couldn't, even as the company's regressive payment practices unwittingly helped alert authors and illustrators to their self-interest as working professionals.

Apart from Brown, few Golden writers were relied upon for the inherent sales appeal of their household names. There was Phyllis McGinley, author of *A Name for Kitty* (1948), known for her *New Yorker* light verse and several picture books published by Lippincott and Viking. And there was Dorothy Kunhardt of *Pat the Bunny* fame, whose endearing boxed set of twelve *Tiny Animal Stories* (illustrated by Garth Williams) was another of 1948's brilliant highlights. Gertrude Crampton, who began her career during the 1930s as a writer of educational materials, rose to prominence as the author of one immensely popular Little Golden story after another, starting with *Tootle* (1945) and *Scuffy the Tugboat* (1946). Helen Palmer, author of *Tommy's Wonderful Rides* (1948), *Johnny's Machines* (1949), and *Bobby and His Airplanes* (1949), had no special claim to literary renown, although she was known within publishing circles both as a gifted editor and as the wife of Theodor Geisel, or Dr. Seuss, whom she had met during their student days at Oxford in the 1920s.

More than a few Little Golden Books were staff-written as timely vehicles for one or another of the contract artists. Ariane and Nicole, the real-life names of Georges Duplaix's two daughters, became two of the pseudonyms under which Duplaix himself occasionally wrote stories. Jane Werner, the acknowledged author of (among many others) *Good Morning and Good Night* (1948), also published as Elsa Jane Werner (*The Little Golden Book of Hymns,* 1947), Monica Hill (*Dale Evans and the Lost Gold Mine,* 1954), Elsa Ruth Nast (*Our Puppy,* 1948), and Annie North Bedford (*The Jolly Barnyard,* 1950). Elsa Nast was the author's mother's

maiden name. The Bedford and Hill names were both in-joke references to Western's California street addresses, first on North Bedford Drive, and later on Santa Monica Boulevard, in Beverly Hills. Kathleen M. Daly succeeded Werner as the Guild's chief in-house writer-in-waiting. Although not a staff member, Edith Osswald, author of *Come Play House* (1948), was a friend and Teachers College colleague of Mary Reed.

Top, left to right: Johnny's Machines *was illustrated by Cornelius DeWitt.* Gaston and Josephine, 1948, by Georges Duplaix, *was illustrated by Feodor Rojankovsky.* Good Morning and Good Night *was illustrated by Eloise Wilkin.* *Bottom, left to right:* The Little Golden Book of Hymns *was illustrated by Corinne Malvern.* Dale Evans and the Lost Gold Mine *was illustrated by Mel Crawford.* The Jolly Barnyard *was illustrated by Tibor Gergely.*

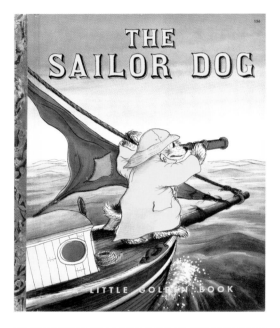

Occasionally, even a near-at-hand child was pressed into service. Margaret Wise Brown gallantly insisted on sharing the royalties for *The Sailor Dog* with a neighbor's son, who, she said, was responsible for the first draft of the story; young Austin Clarke did not, however, share the billing with Brown in the author credits.[31] John Philip Leventhal, a third grader enrolled in Manhattan's Ethical Culture School, fared better in that regard, thanks to the influence of his father.[32] Albert Leventhal had read a class composition of his son's about dinosaurs and decided it might be publishable if expanded. Even family connections apparently had their limits, however. Unlike Clarke, young "J.P." received only a flat-fee payment—a twenty-five-dollar United States Savings Bond—as the author of *From Then to Now* (illustrated by Tibor Gergely, 1954).[33]

Relying on in-house writers and their families and friends was one way to control costs (and maintain the twenty-five-cent price) at a time when the Little Golden line had to contend with its first serious competition. During the immediate postwar years, Golden faced a challenge

not only from the Samuel Lowe Company's line of twenty-five-cent Bonnie Books, but also from Chicago-based publisher Rand McNally's launch of its similar Elf Books series in 1947. By far the most formidable challenge, however, came from Wonder Books, begun in 1946 through a partnership arrangement between Grosset and Dunlap and the Curtis Publishing Company, with distribution handled by Random House. Random's highly competitive president, Bennett Cerf, had long envied his friends and rivals Richard Simon and Max Schuster for the spectacular payoff they'd reaped from their Golden gamble. Wonder Books represented Cerf's attempt to play catch-up.

Not surprisingly, an effort was made to raid the Golden stable, which resulted in Tibor Gergely's and Eloise Wilkin's each illustrating a single title on one of the early Wonder lists and Louise Woodcock's appearing once as author.[34] Ogle and company must have had to scramble to prevent wholesale defections. Perhaps it was with this goal in mind that, during the summer of 1948, Dorothy Bennett made the long journey north to Margaret Wise Brown's primitive Maine summer aerie and, with J. P. Miller at her side, purchased one thousand bricks, several bags of cement, and a trowel and proceeded to build a much-needed fireplace

Facing page, top left: The Sailor Dog, *1953, by Margaret Wise Brown, illustrated by Garth Williams.*
Top right: From The Sailor Dog.

This page: From The Sailor Dog.

in the author's cottage. Brown, who in typical fashion went sailing in Penobscot Bay while her guests did all the backbreaking work, thanked Bennett and Miller afterward by saying that they had given her house "a heart."[35] Ogle and Duplaix continued to tempt her with the promise of substantially increased earnings in return for her agreement to a long-term contract with the Guild. Brown eventually came close to signing such an agreement but thought better of it as negotiations dragged on and the terms seemed to change depending on whether the latest exchange was with Ogle or the often-absent Duplaix.[36]

The Golden juggernaut meanwhile continued to extend its reach as, from 1949, Simon and Schuster licensed the Little Golden name to manufacturers of a dizzying array of children's merchandise, including jewelry, barrettes, wallpaper, T-shirts, fabric, and curtains.[37] That year saw the launch of Les Petits Livres d'Or, French-language editions of Little Golden Books, published by Flammarion, and the finalizing of plans for foreign editions to be published in Germany, Italy, and Spain. Such partnership arrangements were facilitated in part by Western's own evolving international interests as an outgrowth of the company's wartime government contract work. Under the Marshall Plan, Western played a pivotal role in the revival of Italy's publishing industry, providing equipment and technical support to the country's largest house, Mondadori. In the years that followed, Mondadori became the Italian publisher of Golden Books.[38]

Notwithstanding the line's first "real" competition at home, the future of Little Golden Books looked bright indeed. As Western's in-house magazine, the *Westerner,* noted, "The fact remains that more Golden Books are bought in America than the story books of all juvenile publishers combined."[39] In 1942, the sale of one and a half million Little Golden Books had more than sufficed in making a strong impression on the publishing industry; eight years later, Simon and Schuster sold four times as many in February alone.[40]

As the editors at other houses continued to mull over the implications of the Golden challenge, the *Horn Book Magazine* published a satirical commentary on the phenomenon by artist and educator Fritz Eichenberg. Born in Cologne in 1901 into an assimilated Jewish family,

Facing page: A 1947 Little Golden Books display. Courtesy of Steve Santi.

This page, top: The 1955 French edition of The Little Trapper, *1950, by Kathryn Jackson, illustrated by Gustaf Tenggren. Bottom: The Australian edition of* We Help Mommy, *1959, by Jean Cushman, illustrated by Eloise Wilkin.*

Tawny Scrawny Lion lamp, 1972, by the Dolly Toy Co.

Eichenberg, a master wood engraver, had fled Hitler's Germany in 1933 and come to live in New York, where he'd established himself as a printmaker and an illustrator of both literary classics and children's books. A morally engaged artist whose heroes included Goya, Daumier, and Kollwitz, he embraced Quakerism and, in 1949, about the time he wrote the *Horn Book* piece, befriended Dorothy Day and began illustrating for her pacifist *Catholic Worker* newspaper.

In "Artist Through the Looking Glass," Eichenberg recast Lewis Carroll's bewildered heroine as a well-bred college graduate and aspiring illustrator who has found her way to the Platinum and Diamond Book Production Combine Inc., Limited, the "biggest outfit in the country," as a leering art school director has informed her. "They do books for children."

Eichenberg continued:

It was a gigantic enterprise! There was the huge glittering monster reproduction printing and binding combine; there was the invention department; there were the luxurious stables for the hired artists—and, of course, the dungeons, of which we will speak later.

Suspended above this buzzing beehive of activities was the superstructure of the supersales analysis and distribution department. It was outfitted with huge telescopes, radar and X-ray equipment which enabled it to look deep into every prospective reader's mind. Staff psychologists boiled down these findings to the lowest common denominator so that no product could miss its mark. This eliminated the possibility of any kind of flop, failure, or even any slow-selling item.

As for the dungeon:

Deep down under the splendid factory a few rebellious artists were kept on bread and water.

"What have you done, poor souls?" cried Alice.

"Woe is me," a feeble voice replied, "I tried to be original!"[41]

Eichenberg juxtaposed this Orwellian caricature of the Golden operation with a utopian vision of a workshoplike art-for-art's-sake publishing concern that had no exact real-world counterpart. To be sure, the emphasis placed in Eichenberg's imaginary house on leisurely art-making and originality of concept bore some resemblance to the oft-stated goals of the editors at trade houses such as Viking, Scribner, and Harper—as well as the goals of the librarian-critics who judged their books. The essay gave both groups—who together formed the core of the journal's small but devoted readership—much to feel self-satisfied about. But as Eichenberg himself later told Lucille Ogle, the satire's wholesale condemnation of Golden Books was a bit unfair, not to say "juvenile."[42] Perhaps, more than anything, what it showed was the extent to which Golden's success had thrown the established system for publishing and disseminating children's books into a defensive mode.

Just then, as if to bolster the case for any number of Eichenberg's arguments, the nanny employed in Richard Simon's household stood poised to become the author of one of the bestselling Little Golden Books of all time.[43] After remarking to Simon one day on his son's fascination with Band-Aids, Helen Gaspard had gone on to suggest that a Little Golden Book might somehow be fashioned from the material. Simon agreed and encouraged Gaspard to write the story herself. At the same time, he passed the idea on to Albert Leventhal, who presented it to the Sandpiper staff. Soon everyone with an interest in impressing the boss was having a turn. In the end, it was Gaspard who received credit and a modest flat fee as the author of Little Golden Book No. 111—*Doctor Dan the Bandage Man*.

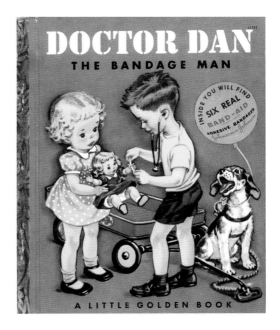

Below: From Doctor Dan the Bandage Man, *1950, by Helen Gaspard, illustrated by Corinne Malvern.*

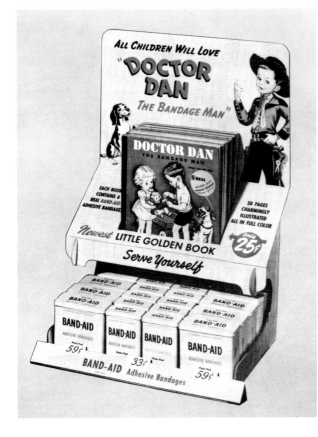

Simon had been quick to recognize a marketing opportunity in the project. With the manuscript in hand, he contacted Johnson & Johnson, the manufacturer of Band-Aids, to gauge possible interest in a collaborative venture. His idea to link two universally recognized brands through a joint sales and advertising campaign was warmly received. In the scheme worked out by the two companies, Johnson & Johnson agreed to supply the publisher with nine million Band-Aids to be inserted, six each, into the books; to advertise *Doctor Dan* in *Life* magazine and, more remarkably, on television; and to order 550,000 copies for sale in drugstores from specially designed counter racks with display space built in for both Band-Aids and books. The first print run was set at 1.5 million— a new Little Golden record. To further pique the public's interest, Simon composed ad copy that told a Thurber-esque backstory, according to which Simon had telegrammed a friend at Johnson & Johnson one day to "PLEASE SHIP TWO MILLION BAND-AIDS IMMEDIATELY"— to which the friend had telegrammed in reply: "BAND-AIDS ON THEIR WAY. WHAT THE HELL HAPPENED TO YOU?"[44]

Top: The Doctor Dan *display.*
Bottom left: Kathryn Jackson's Nurse Nancy, *illustrated by Corinne Malvern, swiftly followed* Doctor Dan *in 1952.*
Bottom right: The Band-Aid assembly line in Western's St. Louis bindery. Both photos from the March 1951 issue of The Westerner.

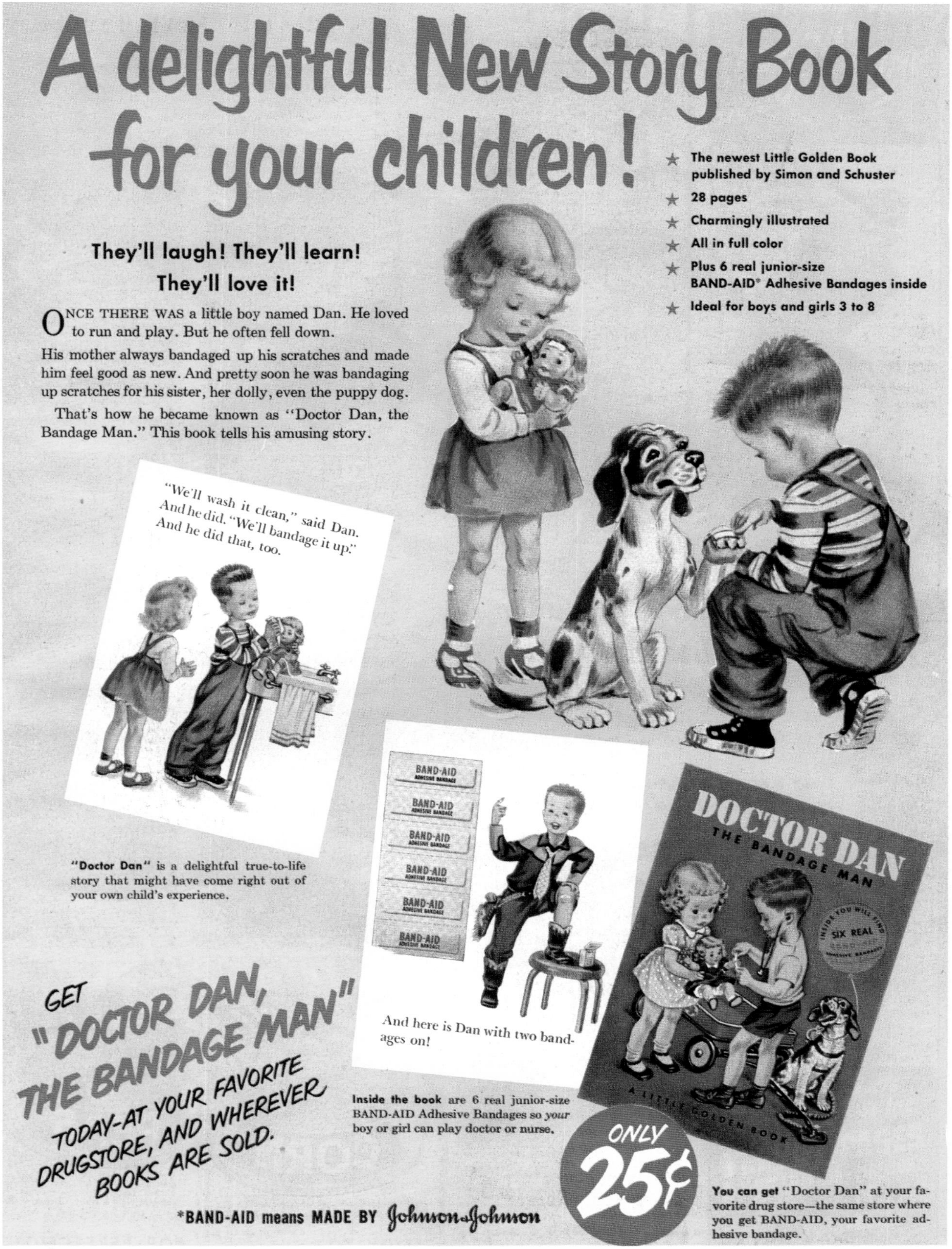

The full-page ad from the February 5, 1951, issue of LIFE.

William Joyce on Garth Williams

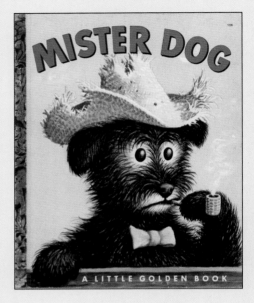

Q: What do you remember about Golden Books from your own childhood?
A: To me, they are like this big lump of warmth. They were my friends! I remember how much I loved the feel of the books, the velvety coarseness of the paper they were printed on, which felt comforting. I loved those little cardboard covers. They weren't delicate, so I didn't have to worry about them. I loved the fact that they didn't have a dust jacket. I hated dust jackets as a kid because you're always supposed to take care of them, not tear them. That is why, now, I always like to have the jacket illustration for a book also printed directly on the cover. It goes back to my memory of Golden Books. And of course, that little strip of gold [on the spine] with the little design: I can't remember what's on the design. But I remember looking at it—forever.

Q: How did Golden Books come into your home?
A: My parents would buy them at the one toy store we had in Shreveport, Louisiana, or at the drugstore.

Q: Did you have many books?
A: No, our parents didn't give us many. Golden Books were about ninety percent of what we had. I remember, for instance, *Doctor Dan the Bandage Man* and *Santa's Toy Shop*. We also had the Tall Books, and a few by Bill Peet. And I had *Where the Wild Things Are,* which I had seen at the library and told my parents I had to have.

Many of my memories of Golden Books are associated with the doctor's office. Our pediatrician had piles of them. There were two things that made going to the doctor a less anxious experience: Golden Books and getting the sucker. At home, I had one of the two Golden Books based on the movie *Babes in Toyland.* My doctor's office was the only place where I could find the second one. The soldiers from the illustrations in those two books show up dead-on in *George Shrinks.*

Q: Is there one Golden artist whose work you especially remember?
A: The worlds Garth Williams created were so appealing that they made me want to go inside them. They appealed to me more than the real world. Everybody looked cheerfully chubby and fuzzy and warm. His characters all looked like they were very pleased and comfortable with who they were. They had such presence. And all their little habitats looked like the nicest, coziest, safest places you could ever find. *Everything* he painted looked good enough to eat, and whenever he actually had food in a painting I wanted that food real bad!

Garth was always jaunty. His illustrations have a musical quality. I always hear little Cab Calloway tunes in my head. When people are running or in motion, it's so blissfully stylized: a combination of weighty and weightless. It's as if they're inflated with helium but it still takes some effort to get around. I guess the best art is always based on contradiction.

Q: Has Williams's work influenced your own?
A: For one thing, when I look at his people—the butcher, for instance, in *Mister Dog,* with that handlebar mustache and straw boater hat—I realize that this has a lot to do with where I got my style. Garth's people look a little antiquated. Like mine, they look to be not from now.

Cold War and Magic Kingdom

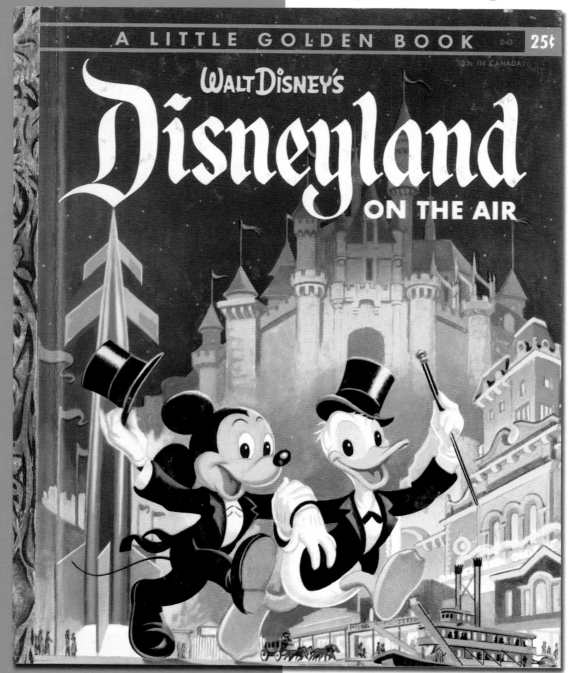

A LITTLE GOLDEN BOOK   D43   25¢
(35c IN CANADA)

WALT DISNEY'S

Disneyland
ON THE AIR

Disneyland on the Air, *1955, by Annie North
Bedford, illustrated by the Walt Disney Studio.*

Golden's on-again-off-again Bank Street collaboration sprang back to life at the start of 1951 with the release of the Little Golden Book *I Can Fly.* The author, Ruth Krauss, was a former art, music, and anthropology student who had joined the Bank Street Writers Laboratory just behind Margaret Wise Brown. Like Brown, Krauss was soon publishing her work with Harper (though apparently with little or no help from the author of *Goodnight Moon,* who seems not to have liked her). Always fortunate in her illustrators, she had already collaborated with the painter Ad Reinhardt and with her husband, comic strip artist Crockett Johnson, when Ursula Nordstrom introduced her to the new Harper wunderkind, a young man from Brooklyn named Maurice Sendak.[1] Krauss and Sendak became friends and worked closely together to create the free-form experiment, based in part on the author's conversations with Bank Street children, called *A Hole Is to Dig* (Harper, 1952).

Left: My Little Golden Book About the Sky, *1956, by Rose Wyler, illustrated by Tibor Gergely.*
Right: Goofy: Movie Star, *1956, by Annie North Bedford, illustrated by the Walt Disney Studio.*

I Can Fly was more than two years in the making. Krauss submitted the manuscript (under the more humdrum title "Birds Can Fly") to the Guild office in late 1948. At only one hundred sixty-one words, the text was brief even for a picture book meant for preschoolers. Having worked out the paging of the book, Krauss typed the few words intended for each double-page spread on separate sheets of paper. When a young Guild secretary pulled the sheaf of nearly blank pages from the envelope, she burst out laughing and summoned her coworkers for a look at what was plainly the work of a lunatic.[2]

The artist chosen to illustrate *I Can Fly* was Mary Blair, a painter and longtime Disney art supervisor who had continued to carry out key assignments for the Disney Studio after leaving California for New York in 1946.[3] Blair was unusual (if not unique) in remaining on the Disney payroll after moving east. That she had managed to do so doubtless attested to Walt Disney's admiration for her work—notwithstanding his pattern of watering down Blair's sophisticated concept paintings with an eye to his mass audience.[4] It was as though Disney regarded Blair as his creative conscience: a force to be reckoned with, if on most occasions only to be suppressed. Veteran Disney animator Marc Davis considered her an "extraordinary artist" who had "spent most of her life being misunderstood." The work of "all the men . . . [at Disney]," Davis observed, ". . . was based on perspective. Mary did things on marvelous flat planes. Walt appreciated this and wanted to see this, but he, not being an artist himself, was never able to instruct the men in how to use [it]. . . . It was tragic because she did [marvelous] things . . . [that] never got on the screen."[5]

Though images composed from flat planes were hard to translate into animation, they worked well on the printed page. So it was logical for Blair to try her hand at book illustration. Published at the start of 1950, *Baby's House* was her debut work in the genre. That February, the *New York Times* praised the book, written by Gelolo McHugh, for catching "the young child's satisfaction in everyday objects as Baby marches through his house, making a joyful inventory of those things which are important in the first years of life."[6] Blair was still shuttling between New York and Southern California. Later that year, when Blair's second child

Top: Ruth Krauss, probably late 1960s. Attributed to Lillian Tonnaire-Taylor. Courtesy of Northeast Children's Literature Collection, University of Connecticut Libraries.
Bottom: Mary Blair, in hat, with Walt Disney, 1964. Courtesy of Kevin Blair.

Facing page: From I Can Fly, *1951.*

was born, the need to reorganize her work life so as to have more time at home became vital. In 1951, *I Can Fly* became the first Little Golden Book to receive an Honor distinction at the prestigious Herald Tribune Children's Spring Book Festival, providing further confirmation that the time might soon be right to resign her highly paid Disney Studio job.[7] She finally did so in February 1953. From then on, working out of the studio in her light-filled, modern Long Island home, Blair devoted herself to a mixture of book illustration, advertising work, and theatrical projects that culminated in her major contribution to Disney's efforts at the 1964–65 New York World's Fair.[8]

This page: Mary Blair, 1950s. Courtesy of Kevin Blair.

Facing page: Images from I Can Fly.

Following pages:
Left: From Mary Blair's The Up and Down Book, *1964.*
Right: Blair's Baby's House, *1950, by Gelolo McHugh.*

Ruth Krauss made sure to send Ursula Nordstrom an early copy of *I Can Fly*. If Krauss had not learned from Margaret Wise Brown to play the Golden card with Nordstrom, she might as well have. Nordstrom and Brown often teased each other about the latter's divided loyalties. Writing to thank Krauss, Harper's editor complimented her on her new work and on the "crazy brain" responsible for its creation. But she could not resist also taking a potshot at Krauss for having shown the poor judgment to publish with a house other than the venerable one for which Nordstrom herself labored. In place of the usual "Dear Ruth," Nordstrom had saluted the author with "Dear Ruthless."[9]

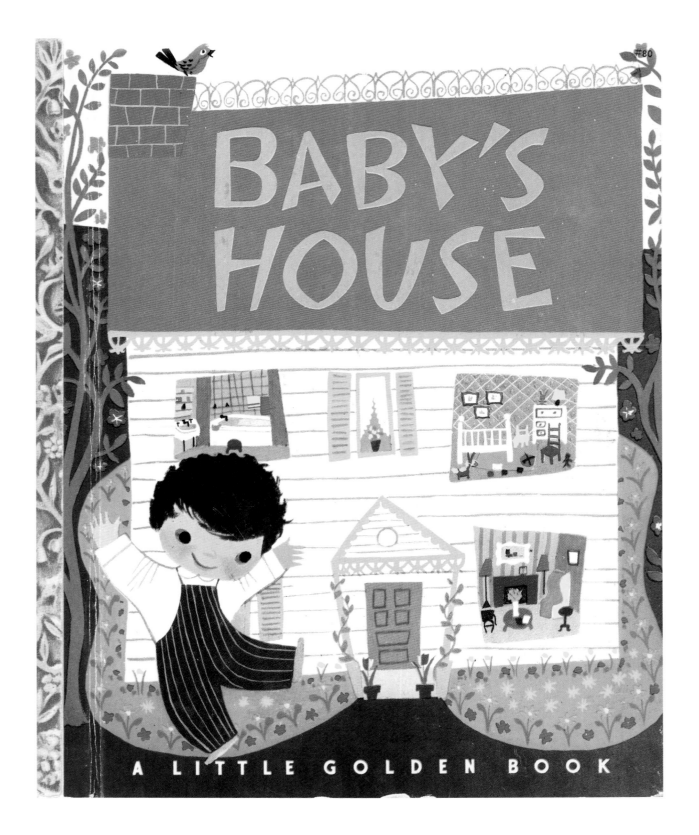

BABY'S
HOUSE

A LITTLE GOLDEN BOOK

Albert R. Leventhal in an undated photograph. Courtesy of Special Collections and University Archives, University of Oregon Libraries.

Facing page: J. Fred Muggs, *1955, by Irwin Shapiro, illustrated by Edwin Schmidt.*

✳

As Western continued to flourish, the need arose for larger, more centrally located, and more impressive quarters than those the company had occupied on lower Fifth Avenue for the past two decades. In late December 1951, the staff of the Artists and Writers Guild and Western's other New York affiliates tagged and crated up their things to make ready for a Cinderella-like transformation: an overnight move to one of New York's most glamorous business addresses, Rockefeller Center's forty-one-story International Building, at 630 Fifth Avenue. Located directly across from St. Patrick's Cathedral, in the heart of midtown Manhattan, the new offices filled half of the sleek skyscraper's many-windowed twenty-eighth floor. Conveniently for the Golden partnership, Simon and Schuster occupied the other half of the same floor, and Essandess's Sandpiper Press was ensconced just one flight below, on twenty-seven. Rising in front of the Fifth Avenue entrance was Lee Lawrie's muscular bronze sculpture of

Atlas holding up the heavens, a bold statement to all comers of their good fortune at merely having found their way to so towering a modern citadel of culture and commerce, a place where the extraordinary routinely happened. The new Guild address boldly trumpeted the fact that Little Golden Books were anything but little.[10] As though to underscore the point, Georges Duplaix papered the walls of his spacious office with a dramatic montage of maps of the world printed by Western for wartime use by the United States military.

In 1954, when Sandpiper needed a new promotion director, Albert Leventhal turned, as he often did, to the sons and daughters of his friends and hired Susan Carr, a Wellesley graduate with a brief stint at Knopf behind her. The new arrival quickly sized up the atmosphere at Sandpiper as "more relaxed and in a way more grown up" than that of her last office, where the polite but nervous talk revolved around the library world and its prim imperatives. At Sandpiper, "there were more men; it was a business."[11] Leventhal in turn doubtless enjoyed the self-assured young woman's tenacious spirit, even as Carr made no secret of her longing to work at a top-flight literary house—Harper, to be precise. When she confronted him one day with a question that she was sure would force him to confess the error of his "mass-market" ways, Leventhal caught her up short with the thoughtfulness of his response. "What would you do," Carr asked, "if the manuscript for *Charlotte's Web* or *Stuart Little* was sent to you?" Leventhal replied, "I would send it on to Ursula Nordstrom. Harper does what it does best and we do what we do best. No publisher can be all things to all people." Carr was impressed—but not persuaded that Sandpiper could ever be the place for her. Three months later, she had her dream job, starting as Harper's reader and rising to become managing editor under Nordstrom herself.[12]

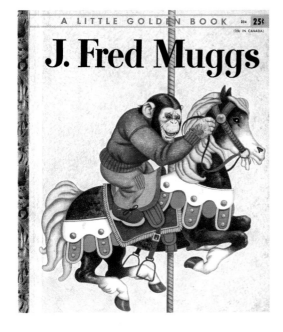

As brief as her sojourn at Sandpiper was, Carr had nonetheless managed to witness the department's single greatest upheaval: the firing of Dorothy Bennett. The younger woman knew from her first day that something was wrong when it became obvious to her that Leventhal had not bothered to tell Bennett in advance about their new promotion director. The frosty welcome from Bennett that greeted Carr that day

E. H. Wadewitz, right, receives a rare "Doscar" award from Roy Disney, President of Walt Disney Productions, in celebration of their twenty-year partnership. From the February 1953 issue of The Westerner.
Below: Davy Crockett: King of the Wild Frontier, *1955, by Irwin Shapiro, illustrations by the Walt Disney Studio, adapted by Mel Crawford.*

Facing page, at left: From Georgie Finds a Grandpa, *1954, by Miriam Young, illustrated by Eloise Wilkin.*
Top: Davy Crockett's Keelboat Race, *1955, by Irwin Shapiro, illustrations by the Walt Disney Studio, adapted by Mel Crawford.*
Middle: Roy Rogers and the Indian Sign, *1956, by Gladys Wyatt, illustrated by Mel Crawford.*
Bottom: Gene Autry and Champion, *1956, by Monica Hill, illustrated by Frank Bolle.*

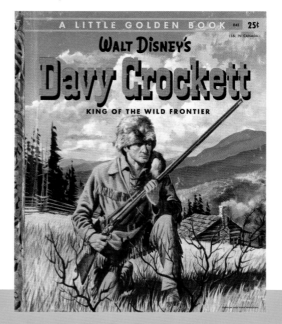

was followed by caustic demands that the newcomer prove herself. Two or three weeks later, a commotion in the hallway heralded the start of a hastily called staff meeting at which Bennett's departure was officially announced. "Dorothy Bennett," Leventhal told the assembled group, "is a perfectionist, which is something that we can no longer afford. From now on, if a book is printed upside down, we will redo it—but nothing short of that!"[13]

Cost- and deadline-related matters had not been the only factors behind Bennett's dismissal. The following year, Simon and Schuster published *J. Fred Muggs,* a Little Golden Book that Bennett had opposed. The title character was the chimpanzee featured, surrealistically, on NBC's *Today Show* as host Dave Garroway's regular sidekick. Bennett had argued that the book amounted to little more than a thinly veiled commercial for NBC's flagship morning program. This was hardly the first time that Bennett had spoken out against Golden Books based on licensed characters and television personalities. After her departure, such books proliferated. It reportedly delighted Bennett, who on leaving Sandpiper found museum education work in California, when the real J. Fred Muggs bit Garroway on camera during a live broadcast and was thereafter banished from television.[14]

It was a mouse, not a monkey, that played a major role in Golden's, and especially in Western's, continuing expansion. In 1953, E. H. Wadewitz, then seventy-five and largely devoted to charity work, drove to Los Angeles to be honored with the Disney Studio's ultimate accolade: a Doscar, the Studio's equivalent of an Academy Award, presented by Walt and Roy. Wadewitz was only the third recipient of the witty statuette featuring an image of Donald Duck.[15] The grand gesture came at a time when Western was once again deepening its relationship with Disney by investing a substantial sum as one of a small group of financial partners in Disney's most ambitious project ever: the long-planned, hugely expensive theme park to be built on 160 acres of Orange County, California, farmland and called Disneyland.[16] In a further strengthening of their bond, the Disneys arranged for Wadewitz's election to the board of directors of Walt Disney Productions.[17]

The following year, as an army of workmen struggled to keep to the park's breakneck construction schedule, Walt, ever the master marketer, served himself up to the American public as the avuncular host of a new hour-long weekly television program, also called *Disneyland*. Not coincidentally, the American Broadcasting Company, which aired the show starting in the fall of 1954, was a one-third-share investor in Disney's park. Designed as a backdoor coming attraction for the park itself, the program offered family entertainment inspired by Disneyland's four distinctive realms—Fantasyland, Adventureland, Tomorrowland, and Frontierland. As the show proved to be a hit and as anticipation of the theme park's opening mounted, Western, with its long-standing licensing agreement with Disney still in force, stood ready to profit handsomely from the sale of book tie-ins. That fall season, when the three-part "Davy Crockett: King of the Wild Frontier" became one of network television's first runaway smash hits, a nationwide "craze" among school-age baby boomers was set in motion. Faux-fur coonskin caps, plastic powder horns, and fringed deerskin zipper

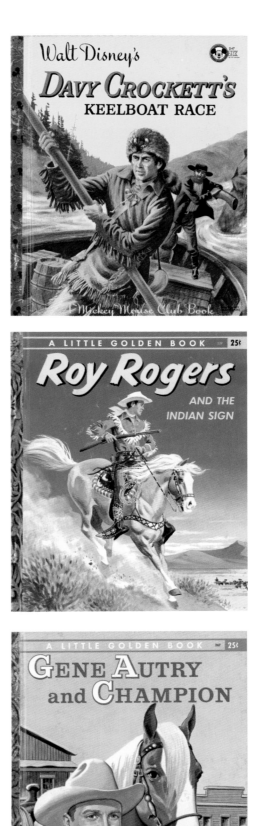

The

WESTERNER

NUMBER 21 ★ AUGUST 1951

jackets suddenly became de rigueur for young suburban boys. If proof was needed of the galvanizing sales power of television, there it was. No sooner had the Crockett trend crystallized than Western swung into action to furnish books—starting with the 1955 Little Golden Book *Walt Disney's Davy Crockett: King of the Wild Frontier*—to be sold along with the rest of the paraphernalia. Guild staff writer Irwin Shapiro received sardonic praise from E. J. Kahn, Jr., in the *New Yorker* for being "one of the busiest of the Crockett chroniclers" and for his "forthright warning to his readers" that his was a "fanciful retelling of the . . . legend."[18]

Against the backdrop of McCarthy-era fear-mongering about espionage, disloyalty, and other forms of "un-American activity," books that safely satisfied American children's natural longing for heroes became a major focus of the Golden list. Books about authentic Wild West heroes such as Annie Oakley and Wyatt Earp, and such modern-day Hollywood facsimiles as Roy Rogers, Dale Evans, and Gene Autry, became Little Golden staples. Many books in this category were illustrated by Mel Crawford, an able freelancer with Disney training, who, having grown up in Oklahoma ranch country and served as a navy fighter pilot, had a bred-in-the-bone understanding of horsemanship, frontier living, and the heat of battle.[19]

Facing page: Roy Rodgers, Western employee, left, and Roy Rogers, "King of the Cowboys," during the latter's surprise visit to Racine. From the August 1951 issue of The Westerner.

This page: Mel Crawford during the mid- to late 1960s. Courtesy of Mel and Ginni Crawford.

The Golden History of the World, *1955, by Jane Werner Watson, illustrated by Cornelius DeWitt.*

Facing page, at left: Martin and Alice Provensen in an undated photograph. Courtesy of Alice Provensen.
At right: The Iliad and the Odyssey, *1956.*

In 1954, Georges Duplaix brought his European perspective to the search for suitable heroes when he proposed that Jane Werner retell *The Iliad* and *The Odyssey* for a young readers' edition in the Giant Golden series. When Werner responded less than enthusiastically to the idea, Duplaix insisted that if she would only spend some time in Greece, she would be sure to get into the proper frame of mind. Werner was feeling a bit drained just then, following the massive effort she had made to complete her soon-to-be-published *Golden History of the World*. Still in a mood to resist, she told Duplaix, "I can think of a couple of reasons for not going," and added dryly, "They're both financial." Duplaix, his back raised, replied with a cutting remark that suddenly made not going unthinkable.

"That," said Duplaix, "is the reasoning of an old man."[20] So off Werner went to Greece. "As a bon voyage gift," she later wrote, "the office group provided me with a staggering bar credit on the *Stella,* accompanied by a card directing me to 'go find your Odysseus.'"[21]

That spring, Werner set sail on what proved to be both a tense and a rewarding tour of the Mediterranean. Her travels took her to Cairo, Jerusalem, Baghdad, Damascus, and Beirut, as well as to various key sites around Greece. She had brief stopovers in Delphi and Mytilene. Transportation to Troy proved too difficult to arrange. The heat was oppressive. Communication in phrase-book Greek was choppy. Werner, in desperate need of solace, regretted not having packed her Bible. To distract herself, she jotted down thoughts for a set of religious books for preschoolers, to be illustrated by Eloise Wilkin: "[I] promise to send you a *Little [Golden] Book of God* soon," she wrote Ogle from Athens on May 23, "and will be thinking of three more." Ever the trouper, she reported good progress on Homer as well: "Got a bit warm doggedly climbing Mt. Lycabettus yesterday, only 900 ft but straight *up*—in the middle of town. But looking *down* on the Acropolis, slightly misty with distance and with the sea a blue haze beyond, it was easier to blot out the modern city . . . and imagine lookouts watching for the approach of the Persian fleet. . . ."[22] It was during this trip that Werner met a fellow American traveler named Earnest Watson, a shy sixty-year-old bachelor and dean of the faculty of the California Institute of Technology. The two fell in love and decided to marry. Later that year [1954], Jane Werner Watson resigned her staff position at Artists and Writers Guild and moved to Southern California to live with her husband.

Watson's Homeric adventure was not yet over, however. Continuing from her new West Coast home to work as the project's editor, Watson reviewed the splendid illustrations prepared for the book by Alice and Martin Provensen. So absorbed in their side of the collaboration had the Provensens become that the couple had produced more and larger paintings than had originally been contracted for. The superlative quality of the art precluded all thought of picking and choosing from their work. This meant, however, that portions of the text would have to be sacrificed, a realization that left Watson in less than the best of moods as she scoured the illustrators' handiwork for flaws. In response to one

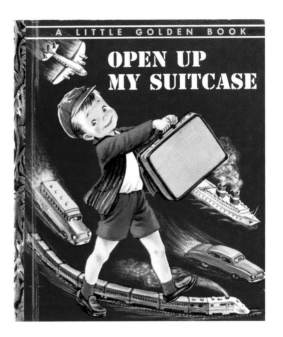

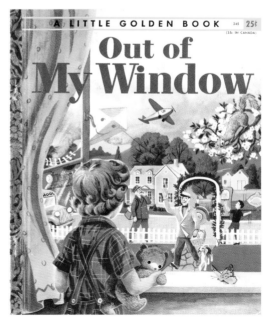

query she raised, Martin, who together with Alice took immense pride in the scrupulous accuracy of their research, wrote:

> Dear Jane,
>
> I understand that you have had considerable doubt as to whether Greek and Trojan warriors rode mounted into battle. We have used as research material a book of reproductions of Greek vase paintings, "Homère, L'ILIADE, illustraté par la céramique grècque," published by Delmas . . . It is quite true that the bulk of paintings show warriors in chariots, but, knowing us, you can understand that we are always drawn to the rare. . . .[23]

Watson continued to write books for a wide range of Golden formats as she and her distinguished husband traveled the world. In this new phase of her life, she allowed herself the luxury of writing only about matters that deeply interested her. Increasingly, Watson pursued the two subjects that concerned her most of all: the need to safeguard the earth's environment and the variety of religious and cultural experience. Among the projects she eventually undertook were a series of beginning readers written specifically for the children of India and the Living in Today's World series aimed at exposing American children to the diversity of life beyond their nation's borders.[24] Gone were the days of laboring entirely in obscurity. In 1958, the *Los Angeles Times* named Watson its woman of the year in literature; two years later, she traveled throughout India in a public role as the wife of the United States Embassy's science attaché.

Throughout the 1950s, both the scope and the scale of Golden's publishing activities continued to work greatly to the company's advantage. If a manuscript or story idea did not suit one line, it might fit another. In 1954, for instance, a Simon and Schuster sales manager encouraged his cousin, a young mother and aspiring lyricist named Alice Low, to submit a song lyric she had written to Little Golden Records.[25] The record was never made, but the lyric became the text of a Little Golden Book, *Open Up My Suitcase* (illustrated by Corinne Malvern, 1954). A second Little Golden Book by Low, *Out of My Window,* illustrated by Polly Jackson, appeared the following year. From this casual beginning, Low went on to pursue a career as a children's book author, which has lasted over fifty years. Time and again, Golden Books, with its rapid-fire production schedule and constant need for new material, proved to be a good starting place for artists and writers.[26]

In 1954, Western's largest printing client, Dell, celebrated its comics division's twenty-fifth anniversary by publishing the 2.5 billionth Dell Comic book. For the comics industry as a whole, however, this was a time of unprecedented public scrutiny and criticism.[27] Librarians had long looked down their noses at the comics as inferior reading matter, the penny dreadfuls of their day. But when psychiatrist Dr. Fredric Wertham, in his bestselling *Seduction of the Innocent*, laid much of the blame for juvenile delinquency at the comics industry's doorstep, nationwide concern was galvanized.[28] Wertham's book prompted a round of congressional hearings, chaired by Democratic senator Estes Kefauver. Before the year was out, the Comics Magazine Association of America adopted a self-censoring code of standards aimed at preempting more drastic governmental action.

Dell's president, Helen Meyer, was quick to defend her company's publications—*Dick Tracy, Popeye,* and Disney Comics, among others—as beyond reproach from the standpoint of morality. Both the public outcry and its sobering consequences seem to have had far less of an economic impact on Dell than on competitors that specialized in more lurid fare. During the mid-1950s, nearly one in every two comics sold in the United States appeared under the Dell imprint. Four years after the debate sparked by Wertham, on November 21, 1958, staffers in Western's Poughkeepsie plant paused to celebrate another comics milestone: the printing of the four billionth Dell Comic book.[29]

As Disneyland's opening day drew near, its telegenic creator solemnly pledged that the park would be "based upon and dedicated to the ideals, the dreams and hard facts that have created America. And it will be uniquely equipped to dramatize these dreams and facts and send them forth as a source of courage and inspiration to all the world."[30]

Perhaps the single most salient "hard fact" brought home by

Helen Meyer. From the May 1949 issue of The Westerner.

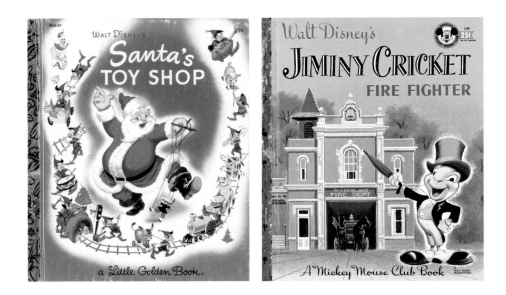

Disney's lavish new entertainment center was the revelation that in the swiftly expanding, consumption-driven postwar American economy, shopping and entertainment were merging into forms of each other. Park-goers out for a day of fun were reminded at every turn of Disney movies and merchandise on which to spend additional money, and of the Disney television program, whose sponsors also hoped to cash in on their association with the Disney legend. Those who strolled along the park's gas lamp–era Main Street, U.S.A.—the very gateway to the park—passed a bookshop stocked entirely with Disney-licensed publications from Whitman, Simon and Schuster, and Dell. Main Street had the quaint, crowd-pleasing look of a nostalgia-drenched historic re-creation; it hardly mattered that real small-town shopping streets of the past had rarely supported a bookseller.

Disneyland opened on schedule on July 17, 1955. Among the attendees at the gala ribbon cutting was a publishing delegation that included Western's president (and E.H.'s son), W. R. Wadewitz; Lucille Ogle; and George Delacorte.[31] The great event was followed that October by the premiere of a second Disney television program, the *Mickey Mouse Club,* broadcast daily in the late afternoon, when schoolchildren were home and their mothers were busy preparing dinner. This show, too, did double duty as a nonstop commercial for the multimillion-dollar park, as well as for all other things Disney. Among the features of that first season was a serialized dramatization of Janette Sebring Lowrey's teen novel *Margaret* (Harper, 1950), retitled *Annette* to serve as a starring vehicle for Annette Funicello, one of the program's lead Mouseketeers.[32] With demand ballooning for Disney-related books, the Guild, meanwhile, added a third floor to its Beverly Hills offices, which now employed a full-time staff of forty-six, most of them artists and writers.

Toward the end of 1955, Richard Scarry, by then the illustrator of fifteen books for Golden and a writer as well, decided that the time had come to renegotiate the terms of his contract with the Guild. Aware that some Golden artists received royalties, he asked Ogle for the same consideration. When the editor readily agreed to this, Scarry asked her why he had not been given a royalty arrangement earlier. "Because you never asked" was all that Ogle, poker-faced, said in reply.[33]

At left: From Scarry's Naughty Bunny, *1959.*

157

In theory, the new agreement, which also released Scarry from his exclusive commitment to Golden, represented a significant gain for the artist. Much to his disappointment, however, he noticed after a time that Ogle was sending him fewer manuscripts to illustrate than she had in the past. The practical effect of this was that Scarry's financial situation grew more precarious than ever.

As Scarry's biographers Ole Risom and Walter Retan observed, it was during this comparative dry spell that he began to think more carefully about books he wished to create on his own, acting as both author and illustrator.[34] In *Naughty Bunny,* for instance, a Little Golden Book from this period, "for the first time, his animal characters emerged as real people, fully clothed and . . . [with] much more personality, [in] drawings [that] are much looser in style."[35] Then, just as the struggling artist began submitting book ideas to other publishers, the ever-alert Ogle, perhaps getting wind of this, "started sending him manuscripts again," according to Risom and Retan. "For the next few years [the Guild] kept him busy creating illustrations for both Little Golden Books and big Golden storybooks."[36]

In 1957, its fiftieth-anniversary year, the Western Printing and Lithographing Company joined the Fortune 500 as one of the nation's largest industrial concerns, achieving the milestone on the strength of annual sales of $63.3 million for 1956.[37] Western was then the world's largest lithographic printer as well as the world's largest producer of children's books and games.[38]

Facing page, top: From Scarry's The Bunny Book, *1955, by Patsy Scarry.*
Bottom: Scarry's The Rooster Struts, *1963 (current edition).*

This page, top left: Sheridan Three Knife Trimmer, Western's bindery.
Top right: Kent ink mixer, Western's Ink Room.
Bottom: Coating machine, Western's Varnishing Department. All photos by James J. Sieger, Racine, 1948. Golden Books archives.

This page, top: The Giant Golden Book of Mathematics, 1958, by Irving Adler, PhD, illustrated by Lowell Hess. Bottom: Jane Werner Watson's The World of Science, 1958, photos by Wilson and MacPherson Hole et al.

Facing page: Exploring Space, 1958, by Rose Wyler, illustrated by Tibor Gergely, cover artwork by George Solonewitsch.

That October, however, the good news was overshadowed by alarming headlines about the Soviet Union's successful launch of *Sputnik I,* an unmanned, rocket-propelled satellite, into earth orbit. Americans were stunned by this graphic evidence of Soviet technological supremacy in the brave new post-Hiroshima world of space-age weaponry. As the national soul-searching that followed resulted in a scathing critique of contemporary American science education, Congress and the president acted to provide schools with the books and other educational materials needed to help close the technology gap.[39] When the National Defense Education Act of 1958 made substantial funding available to schools for the purchase of books about science and mathematics, the Golden backlist already included dozens of suitable titles, ranging from *My Little Golden Book About the Sky* (by Rose Wyler, illustrated by Tibor Gergely, 1956) to *The Golden Guide to Flowers* (written by Herbert S. Zim and Dr. Alexander C. Morris, illustrated by Rudolf Freund, 1950). In fact, few publishers were in a better position to benefit from the federal government's newfound largesse.

The Guild and Sandpiper were quick to build on their advantage. In the new, science-obsessed environment, what book might prove more useful or inspiring than a comprehensive survey of the science-related career opportunities that lay open to young people? It was the perfect project for Jane Werner Watson, whose husband, as dean of the faculty of the California Institute of Technology, was able to arrange for her access to specialists working at the forefront of a wide range of scientific disciplines. The author interviewed the researchers and reported her findings in *The World of Science: Scientists at Work Today in Many Challenging Fields.* In a review published in the *Horn Book Magazine,* Isaac Asimov found the massive volume an exciting piece of work, noting that he had "never read, for this age level, a better description of how computers are programmed." He was also impressed by Watson's consideration of the social and societal aspects of life in the scientific community. "There are many photos of scientists at work, and they are not stereotyped. Some are young and handsome; some are fat and middle-aged; some are women; some Orientals; one is a Negro. The point that science belongs to *everyone* is good, whether made purposely or not."[40]

EXPLORING SPACE

This page, top: Leon Shimkin as executive VP of S&S and president of Pocket Books. From the March 1951 issue of The Westerner.
Bottom: Green Eyes *(current edition), 1953, by A. Birnbaum, was named a 1953* New York Times *Best Illustrated Book and a 1954 Caldecott Honor Book.*

Facing page, top: Charlie, *1970, by Diane Fox Downs, illustrated by Lilian Obligado.*
Below: From Obligado's Little Black Puppy, *1960, by Charlotte Zolotow.*

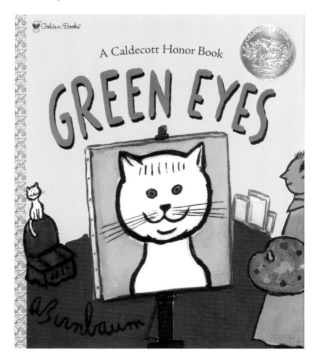

While Western's fortunes continued to soar, 1957 proved to be a year of tumultuous change at Simon and Schuster. First came the death of Marshall Field, the idealistic Chicago-based entrepreneur who had purchased the publishing house from its founders in 1944. (Field had taken an interest in the house largely because of its populist commitment to publishing books that the average American could afford.) Under the terms of the original sale, Richard Simon, Max Schuster, and Leon Shimkin had been granted a first option to repurchase the hardcover side of the firm on preferential terms.[41] When the Field estate put the publisher up for sale, the three men chose to exercise their option. In a separate, unrelated transaction, Shimkin and a junior partner, Jimmy Jacobson, took control of Pocket Books.[42] Not long afterward, ill health forced Simon into retirement, and when Jack Goodman, Albert Leventhal's closest friend at Essandess, died suddenly at the age of forty-eight, Leventhal, in December 1957, decided that, after twenty-four years, the time had come to leave Simon and Schuster and accept the position of vice president and managing director of Western's Artists and Writers Guild.[43]

A press release issued by Simon and Schuster not quite one year later, on November 10, 1958, announced the company's intention to "hereafter concentrate principally on adult and literary publications."[44] With this goal in mind, the house, then run by Max Schuster and Leon Shimkin, reported that it would sell its half ownership in the Golden list to Pocket Books—which was to say to Leon Shimkin. Whatever the meaning of this elaborate dance, Lucille Ogle's position within the Golden hierarchy remained secure. She and Leventhal, who became her immediate superior, drew closer than ever. That month, a new entity, Golden Press, Inc., came into existence as the publisher of all Golden properties.

For once, an official release appears to have given the true explanation for a sell-off. Max Schuster had never cared much for the juveniles side of the business, and Richard Simon's interest in it had at best been lukewarm, a function perhaps of his enjoyment of humorous books in general and of the fun to be had in making serious money from books that rivals such as Bennett Cerf refused to take seriously.[45] To the extent that the move reflected Max Schuster's lifelong aspirations to be known as a "literary" man, it marked the removal of a drag on his reputation. For all Golden's accomplishments, ample reason remained for Schuster to view the matter that way—as a young Argentine-born artist named Lilian Obligado, who came to New York in 1958 seeking illustration work, soon learned. Obligado started her quest by making appointments with two editors: Lucille Ogle of Golden Press and Annis Duff of Viking. Ogle, who was the first to see Obligado, sent her happily away with an assignment. At her next meeting, when the artist innocently mentioned her good fortune to Duff, the latter woman, who as second-in-command under May Massee represented the most Caldecott-bedecked of all New York houses, coldly advised her never again to speak of Viking and Golden Books in the same breath.[46]

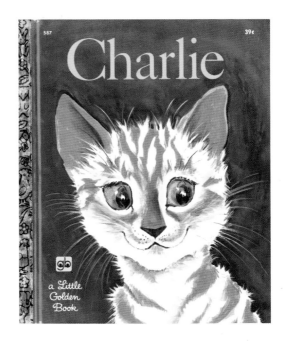

To make up for the loss of Simon and Schuster's contribution to the Golden partnership, Shimkin created a new company, Affiliated Publishers, to provide a sales and marketing apparatus both to Western and to any other publishing client who might wish to make use of its services. Affiliated thus became to the sales and marketing side of the business what Artists and Writers had long been to the editorial side: a hybrid entity aimed at maximizing profitability and efficiency. At the same time, Western purchased the Illinois-based Watkins-Strathmore Company, makers of Magic Slate erasable paper and toys. The acquisition added a popular novelty line to the company's repertoire; far more important, it gave Western its first inroad into the realm of toy jobbers, opening up the nation's toy stores as yet another major outlet for Golden Books.[47]

As the nation's birthrate continued to spiral upward during the 1950s, more and more American parents were coming to consider an encyclopedia an essential piece of household equipment: an omnibus resource for meeting their school-aged children's homework needs and, as the publishers' high-minded sales pitch usually stressed, an "investment" in their children's future. Golden editors thought they saw an important opportunity in the trend and, after conducting extensive research on existing encyclopedia sets, quietly made plans for a more child-focused multivolume set than any currently on the market. The encyclopedia they envisioned was less text heavy than the others, fully illustrated, and priced at a fraction of the usual cost.[48] The author and project editor engaged to pull off this miracle was Dr. Bertha Morris Parker, a veteran teacher at the University of Chicago Laboratory School and a research associate at the Chicago Museum of Natural History. A well-known figure in the educational world, Parker was a past president of the National Council of Elementary Science and the author of more than seventy children's books.

The city of Chicago, with its frontier-spirit openness to untried methods of problem-solving and its wholehearted embrace of democratic values, had long been one of America's centers of progressive education.[49] The laboratory school where Parker distinguished herself was the creation of John Dewey, who, as a rising star in the field of the philosophy of education, had been recruited for the university faculty by, among others, Otho Sprague, local philanthropist and father of Bank Street founder Lucy Sprague Mitchell. Now Parker joined Mitchell on the roster of Golden author-consultants linked to the history-making Chicago/Dewey tradition.

With 1,400 subject entries, more than 6,000 color illustrations, and 375 color maps, the encyclopedia was designed to invite browsing

This page: Bertha Morris Parker (center), probably 1955, as a guest of honor at a retirement tea given by the science department of the University of Chicago. From the October 1955 issue of The Westerner.

Facing page, bottom: The December 1953 issue of The Westerner *profiled the popular "Miss Frances" and heralded Western's new Ding Dong School puzzles and coloring/activity books.*

while serving the school-related needs of children between the ages of eight and twelve.

Ten years in the making, *The Golden Book Encyclopedia* went "into production orbit"—a quaint *Sputnik*-era term—at Western's Poughkeepsie plant in February 1959.[50] From Poughkeepsie, the books made their way to supermarkets and other points of sale all around the United States. The *Encyclopedia* had been chosen as Western's first experiment with a marketing and sales strategy known in the industry as continuity publishing—the timed release of individual volumes in a series in the expectation that the consumer, having been enticed to purchase the first book, would return again and again to complete the set. Over the next two years, the sixteen-volume set sold 60 million copies, making it one of the most commercially successful ventures in modern publishing history.

Perhaps not coincidentally, it was at this time that Western introduced a series of Little Golden Books based on an innovative Chicago-based children's television program, *Ding Dong School*. Off camera, the kindly host of the daily half-hour morning show, known to viewers as Miss Frances, was Dr. Frances Rappaport Horwich, chairperson of the philosophically progressive department of education at Chicago's Roosevelt College (now Roosevelt University).[51] The program first aired locally in 1952 and within months was picked up for national broadcast by NBC. Popularity came with a price tag, however. As the network weighed its options for capitalizing on the show's success, Horwich became embroiled in a series of battles over the number and types of commercials that were appropriate for a children's program. The disagreements culminated in the show's cancellation and its replacement in 1956 by a game show aptly called *The Price Is Right*. Horwich had, however, wisely retained ownership of the rights to the program. In 1959, the first of the Little Golden Books appeared as *Ding Dong School* was having a second life through national syndication.

The *Ding Dong School* books were, for the most part, reissues of titles originated a few years earlier, during the program's initial run, by Rand McNally. Ogle was doubtless pleased to be seizing the advantage

Lucky Rabbit, *1955, by Dr. Frances R. Horwich, illustrated by Ruth Bendel.*

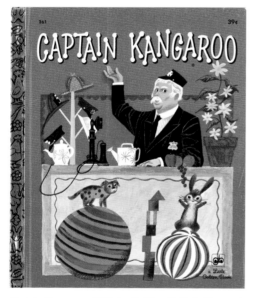

Captain Kangaroo, *1956, by Kathleen N. Daly, illustrated by Art Seiden.*

Facing page, top, left to right: It's Howdy Doody Time, *1955, by Edward Kean, illustrated by Art Seiden;* Woody Woodpecker Takes a Trip, *1961, by Ann McGovern, illustrated by Al White and Ben DeNunez;* Huckleberry Hound Builds a House, *1959, by Ann McGovern, illustrated by Harvey Eisenberg and Al White.*
Middle, left to right: Tom and Jerry, *1951, by MGM Cartoons, illustrations adapted by Don MacLaughlin and Harvey Eisenberg;* Maverick, *1959, by Carl Memling, illustrated by John Leone;* Supercar, *1962, by George Sherman, illustrated by Mel Crawford.*
Bottom, left to right: Steve Canyon, *1959;* Top Cat, *1962, by Carl Memling, illustrated by Hawley Pratt and Al White;* Party in Shariland, *1959, by Ann McGovern, illustrated by Doris and Marion Henderson.*

from one of Golden's stronger competitors, and to be adding the *Ding Dong School* books to a list that already featured titles based on the show's chief rival, CBS's *Captain Kangaroo.* Unafraid of television and, in contrast to most of her publishing colleagues, distinctly curious about its educational possibilities, Ogle also must have been proud to associate Golden with a program as intelligently conceived as Horwich's. Miss Frances' caring, calm on-screen classroom gave many young viewers their first impressions of school. As historians Ted Okuda and Jack Mulqueen have observed, "There was no barrage of cartoons or sponsor promos. Instead, Horwich would converse directly [with] her audience, read a story, or demonstrate an arts-and-crafts project. . . . When she looked into the camera and asked a question, she paused long enough for the viewer to respond."[52] As the *New York Post*'s television critic wrote, Horwich had created the "first network TV program really conceived to meet the preschool child's needs."[53]

Ogle, in any case, was hardly a purist about the new medium. Little Golden Books based on television's first educational children's programming joined others on the list that unabashedly traded on the popularity of licensed characters from the more raucous, "fun" side of television. It is doubtful that Buffalo Bob Smith, the host of the *Howdy Doody Show,* based his programming decisions on anything like an educational philosophy. Yet there on the Golden list he and Howdy Doody were too, right alongside Huckleberry Hound, Woody Woodpecker, and Steve Canyon.

By 1959, more than 150 Little Golden Books had sold one million or more copies, and over 40 percent of the more than 1,000 books published under the Golden imprint were available in foreign editions, some in as many as thirteen languages. That year, Golden Press also became the publisher of Betty Crocker cookbooks. Acquiring the Crocker line not only was profitable in the usual sense, but it also strengthened Golden's reputation as a publisher that understood and serviced the practical needs of families.[54] With the first generation of Little Golden Books readers in their teens and fast approaching the time when they themselves would become parents, the move once again demonstrated the extent to which a unified vision still guided the growth of the list.

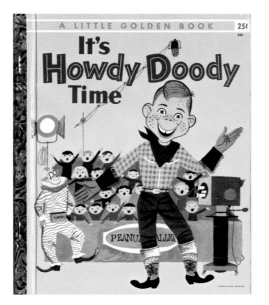

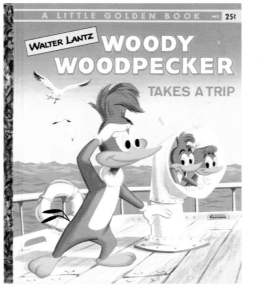

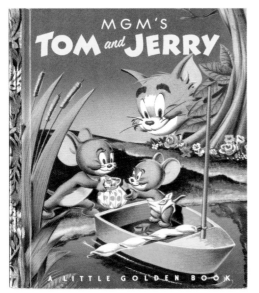

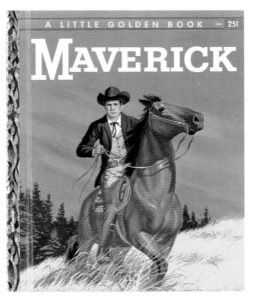

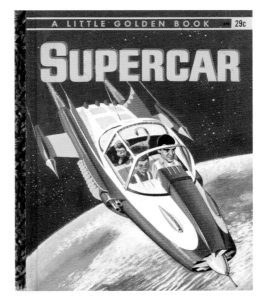

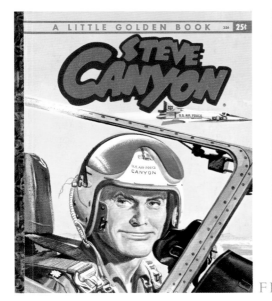

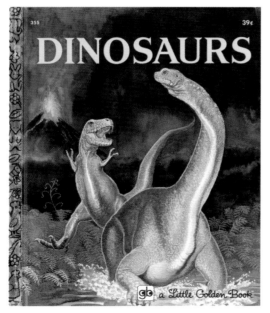

Notwithstanding such well-laid plans, by the end of the decade, persistent inflation combined with increased industry competition to make Golden's long-term outlook appear less certain than it had at any time in the recent past. In 1957, shortly before his departure from Simon and Schuster, Albert Leventhal foresaw the coming trouble: "It takes a vast amount of intestinal fortitude to keep publishing good 25¢ books for children. Plate costs are high and the printings, by the very nature of the enterprise, must be enormous. First printing runs of 500,000 are considered modest for a new Little Golden Book, and many are astronomical. It is our opinion that the near future will see a period of overproduction and overexpansion in the industry, followed by the inevitable shake-out."[55]

Partly as a hedge against that eventuality, Leventhal and Ogle increasingly concentrated their efforts on books addressed to the nation's millions of schoolchildren. The elaborately researched and illustrated larger-format books that poured forth each season from Golden Press spanned the Dewey decimal system. One such book, *Dinosaurs and Other Prehistoric Reptiles* (a Giant Golden Book by Jane Werner Watson, illustrated by Rudolph F. Zallinger, 1960), typified the publisher's knack for correctly reading and building upon a popular trend.

Rudolph F. Zallinger was the preeminent artist in the field of paleontology and the recipient of a Pulitzer prize for the great 110-foot-long by 16-foot-high mural *The Age of Reptiles,* which he had created for the Peabody Museum of Natural History at Yale University in the 1940s. When he began work on the mural, the study of dinosaurs had long been out of fashion with scientists, who assumed that everything worth knowing about the subject had been discovered by 1918.[56] Remarkably, it was the widespread interest generated by Zallinger's epic artwork that finally compelled a scientific reassessment. In September 1953, a *Life* magazine cover story by staff writer Lincoln Barnett, with illustrations by Zallinger, James Lewicki and Antonio Petruccelli based on the mural, further piqued the public's curiosity—and set a new generation of paleontologists on the paths to their vocations.[57] Watson's Giant *Dinosaurs and Other Prehistoric Reptiles* and a Little Golden Book written by her that

DINOSAURS
and Other Prehistoric Reptiles

A GIANT GOLDEN BOOK

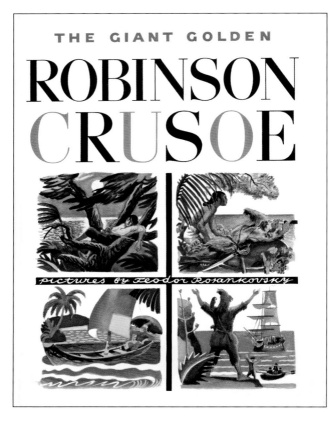

year (*Dinosaurs,* illustrated by William de J. Rutherfoord) were among the first children's books that young readers of the *Life* article could turn to for additional information.

The swift-paced narrative of *Dinosaurs and Other Prehistoric Reptiles* epitomized Watson's talent for presenting complex subject matter in concrete yet never entirely predictable terms: "Men," the author noted, "learned about dinosaurs from fossils in rocks. It was a bit like learning to read. The rocks of earth are like a huge book. The rock layers are its pages. Hidden in them is the story of the earth's past. But to learn that story, men had to learn to read the book of the rocks."[58]

Big and Giant Goldens, including several illustrated by the veteran artists first associated with the line, appeared in profusion in 1960. Feodor Rojankovsky—who won the 1956 Caldecott Medal for a book published by Harcourt Brace (*Frog Went A-Courtin'*, retold by John Langstaff, 1955)—realized a childhood wish as the illustrator of the Golden Press edition of Daniel Defoe's *Robinson Crusoe*. The project had special meaning for Rojankovsky not only because, like Crusoe, he had been a wanderer compelled by circumstance to remake his life in strange

new surroundings, but also because when he was eight or nine, he and his younger sister Tatiana had joined forces to illustrate the book on their own.[59] As the illustrator of the Golden edition, Rojankovsky returned to his very beginnings as an artist.

In depicting the island setting of Crusoe's adventures, Rojankovsky incorporated memories of the lush tropical Florida landscapes that Georges Duplaix had introduced him to during a visit to Duplaix's Palm Beach home after the war. For a time, Rojankovsky owned a not-very-Crusoe-like home of his own on neighboring beachfront property.[60] He soon grew bored there, however, and gave up his Florida retreat for a more congenial one in the south of France. Visual details of the exquisite Mediterranean seaside village of La Favière, where many Russian artists, writers, and musicians came together to create a semblance of their lost world, also found their way into the illustrations of *The Giant Golden Robinson Crusoe*.[61]

During the early months of 1960, as Rojankovsky awaited publication of *Robinson Crusoe*, Gustaf Tenggren, wintering in La Jolla, California, sketched the illustrations for *Canterbury Tales*, and Herbert S. Zim, happily ensconced in his own tropical outpost in the Florida Keys, was blasting ahead with the editorial work for the monumental sixteen-volume *Golden Encyclopedia of Natural Science*. Not even the destructive force of Hurricane Donna, which leveled Zim's office that September, could compel more than a few weeks' delay in the protean science educator's fever-pitch production schedule. By November, Zim had moved into new quarters more than twice the size of his original office and, with the help of his dedicated authors and staff, made substantial progress on encyclopedia volumes devoted to fishes, mammals, trees, flowers, reptiles and amphibians, nonflowering plants, and useful plants.[62]

Before the year was out, another regular contributor to the Golden list experienced a triumph in an altogether different realm. In October 1960, the Vogue Dolls toy company introduced Baby Dear, a "soft, cuddly" vinyl doll styled to resemble a one-month-old. Twenty years in the making, the doll, which won instant approval from girls for its expressive face and the uncannily lifelike feel of its skin, was the work of

Facing page, bottom: From Rojankovsky's The Giant Golden Robinson Crusoe, *1960, by Daniel Defoe, adapted by Anne Terry White.*

This page, top: Tenggren's The Canterbury Tales of Geoffrey Chaucer, *1961, selected and adapted by A. Kent Hieatt and Constance Hieatt.*
Bottom: Dr. Herbert S. Zim. From the March 1963 issue of The Westerner.

At right: Eloise Wilkin working on what would become the Baby Dear doll, 1951. Courtesy of and copyright by Deborah Wilkin Springett.

Facing page, top: Feodor Rojankovsky did the cover and endpaper artwork for the Treasury.
Bottom: From The Seven Sneezes.

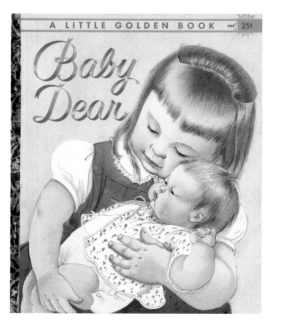

Eloise Wilkin. In honor of the new arrival, FAO Schwarz transformed its corner display window on New York's Fifth Avenue into a make-believe nursery that appeared to be literally crawling with the realistic dolls. Crowds gathered to take in the charming spectacle.

Soviet Premier Nikita Khrushchev was in town just then to address the opening session of the United Nations General Assembly. It was on this occasion that the Soviet leader famously pounded the table before him with a shoe in a bellicose show of displeasure over anti-Soviet statements made by the head of the Philippine delegation. Then, in a surreal time-out from Cold War brinkmanship, Khruschchev and members of his delegation ventured out on a shopping spree and, after stopping at Schwarz, came away with thirteen of the adorable Wilkin dolls to take back home to Moscow. By Christmas, 100,000 Baby Dears had been sold. Although Golden Press had no financial stake in the doll, the appearance of a Little Golden Book, also called *Baby Dear* (1962), illustrated by Wilkin and written by her sister, Esther, was not long in coming.[63]

As though to put a cap on a year of impressive achievements, a retrospective *Treasury of Little Golden Books*—a gathering of forty-eight previously published stories (and selected illustrations) dating from 1942 onward—appeared on store shelves in time for the holidays. Perhaps the most striking thing about the volume was that its compiler was Ellen Lewis Buell, the children's book editor of the *New York Times Book Review*. As Buell explained in her foreword, she herself had proposed the project after realizing that, notwithstanding the reservations she had expressed about the line over the years, Little Golden Books had clearly proved their appeal to children. "I remember one little New York girl," wrote Buell, "who . . . would set out expectantly every Saturday morning with her father to the nearby tobacco store. He bought a cigar and she proudly carried home a Little Golden Book. These Saturday walks were important occasions for both—a shared experience and the beginning of one child's everlasting devotion to books. . . . There were, too, the happy absurdities of 'The Seven Sneezes' and 'Little Boy with a Big Horn,' the antic action of 'The Happy Man and His Dump Truck'—one little boy asked for six copies of that, one for every room in the house. And then there was 'The New House in the Forest' and 'Seven Little Postmen,' so disarming that no child would ever suspect that he was having first lessons in social studies." The *Treasury*, Buell continued, represented her best judgment as to which of the books deserved to "be collected and preserved in more enduring form."[64] As of 1960, 450 Little Golden Books had been published in all. Nine of the forty-eight texts Buell chose were the work of Margaret Wise Brown (either wholly so or in collaboration with Edith Thacher Hurd); seven were by Jane Werner Watson.

On receiving a copy of the collection, Watson wrote Ogle from California to say that, although proud of her strong showing, she regretted seeing the unprepossessing originals conflated for the sake of canonization in a ponderous tome. Ogle replied that, though in theory she heartily agreed, she had nonetheless found Buell's offer to edit such a book irresistible. "Since she had always been so nasty to us," Ogle confided to her old colleague with a wink and a nod, "we thought this would butter her up a bit."[65]

Harry Bliss Looks at *I Can Fly*

Current edition.

Q: Did you have Little Golden Books as a child?
A: No, I discovered them for myself much later, in a bookstore. *I Can Fly* was the one that pulled me in.

Q: What especially interests you about that book now?
A: The overwhelming thing for me is Mary Blair's design sense, her orchestration of color, shape, and drawing. There's a rhythm to it. It flows like a great piece of music.

In the page for "Crunch crunch crunch," for example, there are not less than four viewpoints: she's taken the table and pressed it flat; she's tilted the plate, so we can see what the girl's eating; with the door, she's given us perspective, so we're going back in space; and then there's a horizon line, on which the goat is happily perched. On the page for "A clam is what I am," she gives the clam and the little girl's hat a similar pinstripe pattern and color scheme. And on the page that reads, "Pitter, pitter, pat, / I can walk like a cat," she has designed the table to echo the little cat's face. The knobs are kind of like eyes. When I look at this page, I'm reminded of Picasso's *The Three Musicians*. There is a similar harmony in the way the shapes and colors work in concert with one another.

Q: So you see the influence of Cubism on Blair's illustration.
A: Absolutely.

Q: At the same time, her work is very decorative.
A: I said to my wife the other day, "If you're ever unsure [of] what to wear, just pick up *I Can Fly.*" Blair really understood what does and does not go together.

Q: What else appeals to you about Blair's illustrations?
A: Her use of white space is brilliant. She knows how to let the text breathe, how to go with the simplicity of the text. It's all very sophisticated, but at the same time totally accessible. And I love the last spread of *I Can Fly*, where she brings the whole cast of characters back together. I know that influenced me when I illustrated William Steig's *Where Would You Rather Be?* And that pillow—the way she indicates the form with just a few lines—I marvel at the utter simplicity of it!

175

Part Six

"We *Are* Publishers. . . ."

The Big Tidy-Up, *1970, by Norah Smaridge, illustrated by Les Gray.*

For Western, 1960 had been another banner year, with sales up from 1959 by a remarkable 33 percent—the fifty-third consecutive annual increase. As the company snapped up whole or part ownership of publishing houses in France and Switzerland, and as Golden Press reaped record profits from *The Golden Book Encyclopedia,* the board of directors voted to rename the company Western Publishing Company, Inc. The new name acknowledged the new reality—the historic reversal in the relative importance of publishing and printing within the firm. The Western Printing and Lithographing Company was from then on to have the status of a mere subsidiary. "Can you imagine that?" Lucille Ogle crowed in a letter to Jane Werner Watson.[1] In July, the board voted to make a minority interest of company shares available to outside investors through the over-the-counter market.[2] Ogle urged Watson to take whatever cash she and her husband had on hand and invest in the stock, which the editor

Left: Hilary Knight's Mother Goose, *1962.*
Right: Knight's The Circus Is Coming!, *1978.*

December 9, 1960

Dear Miss Blair,

How perfectly sweet of you
to send Caroline the autographed copy
of one of her favorite books! This
we will treasure.

Sincerely,

Jacqueline Kennedy
Mrs. John F. Kennedy

3307 N Street, N. W.
Washington, D. C.

Courtesy of Kevin Blair.

Facing page: Photo by Jacques Lowe. Used with the permission of Woodfin Camp/the Estate of Jacques Lowe.

predicted would trade at between $30 and $40 a share. When the stock opened at $86, many people associated with Western, not even counting the company's more senior executives, became instant millionaires.[3]

The election of John F. Kennedy as president of the United States that November was widely hailed as good news for publishers. Not only was Kennedy known, in striking contrast to his immediate predecessor, to read books, he was an author as well, and a Pulitzer prize winner in biography for *Profiles in Courage*. Ruth Krauss happened to be visiting the new president's home city of Boston on Sunday, April 2, 1961, when she opened *Parade* magazine to a puff piece about "the little girl in the White House," Caroline Kennedy, and had her own warm feelings about the new administration bolstered.[4] To Krauss' astonishment, there on the page before her was a photograph of the president's daughter sitting beside the First Lady, holding up a copy of *I Can Fly*.[5]

Heady with the impact of this priceless piece of bolt-from-the-blue publicity, one Golden Press staffer piped up at an editorial meeting, "Can't we find *more* books like *I Can Fly*?"

Ogle, suddenly reminded of another incident involving the Krauss-Blair book, was less sanguine: "Don't you recall that little girl?" she prompted. "You know, the one who thought she really *could* fly?"[6]

That June, Ogle and her colleagues once again packed up their offices, this time for a move to the gleaming new Western Publishing Building, an impressive glass-box skyscraper at 850 Third Avenue, a few blocks east of Rockefeller Center, in a neighborhood that was becoming the city's latest Publishers Row. "The offices are just lovely," reported Golden Press rights manager Hazel Jacobson to Jane Werner Watson, in California, "(except for the reception room, which looks like a bar) . . . and the elevator foyer (which looks like the entrance to a basement room or lavatory." All else was "light, bright, and comfortable."[7] Western's far-flung expansion meanwhile continued at a feverish rate. That year, it acquired the Capitol Publishing Company, a maker of educational kits and teaching materials, and Odyssey Press, a publisher of high school and college textbooks, both based in New York, as well as an advertising printing company headquartered in Detroit.[8]

New York

OFFICES TO HAVE NEW HOME

Facilities Will Be Housed in Building Now Under Construction

WESTERN AND SEVERAL of its subsidiaries which maintain office quarters at several locations in New York City have made plans to occupy important office space in a new building now under construction at 850 Third Ave., New York City. Occupancy is slated for April, 1961.

The contemplated move to 850 Third Ave. will enable our Company to combine many operations and activities in one location which, according to Western officials, should contribute greatly to the efficiency and close liaison and coordination that is desirable among our New York offices.

Western and its subsidiaries have long been identified in the printing and publishing circles of New York City and currently have offices at several prominent locations there.

The offices of Artists and Writers Press, Inc., a Western subsidiary, and Golden Press, Inc., an affiliated, jointly-owned company, are located at 630 Fifth Ave. Sales offices of Whitman Publishing Co., another subsidiary, and of a Western Commercial Sales Division are at 415 Madison Ave. In the same building are the Newsstand Division, which creates and produces comic magazines and newsstand books for Dell Publishing Co., and the Industrial Books Division which devises special books for commercial and cooperative publishing purposes. A sales office for our subsidiary Kable Printing Co. is maintained at 60 East 42nd St.

After the consolidation move is made in April, 1961, all of the Company's New York City operations with one exception will be concentrated in the 35,000 square feet of the building that Western intends to occupy at the start. In all, the Company has arranged for the leasing of three floors in the new structure. Display facilities which Whitman Publishing Co. has maintained for many years at 200 Fifth Ave. will be continued at that location for the convenience of buyers in the juvenile book, game and toy field.

The new office building at 850 Third Ave. is located between 51st and 52nd Streets in the midst of a fast-exploding area of modern business development. Western's offices will be extremely convenient to important publishing, advertising and printing contacts.

Pictured is a drawing of the new building now under construction at 850 Third Ave., New York City. Western will lease three floors in the building. Occupancy is slated for April, 1961.

12

From the May 1960 issue of The Westerner.

Facing page: From Richard Scarry's Best Word Book Ever, *1963.*

Years later, Grace Clarke, who worked in the art department under Ole Risom, recalled veteran illustrator J. P. Miller's occasional visits to the new offices. Wracked with self-doubt and genuinely unaware of the extent of his talent, Miller would always hesitate to turn in the artwork for a book, feeling that more work surely remained to be done. Faced with Western's unforgiving production deadlines, Clarke finally suggested one day that Miller bring his brushes and a water jar to the office along with the paintings that were not quite to his liking. Miller agreed to the plan and was given a quiet place in which to apply finishing touches before at last surrendering the illustrations to Clarke.

Over the fall and winter of 1962, Risom himself was hard at work with Miller's old friend Richard Scarry on the project that would transform Scarry's career. The "Scarry Word Book," as it was provisionally named in the Western contract Scarry had signed that August, had first been offered to Doubleday, the publisher of a recent series of books by him about "Tinker and Tanker." Only an upheaval at Doubleday that had resulted in the departure of Scarry's trusted editor there had prompted the artist's return to Western. As work on the project proceeded, a casual remark by Albert Leventhal—"That's the best word book ever!"—furnished the catchier title.[9] It was also the publisher's idea to incorporate the artist's name into the title. Thus began the branding of Richard Scarry that over the next several years would make the reclusive illustrator's name nearly as well known to book buyers around the world as that of Dr. Seuss.

MEALTIME

The Pig family is having a special holiday meal. There is so much good food to enjoy! What do you see on the table that you like to eat?

turkey

milk pitcher

cake

carving knife and fork

roast beef

meat platter

tablespoon

coffeepot

squash

baked potatoes

green beans

gelatine

cranberry sauce

mashed potatoes

teapot

saltshaker

beets

onions

pepper shaker

ice cream

fork

dinner plate

glass

cream pitcher

peas

butter

steak

soup

knife

spoon

cup

saucer

salad

pie

rye bread

white bread

rolls

napkin

sugar bowl

rake

leaves

From Richard Scarry's Best Word Book Ever.

Facing page, bottom left: Detail of an illustration from
A Visit to the Children's Zoo.
Right: The revised illustration.

Published in the fall of 1963, in the same season as Maurice Sendak's *Where the Wild Things Are, Richard Scarry's Best Word Book Ever* came as a complete surprise to readers familiar with the artist's previous work, and greatly expanded his audience. Scarry unveiled more than a new, more relaxed and playful illustration style across the expanse of the book's ample 10-1/2 x 11-5/8-inch pages: here too was a fresh approach to early learning that combined the best aspects of a first reference resource with those of a sheer flight of fancy. The busy, all-over quality of Scarry's colorful, flat, emotionally upbeat art—the impression it gave that no bit of available space had been left unfilled—doubtless reflected the influence of Ole Risom, who kept a sign in his office that read: "White space is for ad agencies."[10] Treating each page as valuable real estate, Scarry had given his illustrations the festive atmosphere and compressed design of a theme park. The overall effect translated for parents to good value, and for children to a bounty of worldly possibility to explore.

Scarry's distinctive plan for organizing the material—by concept categories ("Summer," "Parts of the Body," and the like) rather than alphabetically by word—also drew praise from progressive educators, who welcomed the book as a new tool with which to highlight for preschoolers the myriad human and material interrelationships that compose the fabric of everyday experience. Scarry's alternative to alphabetization served a long-term sales and marketing objective as well: it meant that the book could be translated into any language and published anywhere in the world without the need to reorder the contents.[11]

In 1964, Western agreed to buy out Pocket Books' 50 percent ownership share in the Golden Press to become, for the first time in its history, the sole proprietor of the Little Golden Book list and of all the publishing properties associated with it. That year, the company reorganized its sales operation, acquired half ownership in Golden's British publisher, and introduced Golden Stamp Books, paperbound Golden Shape Books, and the *Golden Magazine,* for grade-school-aged subscribers.[12] It was all in a day's work for the executives in New York and Racine.

No one seems to have anticipated the coming trouble.

On August 6, 1964, Whitney M. Young, Jr., executive director of the National Urban League, published an essay in his nationally syndicated column that profoundly disturbed the juvenile publishing world as a whole, but in particular those at Western, as two of its books bore the brunt of the civil rights leader's criticism. Young began the piece by declaring, "There is a segregated zoo in the heart of New York City. No Negro child has ever been there and, from the look of it, none may ever get in.

"The zoo exists in a book, a book for children. It is typical of the thousands of books published annually by the children's book divisions of some of our most respected and venerable publishing houses, concentrated in New York."

Young went on to identify the offending volume as a Little Golden Book called *A Visit to the Children's Zoo* (by Barbara Shook Hazen, illustrated by Mel Crawford, 1963). Although the setting, he noted, was "the real-life zoo in Central Park," it had not been portrayed "in a real-life way . . . The real zoo, you see, is integrated. It teems with Negro and white parents who have brought their children to inspect the miniature castle, slide down the Rabbit-Hole, visit a real farm . . . But in

To market, to market to buy a fat pig,
Home again, home again,
jiggety-jig;
To market, to market to buy a fat hog,
Home again, home again,
jiggety-jog.

The original illustration on page 63 of The Tall Book of
Mother Goose.

Facing page: The revised illustration.

the book there is not a black face anywhere." Accusing the author, illustrator, and publisher of a "crime of omission," Young insisted that his purpose in doing so was not to lay blame on a few individuals, but rather to highlight the complicity of the "entire publishing industry" in such matters. He then discussed the prevalence of racial stereotyping in books, which, as an overt expression of attitudes toward race, he considered an even more serious offense. Young cited as an example of racist imagery Feodor Rojankovsky's illustration in *The Tall Book of Mother Goose* for the rhyme "To Market, to Market," in which a stout black nanny in a red bandanna was depicted minding a little white girl. Young, not surprisingly, seems to have been unaware of the behind-the-scenes relationship that linked *Mother Goose,* as an editorial project of the Artists and Writers Guild, to the creators of Little Golden Books. He put down the offending illustration to the discredit of the house of record, Harper and Brothers—"one of the country's leading publishers"—in an attempt to demonstrate that the problem was indeed rampant throughout the industry, from high end to low.[13]

Young's main point was right, however, despite the fact that only a year earlier, *The Snowy Day,* an unself-conscious depiction of a black child's enjoyment of a snow-blanketed city landscape, had won the Caldecott Medal. In 1964, it was far from clear whether the award for that picture book—the work, as it happened, of a white artist—represented anything more than the exception that proved the rule. Stung by the public dressing-down, Albert Leventhal circulated a memo acknowledging the truth of Young's complaint and urging his staff to immediately set about doing all they could to redress the company's past insensitivities. Among the ideas debated—and rejected—at a senior staff meeting was one to selectively "screen in" darker skin pigmentations in the illustrations of books already published on the Golden list.[14] The group concluded that merely fiddling with the earlier books would not work.

Tensions ran high. Lucille Ogle at first bristled at the harshness of Young's critique, but she quickly came to accept its essential validity. Responding to an August 10 memo from Racine, to which a photocopy of the Young commentary was attached, Ogle replied brusquely that she had visited the Central Park Zoo the previous Sunday, "and there were no negro children there." Unsure for once just what she thought, Ogle added, "There were lots outside but they didn't have the 10¢ to get inside. This article does point up a very serious problem."[15]

Ogle was among those who quickly recognized that righting so fundamental a wrong was not going to be a simple matter of substituting dark-skinned faces for white ones in an illustration. She was still struggling with the alternatives when, the following spring, she learned that *The Tall Book of Mother Goose* was due to go back to press for a printing of 50,000 copies, 10,000 of which had been earmarked for sale to public schools. Recalling Young's stinging words, Ogle realized that the illustration he had objected to would somehow *have* to be changed before the books were bound and shipped. The Harper editor responsible for the Tall Book series, Ferd Monjo, had come to the same panicked realization. On June 8, 1965, Ogle wrote Feodor Rojankovsky in France with an urgent request for him to "redraw the drawing," to replace "the beautiful voluptuous creature which now graces the page" with a picture of a white person, perhaps the little girl's father or mother.[16] Rojankovsky did as he was asked, substituting for the offending image a sequence of small drawings of a doughty Mary Poppins–like figure with a basket and an umbrella, and a larger painting of the pig the woman brought home.

Of the Golden artists belonging to the older generation, Eloise Wilkin responded most vigorously to the call for racial inclusiveness in books. A devout Catholic, Wilkin considered the social and political work she undertook from time to time—as a volunteer in an upstate New York soup kitchen and, a bit later, as a demonstrator against the Vietnam War—an expression of her religious devotion.[17] Wilkin's illustrations for Clara Cassidy's *We Like Kindergarten* (1965), in which she depicted a racially integrated classroom, were her first paintings to express her concern about the issue.

Younger illustrators also contributed to the effort, as in *The Wonderful School* (written by May Justus, 1969), another story about a preschool or kindergarten class, this one featuring footloose, Bemelmans-inspired paintings by Hilde Hoffmann. Meanwhile, encouraged by the poet

TO MARKET,
TO MARKET

To market,

to market

to buy a fat pig,

Home again,

home again,

jiggety-jig;
To market, to market to buy a fat hog,
Home again, home again,
jiggety-jog.

and political activist Lilian Moore, Ogle herself became an early supporter of the Council on Interracial Books for Children, a nonprofit publishing watchdog group. Ogle also tried, apparently unsuccessfully, to interest Western's corporate management in contributing either money or printing services to the organization.[18] The issue of racial inclusiveness continued both to intrigue and to trouble her. She had worked through many knotty problems in the past. But as Ogle wrote Dr. Irving Adler, a civil rights activist and coauthor with his wife, Ruth Adler, of numerous juvenile science books, "This business of making books that are truly integrated is the most challenging job I have ever attempted in publishing."[19]

In July 1966, Ogle vacationed in northern Europe with Herbert S. Zim and his wife, anthropologist and author Sonia Bleeker. Writing afterward about the trip to an old acquaintance, she casually outlined their breakneck itinerary: "We went on the North Cape cruise to see the midnight sun. Then we went to the meeting of the IUCN (International Union for the Conservation of Nature) in Lucerne and went on a botanical junket and also a bird-watching one in the Alps. They were both great. Then we went

187

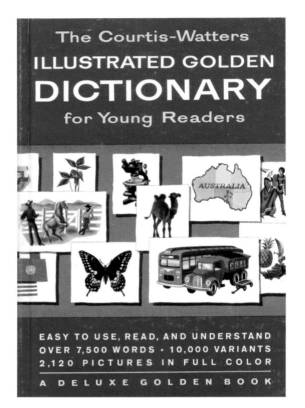

Dr. Stuart A. Courtis in an undated photograph. Courtesy of Special Collections and University Archives, University of Oregon Libraries.

Facing page, top: Joe Kaufman's Wings, Paws, Hoofs, and Flippers, *1981, was one of Kaufman's many Golden titles.*

on a bird cruise around the islands of Scotland conducted by the Scottish Ornithological Society as a pre-trip for the International Ornithological meeting in Oxford."[20] Much to her regret, Ogle had had to return to the office rather than continue to the Oxford event, which in addition to the Zims was attended by Arthur Singer and Oliver Austin, among other Golden nature authors and artists. Even so, the time away had been "wonderful," as she wrote illustrator Cornelius DeWitt the following month. "Somehow, out in the wild like that, you do forget the stresses and strains of modern living, and realize that none of us need as much as we thought we needed. In fact, a trip like that peels one down to size, and that's good."[21]

As if to balance out this object lesson in humility, on her return to New York, Ogle found in her mail a charming validation of the breadth and significance of her publishing career. Among the letters on her desk was one from Dr. Stuart A. Courtis, a renowned University of Michigan education professor, who thirty years earlier, with Ogle as his editor, had pioneered the genre of the picture dictionary for beginning readers. Many years had passed since Ogle had last heard from Courtis, who reported now that at ninety-two he had finally forsaken the Midwest and moved into a retirement home in Northern California, the "land of sunshine and flowers," as he wryly summed up his pleasant new surroundings in a subsequent letter.[22]

The old professor's sudden reemergence filled Ogle with a flood of nostalgic memories, as she and the dapper gentleman with the rounded spectacles and dagger goatee went back a long way together professionally. They had discussed the idea for a young child's dictionary shortly before the editor quit her job at Harter and left Cleveland for New York. Ogle had taken Courtis' innovative plan along with her: the *Picture Dictionary* was the first project she had signed up at the Artists and Writers Guild. Whitman had published the *Children's Picture Dictionary,* coauthored by Garnette Watters, in 1939, and remarkably, the book was still in print. (Courtis later coauthored a similar work, *The Illustrated Golden Dictionary for Young Readers,* with Watters for the Golden imprint. Published in 1951, it too enjoyed great longevity.) "It's wonderful," Ogle wrote back warmly, "to see something still selling that I started working on the very first day I worked for Western, which will be thirty years ago come September 15th."[23]

In the early months of 1967, Golden executives found themselves locked in a bitter struggle with Random House for the services of their most profitable artist.[24] Richard Scarry had followed up on the tremendous popular success of his *Best Word Book Ever* with (among others) *Richard Scarry's Animal Mother Goose* (1964), *Richard Scarry's Busy, Busy World* (1965), and *Richard Scarry's Storybook Dictionary* (1966), all of which had enhanced his reputation as a bestselling (if not prizewinning) illustrator. Having more than proved his worth in the marketplace, Scarry decided that it was once again time to review his contract. The battle was joined when his attorney simultaneously submitted plans for the artist's next large-format book to Western and Random House, inviting both firms to bid for the privilege of publishing it. Resentful at having been put in so tenuous a position by an artist whose career he had done much to nurture over the years, Albert Leventhal angrily refused to play the game. Further souring his mood was the fact that the new head of Random House, Robert Bernstein, had begun his career at Simon and Schuster as one of Leventhal's own sales managers. By the time Leventhal reconsidered the matter, the chance to keep Scarry at Western had passed. Ironically, the aim of the project that had precipitated this clash of publishing titans, called *What Do People Do All Day?* (Random House, 1968), was to give young children a lighthearted view of how grown-ups make their money.

Scarry had laid out the dummy for the new book in his signature format—the oversized, near-square design of all his recent Golden bestsellers. His new publisher had no reason to suggest otherwise—not, that is, until the time came to set the manufacturing arrangements for the book, and Random House staffers learned to their horror that only one bindery—Western, of course—had the right machinery for binding a book of those particular dimensions. For the sake of avoiding a potentially awkward negotiation, Scarry agreed to return to his drawing table and resize the art.[25]

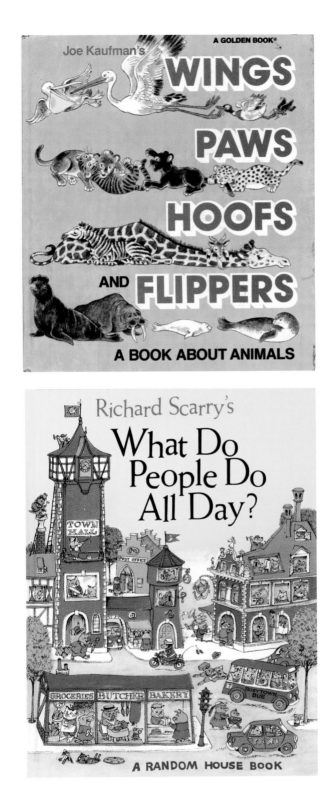

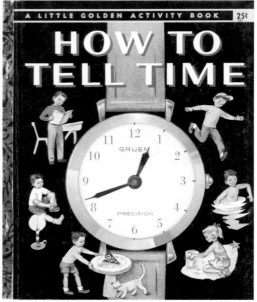

The loss of Scarry to Random House made for a most unwelcome start to Little Golden Books' twenty-fifth anniversary year of 1967. Even so, Western had much to celebrate. By 1967, more than two hundred books on the Golden list had surpassed the million-copy sales mark.[26] Books originated by the Guild and its successor, Golden Press, were in print in twenty-six languages, including Hebrew, Turkish, Hindi, Japanese, Chinese, and Tagalog, as well as all major European languages. That October, the publisher issued a commemorative edition of *The Poky Little Puppy* with the wide-eyed hero's paw-print "autograph" stamped on the cover. In a note to Lucille Ogle thanking her for a copy of the special edition, Mollie Tenggren, the illustrator's wife and business manager, wrote that at twenty-five the little dog still seemed more frisky than poky to her, at least from a sales perspective. Her husband, she added, not a famously sentimental man, particularly enjoyed the distinction of having illustrated one of the few books in history to have given the Holy Bible a run for its money.[27]

That year, time itself was the theme of *The Golden Hours Library*, an elaborately engineered, immensely appealing novelty composed of twelve small picture books housed behind the pendulum of a Chippendale-style cardboard clock. The three-dimensional clock face had plastic hour and minute hands that a child could set and reset manually. The twelve books—one for each waking hour of a small child's day—were a selection of reformatted Little Golden favorites, including, of course, Jane Werner Watson's *How to Tell Time* (illustrated by Eleanor Dart, 1957).

Not every special project undertaken by Golden worked so well. A collaboration envisioned with anthropologist Margaret Mead failed to make it past the talking stage. Memories of the aborted series, which came to be known around the office as "Little Silver Books for Little Psychopaths," gave Jane Werner Watson pause when, in the fall of 1968, she was asked to begin preliminary work on a set of books based on psychological research being conducted at the famed Menninger Clinic of Topeka, Kansas.[28]

By the 1960s, the progressive educators' approach to understanding early cognitive development had long since entered the mainstream, and the frontier for those interested in children's internal development had shifted to the emotional and therapeutic spheres. As undergraduate psychology courses demystified the entire field for growing numbers of Americans, and as seeing a therapist began to lose its stigma, experts in childhood development urged that children's books be given a more definite role in helping young people to "cope" with their emotional growing pains. Catching the first wave of interest in what would come to be known as bibliotherapy, the Menninger "Read Together" books to which Watson had been assigned were intended to serve as conversation starters between young children and their parents on a range of topics related to self-esteem and feelings. The flavor of the series is indicated by the first four titles: *I'm a Boy, I'm a Girl, Sometimes I Get Angry,* and *Look at Me Now!*

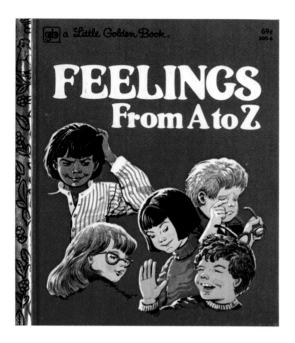

Feelings from A to Z, *1979, by Pat Visser, illustrated by Rod Ruth.*
Below: *Lucille Ogle at her retirement party, 1969. Courtesy of and copyright by Deborah Wilkin Springett.*

The plan was for Dr. Robert E. Switzer, director of the Menninger Clinic's Children's Division, and his colleague Dr. J. Cotter Hirschberg to prepare a first draft for Watson to recast in language appropriate for young readers. Watson's wariness dissolved on first contact with the two good doctors. "Switz" and Hirschberg could hardly have been more congenial or responsive collaborators. When a problem did arise, it had nothing to do with their three-way partnership. If anything, the doctors and Watson drew even closer together when, after a considerable investment of time and effort on all their parts, Watson was suddenly informed that Western executives had decided to postpone the Menninger series indefinitely.

Western just then was still adjusting to the consequences of a tumultuous administrative restructuring begun a few years earlier. A new president, wishing to impose order on the sprawling operation, had hired the McKinsey management consulting firm to evaluate the productivity levels of each division within the company. Salaries were to be reviewed based on the findings. Among those rankled by the wholesale house-cleaning was Albert Leventhal, who argued in vain that the productivity of "creative people," such as those with whom he worked, could not be quantified with anything like the precision that could be applied to the work of pressmen and binders.[29] When all was said and done, both Leventhal and Lucille Ogle were among those who left the newly

WESTERN PRINTING LUCILLE OGLE 20 YEARS

To Lucille with love Sep. 15, 1956 Tibor

reconfigured company at the end of 1968, just as work on the Menninger books was starting.

When Jane Werner Watson received word from Racine of the series' postponement, she was unsure how to break the news to the doctors. Torn between conflicting urges to reassure her friends and to offer them the blunt assessment to which her knowledge of the turmoil at Western clearly pointed, she wrote Switzer and Hirschberg in January 1970, "Earnest and I feel strongly that there is not only a market but a genuine need for these little books." Having said that, however, she acknowledged that the immediate prospects for the books looked grim.[30] As Watson went on to explain in a second letter, written less than two weeks later, Western's new president, Jerry Slade, was "an outsider to what had been a close-knit, 'family' organization. . . . We soon heard . . . that the plan of the parent organization was to downgrade the Golden Book operation to the level of the Whitman books, which seemed such madness that at first hearing we did not believe it. But as the top creative spirits of the organization have drifted away and we have become aware of other developments, we have been forced to accept that something like this is indeed underway."[31]

Amid all the internal chaos alluded to by Watson, Western, in the fall of 1969, made a dramatic foray into television advertising, mounting a nine-week prime-time campaign for Little Golden Books, highlighting three Richard Scarry titles.[32] The company, it seemed, had resolved to do everything in its power to repair its damaged relations with its best-selling artist. Scarry, then living in Switzerland, was unlikely to see the commercials, but his attorney was sure to see them, as of course were the people at Random House. That October, Scarry agreed to meet with a delegation from Western at the Frankfurt International Book Fair. During the course of a tense exchange, the artist seemed to open the door to a resumption of work with the house, albeit in a limited way. According to Ray Butman, Western's director of rights and royalties, who took part in the meeting, Scarry made it clear that he "felt abused by Western."[33] The publisher's emissaries, in turn, acknowledged that they had "embarrassed themselves in the book trade" through their loss of an author "as valuable as him." In the end, marketplace realities led to a new agreement after Scarry realized that his long Western backlist was far likelier to continue receiving preferred treatment from booksellers if Western's salesmen also had an occasional new title to offer them to help spur reorders.

Earlier that year, the Disney Studio awarded Lucille Ogle its Mousecar statuette (an honor ranking just below that of the rarely conferred Doscar) in a valedictory gesture marking her retirement from Western the previous December.[34] For the few remaining people who could trace their Golden Books connection to the line's very beginnings, it was a time of farewells. Gustaf Tenggren died on April 6, 1970. Feodor

The New Baby (1948) exemplifies how Little Golden Books
often reflected social change.
Below, Eloise Wilkin's original portrayal of Mike's "mummy," in
which she doesn't appear to be expecting the baby that she delivers
days after this scene takes place.

Facing page: Wilkin's more realistic portrayal of the same scene for
the reillustrated 1975 edition.
Top to bottom: The 1948 cover; a revised 1954 cover;
the 1975 cover.

Rojankovsky followed on October 12. As the loss of both Lucille Ogle and Albert Leventhal came increasingly to be felt in a general weakening of the company's editorial focus, the executives in Racine began in early 1971 to court Jane Werner Watson to return as a consultant.[35] Later that year, Watson agreed to do so.[36] As for the Menninger "Read Together" books, Western finally published the series' first four titles in 1971, followed by four more the next year, to strong reviews.[37]

By the late 1960s, the size and complexity of Western's many businesses were becoming more of a burden than an advantage. The new president's efficiency experts might have found better ways to coordinate some of the company's hydralike operations. But in 1972, after a substantial portion of the New York office's editorial authority was reassigned to a newly constituted "creative group" in Racine, several more disappointed key New York staff members left the company. Included in this group were art director Ole Risom and his able assistant, Grace Clarke, both of whom Random House was only too happy to hire.

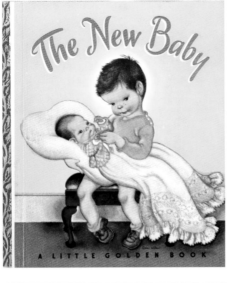

Without the benefit of Ogle's perceptive eye and force of personality, the Golden lists of the 1970s served far less often than in the past as a platform for launching brilliant careers in illustration. (Another reason for the change was that even beginning artists were becoming more aware of their options and thus less likely to sign with a house that offered primarily work for hire.) New work by veteran Golden illustrators Eloise Wilkin and Aurelius Battaglia, and by two discoveries of the previous decade—Joe Kaufman and Jan Pfloog—provided most of the bright spots during a decade largely dominated by derivative licensed-character material. Mercer Mayer made an awkward debut at Golden with *One Monster After Another* (1974), a picture book that drew widespread criticism for its resemblance to Maurice Sendak's *Where the Wild Things Are,* the 1964 Caldecott Medal winner. Mayer was hardly the only illustrator to lose his way in the dark recesses of Sendak's long shadow; to his credit, he later reemerged from the influence of others to create the popular Little Critter series for Golden in an unself-consciously amusing style that was clearly his own.

Among Ole Risom's last projects before departing for Random House was one that left Golden with the odd distinction of having published the first American-market scratch-and-sniff book, Patricia Scarry's *The Sweet Smell of Christmas* (illustrated by J. P. Miller, 1970), a special-effect novelty made possible by the "micro-encapsulation" process, developed by 3M, of applying a fragrance label to the printed page.[38] The project was a typical creation of the workshop run by art director Ole Risom, the Danish-born populist who took unabashed pride in devising book/toy hybrids that children enjoyed, whatever critics might say about them.[39]

A native of Copenhagen, Risom had learned the book trade at Bonniers publishing house in Sweden before immigrating to the United States in 1940.[40] After serving in the United States Army in Europe during the war, he worked at *McCall's* and *Better Living,* then entered the children's book field in 1952 as art director of the Artists and Writers Guild. He remained at the Guild for the next two decades. Risom's warm friendship and intimate working relationship with Richard

Scarry made his departure for Random House inevitable once Scarry himself drifted away from Western. Other notable 1970s Golden titles that bore the playful Risom stamp included Scarry's last two major works for the house, *Richard Scarry's Cars and Trucks and Things That Go* (1974) and *Richard Scarry's Animal Nursery Tales* (1975), and several repackagings of earlier Scarry material aimed at maintaining interest in the artist's Golden backlist.

During the 1970s, feminist critics for the first time called attention to outmoded gender stereotypes in the stories and illustrations published by Golden. Partly because of their outsized popularity, Scarry's books became a lightning rod for such criticism. After first reacting dismissively to the letters that began pouring into Western's offices, the artist finally agreed to revise the cover and some of the interior illustrations for his most popular title. On the cover of the new edition of *Richard Scarry's Best Word Book Ever,* a bunny in a man's suit helps out in the kitchen; a cat in a blue dress drives her own car. All in all, it was a minimal concession to changing times. In the decade to come, the criticism that prompted it would compel Golden editors to take a fresh look at other books long considered standard-bearers of the list.[41]

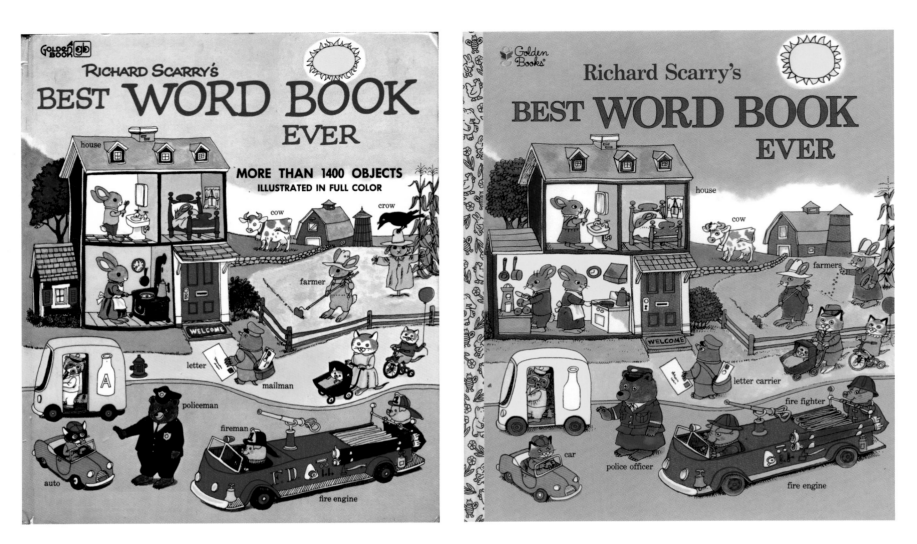

Top left: The original Best Word Book Ever *cover.*
Right: Richard Scarry's revised cover for the 1980 edition.

Facing page: From The Monster at the End of This Book, *1971, by Jon Stone, illustrated by Michael Smollin.*

During the inflation-troubled 1970s, children's paperbacks finally won acceptance for purchase by budget-strapped libraries and schools. The trend signaled a dramatic revamping of librarians' and educators' long-standing assumptions about the worth of lower-priced, more ephemeral books to their collections. Against the backdrop of this newly flexible attitude, the populist logic that had fired the creation of Little Golden Books a generation earlier came into clearer focus for critics as well. In an essay titled "All That's Golden Is Not Glitter," Selma G. Lanes displayed a degree of open-mindedness about the significance and extent of Little Golden Books' impact on juvenile publishing and children's culture that must have startled Ogle, Leventhal, and their former colleagues every bit as much as it gratified them.[42] Five years later, the reappraisal continued on a grander scale in Barbara Bader's sweeping historical survey, *American Picturebooks from Noah's Ark to the Beast Within* (Macmillan, 1976). Commenting on the vagaries of the Golden sales rotation system and byzantine history of reformattings, Bader concluded, "The material is mined, but it stays alive; and much of it is alive, the product of an authentic popularizing impulse and auspicious circumstances."[43] In an elegant turn of the wheel, Macmillan published the Bader book under the editorial supervision of Susan Carr Hirschman, the same editor who, as Susan Carr, had twenty years earlier challenged the legitimacy of Albert Leventhal's mass-market philosophy, only to come away impressed by the underlying integrity of his vision.

Whatever the decade's fever-pitch embrace of paperback publishing might have contributed to Golden's long-term reputation, the change posed an immediate threat to Western, undercutting as it did the publisher's position as the preeminent source of inexpensive good-quality children's books. The new paperbacks made Golden Books less special.[44] Western responded to the challenge in part by exploiting with ever-greater ferocity another of its major strengths, its collection of lucrative character licenses, and by setting out to increase its dominance in that domain. In 1971, the publisher made its first licensing agreement with Children's Television Workshop, the producer of *Sesame Street*. Much to its dismay, however, Western found that it had not acted quickly enough to acquire exclusive publication rights to Jim Henson's Muppets. Random House—Western's archrival—had already locked up rights in certain price categories.[45] Two years later, the company had better luck with Little Lulu, a cartoon character with which Western had been associated, in a more limited way, since the mid-forties. Once known as a "family of families," Western now seemed bent on becoming the brand of brands.

Consolidation and the quest for steady, predictable growth were the new corporate watchwords.

Oh, I am so embarrassed....

Examples of Golden titles from the 1960s and 1970s.
Clockwise from top left: Bow Wow! Meow!, *1963, by Melanie Bellah, illustrated by Trina Schart Hyman;* The Jetsons, *1962, by Carl Memling,*
illustrated by Al White and Hawley Pratt; Donny and Marie: The Top Secret Project, *1977, by Laura French, illustrated by Jan Neely; Jack Kent's*
There's No Such Thing as a Dragon, *1975 (current edition).*

From Bow Wow! Meow!

Top: *Walter Retan in an undated photograph.*
Courtesy of Elizabeth Retan.
Bottom: Animal Friends and Neighbors, *1973, by Jan Pfloog.*

Facing page: *From* The Tale of Peter Rabbit, *1993, illustrated by Cyndy Szekeres.*

In 1975, Western finally retired the Whitman imprint; from then on all publications would bear the Golden name.[46] The following January, the renewal of Western's long-standing contract with Dell went into effect in an agreement valued at more than $50 million, the largest in Western's history. The company that had printed all Dell paperbacks since 1942 could count on continuing to do so for at least the next ten years.[47] While positive developments such as these were a reflection more of management diligence than of the kind of history-making innovation upon which Western first built its reputation, the company kept on an upward path in annual sales, realizing an 11 percent rise in 1977, to $263 million. A year later, sales rose yet again, to $275 million.

From Western's earliest days, timely acquisitions had done much to fuel the company's impressive growth. During the late 1970s, an overheated time of corporate mergers and acquisitions, the publisher suddenly found itself on the other side of the buyout equation. In 1979, Mattel, Inc., the world's largest toy manufacturer, acquired Western in a stock swap arrangement that took effect in June of that year.[48] As a new set of efficiency experts swept through the company's offices, Mattel's elaborate market research techniques were introduced to streamline the company's activities. It was decided that Western's corporate headquarters would remain in Racine, and that editorial work, which had only recently been reassigned to the New York office, would continue to be conducted in New York, under the direction of Walter Retan.

In a stunning coup finalized just months before the Mattel takeover, Western had hired Retan away from Random House to head its publishing program. Arriving to a broad mandate to revive and expand the core list of books upon which Golden had built its reputation, Retan was given the budgetary authority to assemble a first-rate editorial staff that included alumni from Random, Harper, and other respected houses. Retan understood the problem he had inherited. As he told a reporter in 1981, "Little Golden Books over the last twelve years have gotten into an assembly-line kind of production, and we want to correct that immediately."[49]

He came prepared to experiment. Hoping to build on the growing popularity of preschool education and on the advent of a second postwar baby boom, Retan introduced First Little Golden Books, a smaller-format line for children even younger than those who enjoyed Little Goldens. He also initiated a comprehensive review of the entire Golden backlist with the goal of rooting out outdated stereotypical references. Under the new regime, "fireman" became "firefighter," and "policeman" became "police officer."[50] In an effort to lift the line's reputation, Western signed Cyndy Szekeres, a well-regarded picture book artist long associated with Random House, to an exclusive contract. To encourage others to follow Szekeres, Retan for the first time made it standard policy to pay at least a modest royalty to Golden's authors and artists and to return illustrators' original artwork rather than claiming it as company property.[51] In addition, Retan tried for the first time to insert Western into the young adult fiction market, persuading Jean Little and Louis Sachar, among others, to publish on the list. (Slow in starting, the project was abruptly canceled before any of the books appeared; as a result, the effort achieved the opposite of the intended effect by further undermining Western's credibility as a "literary" house.)[52]

For Retan, coming as he had from a mainstream trade house, life at Western required cultural adjustments that in the end proved too much to bear. The tremendous volume and frenzied pace of the work were hard to adapt to for someone accustomed to Random's more individualized and somewhat more leisurely approach to publishing. Making matters worse, the new Mattel-directed marketing staff in Racine felt free to override his authority. After a few fitful years, Retan had had enough. In 1983, he and his art director, Grace Clarke—the same Grace Clarke who had left Western once before for Random House—put corporate politics behind them forever to start their own independent book-packaging company.

Retan was succeeded by Doris Duenewald, a colorful publishing veteran with a patrician manner, a salty wit, and a flair for dressing glamorously for the office in Chanel suits accessorized with elegant furs and jewels.[53] The daughter of the founder of an eponymous printing company long associated with the book trade, Duenewald had grown up around printer's inks and pressrooms and spent most of her own career at Grosset and Dunlap trying to replicate, on a somewhat smaller scale, Lucille Ogle's

Top: Doris Duenewald, 1985. Courtesy of Aimee Garn.

Facing page: From The Good-By Day.

stellar successes at the Guild. A firm believer in the value of putting good-quality books into the hands of the largest number of children possible, she thrilled at the prospect of donning Ogle's considerable mantle.

Determined to make a grand entrance, Duenewald turned up the already frantic pace of editorial production, canceled projects (including the young adult fiction series) that had yet to realize their promise, and spoke fervently to the staff about her vision for a type of publishing that she called "mass trade"—a hybrid form that aimed (as Little Golden Books had from the very beginning) at combining the best qualities of trade and mass market books at affordable prices. Notwithstanding the renewed vigor she brought to the publishing operation, the company's reputation suffered another blow when Mattel decided to shed its recent acquisition and sold Western in 1984 to a group of private investors led by New York businessman Richard A. Bernstein.

Throughout the upheaval, Duenewald held her ground. Her quick, agile approach to bookmaking served her well in dealing with some of the problems that confronted her. When she noticed that a "really adorable book" called *The Scarebunny* (written by Dorothy Kunhardt, illustrated by Kathy Wilburn, 1985) was not selling as well as she thought it should, she renamed it *The Friendly Bunny.* On store racks within months, copies of the new version sold briskly.[54] Duenewald continued to search for new ways to recapture the former glory of the line. It was with this overarching goal in mind that, in 1985, she introduced Little Golden Book Special Editions, jacketed picture books to be sold to the bookstore trade. An ingenious strategy underlay the plan. The higher price ($4.95 at a time when clothbound trade picture books typically sold for between $9.95 and $11.95) and the traditional dust jacket were both calculated to attract more established authors and illustrators to the list. Because the books were otherwise nearly identical in format to the ninety-nine-cent Little Golden Books, a Special title could, once its sales potential had been reached, be reintroduced for a second life on the lower-priced list. Emily Arnold McCully, Wendy Watson, and Jan Wahl all took a chance on this worthy experiment, which ultimately failed, at least in part because of the difficulty of overcoming the still deeply ingrained resistance of booksellers to the Golden brand.[55]

Duenewald's efforts to overcome that resistance were hardly helped when Western's chairman, Richard Bernstein, a real estate investor with no prior experience in publishing, glibly remarked to the *Wall Street Journal* in a 1987 interview, "We're really not publishers. We do a tonnage business."[56] In one ill-considered bold stroke, Bernstein had as much as confirmed the worst suspicions of the company's critics and seriously undermined his publisher's program. The next year, Duenewald used a *New York Times Book Review* essay for which she was interviewed as a public platform from which to counter the remarkable assertion of her boss. "We are publishers," she declared, "and we care mightily about the quality of our art and the quality of our writing."[57]

Duenewald had other problems to contend with. In 1984, her first year at Western, she had published a Little Golden Book called *The Good-by Day* (written by Leone Castell Anderson, illustrated by Eugenie), about two best friends, one of whom was about to move. The cover illustration depicted the friends—one a white girl and the other a black girl—playing together for the last time. At a subsequent "line review" meeting, attended by both Duenewald's editorial staff and the Racine-based marketers, for the purpose of jointly assessing the strengths and weaknesses of the entire list, one of the visitors from Wisconsin questioned the rationale for the book. "We never see white children and black children playing together," he told the group by way of making his point. To the New Yorkers in the room, the comment highlighted the worst aspects of the growing divide between Western's two power centers—a rift arising in part from different sets of cultural experiences and expectations, and in part from the difficulties inherent in reconciling a strictly marketing-based approach to publishing with the editorially based approach that Duenewald was intent on pursuing.[58]

Dan Yaccarino remembers J. P. Miller's *Little Red Hen*

The Little Red Hen, *1954, illustrated by J. P. Miller.*

Q: What makes you such a fan of J. P. Miller's work?
A: Miller was a brave artist in that he abstracted things to a certain degree and left it to the viewer to decipher the image. He took a cue from Picasso, weaving Cubist ideas about perspective into his illustrations and making it fun. Miller always made it his own. He worked over such a wide range. He could do total painting, covering every inch of the page with paint, creating a sense of volume, indicating a light source and secondary and tertiary shadows. Yet he also had the guts to take bits and pieces of a scene and flatten them out completely.

I find that an illustrator is usually either on the side of straight painting or on the side of abstraction. Gergely, for instance, didn't abstract anything, whereas Mary Blair did *a lot* of that, reducing things to flat areas of shapes, color, and line. The unique thing about Miller is that he brought the two possibilities together—often in the same image, which I think is amazing. Look at the illustration in *Little Red Hen* of the hen holding the rolling pin in the kitchen. Miller gave the hen dimensionality. He gave her color. He gave her texture in the way he painted the feathers. And yet right behind her he placed a little square that we still somehow know is a potholder and indicated a vase by just a white blob with very little modeling. How many artists can do that?

Q: Why does *Little Red Hen* stand out for you among Miller's books?
A: It has all the elements in it. He gives a straightforward retelling of the story, but in the illustrations he goes off in all sorts of directions. We're told that the other animals are lazy. But we're *shown* them playing the flute, fishing, catching butterflies, playing pirate. You can tell Miller had a good time and you come away feeling the same way.

I get caught up in all the funny little details. In the scene where the pig is fiddling, for instance, Miller has a half-eaten watermelon, a thermos, a basket, a little pipe. There's a bug on the pig's head. The branch over his head indicates that he's in the shade. His eyes are closed, suggesting that he's relaxed and enjoying himself. There's so much personality in that pig and the cat shown across from him, fishing. It's so lovely. The sinker on the cat's fishing line is drawn in a kind of shorthand; still, you can see exactly how it works. Miller must have gone out and researched it. The fish is gorgeous, even though it's such a minor, throwaway element of the picture. Miller was inviting us to be distracted: to let our minds wander through his pictures, and I find there's always something new to notice in them.

Part Seven

Circles

Dan Yaccarino's Mother Goose, *2003.*

By the 1980s, Golden Books had played a major role in introducing books and reading to two generations of children. Millions of Americans—and millions of other people scattered throughout the world—harbored not only fond but also formative memories of the brightly trimmed, cheerfully illustrated, ubiquitous books. Whatever the future might hold in store for the line, the deep emotional imprint made by the early Golden classics had long since left an indelible mark on mainstream American culture. Baby boomers, now parents themselves, remembered and were palpably nostalgic for the books. Eager to capitalize on this phenomenon, Western found the perfect moment to do so. On the morning of November 20, 1986, work briefly came to a halt at the company's Racine headquarters so that the entire staff could assemble in the second-floor bindery. There, with everyone gathered within view of Line 60, the crowd roared its approval as Joseph A. Marino, Western's president and chief executive officer, held aloft

Left: The Boy and the Tigers, *2004, by Helen Bannerman, illustrated by Valeria Petrone.*
Right: I'm a Truck, *2005, by Dennis Shealy, illustrated by Bob Staake.*

the one billionth Little Golden Book, just off the assembly line. The book chosen for the honor was, quite naturally, *The Poky Little Puppy,* the consistent number one Golden bestseller. A notary summoned for the occasion ceremoniously affixed her stamp to the special copy of the special book. The celebration continued as the book was then spirited away and flown to New York, where the actor Tony Randall, seated in an outsized "storytelling chair" that was a gift from Western, read it to a group of children gathered at, of all places, the New York Public Library's Central Children's Room.[1] Few of those present were old enough to appreciate the extreme irony of the setting.

Koko, the gorilla famous for communicating in American Sign Language—and for requesting, and getting, a real cat to keep as a pet—listens intently as Dr. Francine Patterson reads one of Koko's favorite stories, "The Three Little Kittens," from the Golden Book Three Bedtime Stories. *Photo by Ronald H. Cohn from* Koko's Kitten *by Dr. Francine Patterson. Photograph copyright © Ronald Cohn/The Gorilla Foundation/National Geographic Society. Used by permission of Scholastic Inc.*

GOLDEN LEGACY

Before 1986 was out, Richard Bernstein took Western public for the second time in its history, this time on the New York Stock Exchange, where a far larger percentage of shares were put up for sale than had been the case in 1960. Bernstein and his original investment partners profited substantially from the move, but the company was drifting into trouble. The once dynamic Poughkeepsie printing plant now lumbered along with outmoded equipment. Western's massive sales apparatus was not adjusting well to major changes in the market, notably the advent of big discount chains such as Kmart.[2] Even so, with a second postwar baby boom in full swing, the demand for children's books remained strong. For a time, Western's stock increased in value.[3] In May 1988, the *New York Times* reported that talks were under way about a possible merger between Western and Gulf & Western, a conglomerate with interests in the entertainment, financial services, and publishing businesses. Gulf & Western had entered the book-publishing industry in 1975 when it had acquired Simon and Schuster. Thus, had the negotiations with Western not broken off, the new umbrella corporation would have reunited the original partners in the creation of Little Golden Books.[4]

Three Bedtime Stories, *1958, illustrated by Garth Williams.*

By then, Doris Duenewald had retired, and her handpicked successor, Robin Warner, had come from Simon and Schuster, determined to make peace with the Racine-based sales-and-marketing side of the company. To that end, Warner flew to Wisconsin as often as once a week, taking the corporate jet that Richard Bernstein had emblazoned with a jaunty super-graphic of the Poky Little Puppy. At first, these efforts paid off by helping to build a more cooperative relationship between the company's two power centers. With the advent of computerized inventory control, Western began tracking the store-by-store sale of each of its numerous titles rather than simply keeping tabs on the overall sale of the book assortments it shipped to retailers. Warner's eagerness to learn from the data impressed the people in Racine.[5] At the same time, however, Bernstein was hiring other executives, who arrived with no publishing experience and who instituted policies that bloated

The 1992 boxed set issued for the Little Golden Books'
fiftieth anniversary.

Facing page: From The Shy Little Kitten.

Western's inventory, tying up large sums of money that might have
been better spent for other purposes.

During the early 1990s, in a new variation on its pattern of
servicing other publishers in tandem with its own publishing operation,
Western ventured into the business of bookselling. In September 1992, in
partnership with Toys "R" Us, the company opened the first two of what
it hoped would become a chain of hundreds of boutique-like Books "R"
Us stores-within-stores, stocked and serviced by Western employees and
offering an assortment of both Western's and other publishers' most popular titles. While some in the industry expressed concern that traditional
booksellers might be harmed by such a partnership of giants, others noted
that, in a children's book market that had more than doubled between
1986 and 1992 to cross the $1 billion mark in total annual sales, room
enough might remain for all comers to prosper. The experiment, which
lasted just over a year, proved in the end to be too costly to justify.[6]

As Western sought new ways to flex its muscle in the marketplace, the publisher also looked to freshen its image in time for the fall
1992 celebration of Little Golden Books' fiftieth anniversary. With a view
to showing that better times lay ahead for the house, Western commis-
sioned Little Golden Books by James Marshall and Anita Lobel—two
artists long associated with the upmarket trade—as well as by Golden
standbys Joan Walsh Anglund, Richard Scarry, Mercer Mayer, and Cyndy
Szekeres. It also issued an elegant boxed set of facsimile editions of the
original twelve history-making titles. Advertisements, media events, and
consumer sweepstakes and giveaways all took their places in a coordinated
effort aimed at capitalizing on the extraordinary fact that whatever
Western's short-term financial difficulties might be, Golden Books
remained one of the world's best-known brands, a name recognized,
according to one estimate, by more than 90 percent of the American
public. Far fewer Americans could be counted on to name their own
congressman or to point out Wisconsin on a map.

Even Richard Bernstein prepped for the occasion, sitting for a
Publishers Weekly interview with a quotable catchphrase at the tip of his
tongue: "Books . . . for the masses, not the classes." That, ventured

Bernstein, was what Golden Books had always been about. He proceeded to expound in grandiose terms on the company's latest expansion plans and, in particular, on his own determination to "control the process, from the mill to the till."[7] Two years later, however, the talk was of divestiture. In an effort to stanch its hemorrhaging financial assets and appease stockholders, Western sold off its games and puzzles division—a mainstay since the Great Depression years—to Hasbro, Inc., for $105 million. Despite this move, in 1995, the company's losses had passed $30 million, and they continued to rise.[8] Soon the publishing and investment communities were aswirl with speculation about a possible sale or merger.[9]

This time, the rumors of an impending transfer of ownership attracted more than the usual business-page media coverage. This was due only in part to the amusing incongruity of a publisher long identified in the public mind with such amiable icons as the Poky Little Puppy and Tawny Scrawny Lion having suddenly become the target of a high-stakes takeover bid. Also of special interest was the suitor being mentioned: Richard E. Snyder, one of publishing's most aggressive, flamboyant, and (until his recent fall from grace as head of Simon and Schuster upon its acquisition by Viacom) powerful players. Accustomed to living a life of baronial splendor and striking rich, high-profile deals with the likes of Bob Woodward, Mary Higgins Clark, and Rush Limbaugh, Snyder seemed a most unlikely candidate to revive Poky and company's sagging fortunes—even though he too had begun his publishing career as one of Albert Leventhal's protégés. What could Snyder, the "little Napoleon of publishing," possibly be planning?[10] Snyder was more than eager to respond to that question in the pages of the *New York Times Magazine*.

"Golden Books!" he rhapsodized to his celebrity interviewer,

PBS *NewsHour* essayist Roger Rosenblatt, shortly before Snyder and a small group of investment partners, including Warburg Pincus Ventures and media mogul Barry Diller, assumed control of the company in May 1996. "The name is priceless. No one buys an S. & S. book or a Random House book because of the name. It's because of the author or subject. But every mother alive has read Golden Books to a child and will buy them for her children . . . We have the only brand name that counts!"

In a lengthy profile that explored the quirky logic behind the sixty-two-year-old publisher's autumnal career move, Rosenblatt described Western as a "drowsy, midsize, $400 million enterprise" and quoted Snyder as quaintly characterizing his new fiefdom as a "handyman's fixer-upper."[11] To be sure, Snyder appreciated more than most publishers the true extent of Western's publishing legacy: the company's decades-long dominance of the mass-market segment of juvenile publishing that it had pioneered; its lucrative history of alliances with such partners and clients as Simon and Schuster and Dell; and in particular, its supporting, and at times vital, role in the rise of the Disney empire. Renaming the company Golden Books Family Entertainment, he seemed intent on reclaiming the epic reach of the Golden Press during the halcyon late fifties. Or on becoming the next Walt Disney. Or both. Or so Snyder intimated to the press and stockholders.

Reverting, as head of a publishing house still in deep financial trouble, to his old, imperial management style, Snyder proceeded to institute a new regime of "restructuring" measures, which were intended to slow, but which in fact accelerated, the company's losses. He sold Western warehouses and printing plants in Maryland and Kansas, acquired veteran puppeteer Shari Lewis' television production company, considered purchasing Canada's Nelvana animation studio, and created an adult trade imprint, led by former Simon and Schuster editor Robert Asahina, which launched its inaugural list in the fall of 1997 with Stephen R. Covey's *The Seven Habits of Highly Effective Families*. Propitiously, the Covey book debuted as No. 4 on the *New York Times* bestseller list for November 16. But in less than two years, Snyder, desperate to raise cash, sold off the Golden Books Adult Publishing Group to St. Martin's Press.

Facing page: Photo of Richard Snyder from the Golden Books Family Entertainment 1996 annual report (in the background, some headlines from 1995 through 1998).

Fitted out—ludicrously, considering the company's overall financial situation—with a corporate chef and a chauffeur, he arranged matters to ensure himself a substantial payoff regardless of the outcome.[12]

Before long, the business press was all over the company's distressed balance sheets and plummeting stock price. By the fall of 1998, bankruptcy had become a question only of time. The court filing came the following February. In a development that further undermined the company's chances of recovery, Golden lost the Disney license to Random House in April 2000, ending one of the oldest, most profitable, and most symbolically important relationships in Golden's history. In August 2001, after a ruling in the U.S. Bankruptcy Court in Delaware,

Golden accepted a joint bid by Random House and Classic Media to acquire its assets. When a last-minute competing offer from HarperCollins and the DIC television production company delayed the resolution of the sorry situation, *Publishers Weekly* noted that "like the Poky Little Puppy character that helped make it famous, Golden Books [had] gotten waylaid several times on its path to a final sale." The trade journal went on to speculate about why bidders would vie for a company in so much trouble. The magazine concluded that there was still "something about what Golden does. The ability to license characters to TV and movie studios makes the Golden deal not just a sideline but an attempt at diversification. At a time when characters are more license ready, and consumer book-buying is more tenuous than ever, this could be an important . . . way to keep revenues high."[13]

Serendipitously, the latest attempt to breathe new life into one of modern publishing history's most fruitful experiments came at a time when a gifted group of working illustrators—grown-up children of the baby boom generation—were absorbed in looking back at the Golden Books of their childhoods for renewed inspiration. The effort by Random House also came just as the picture book as an art form was becoming increasingly top-heavy with technical virtuosity and with a sense of its own artistic self-importance, when what was perhaps most needed for children's sake was a return to simpler, less imposing books

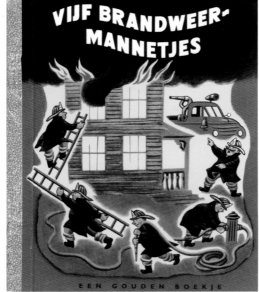

that, much as the first Little Goldens had done, aimed at achieving an authentic child-centered focus. So it seemed a promising and timely development when Random House committed itself both to reissuing many of the classic Golden titles and to publishing new books written, illustrated, and designed in an updated interpretation of their stylish but unpretentious manner.

People in many quarters were taking a closer look at the older books. In 2004, exhibitions of original art from Golden Books at Manhattan's National Arts Club and the New York Public Library did more than stir feelings of nostalgia in visitors.[14] Viewers of the two shows marveled at the high degree of artistry that had gone into making the low-priced books. A year earlier, a similar exhibition in the Netherlands had marked the fiftieth anniversary of Little Golden Books' first appearance in that country. Welcomed by the postwar Dutch as good-natured, energetic children's fare from the land of their American liberators, the Golden line—led in popularity by *Five Little Firemen* and *The Taxi That Hurried*—quickly came to occupy an honored place in Dutch family life.[15] Only the Japanese, with their elaborate postwar history of embracing elements of Western culture, matched the Dutch people's enthusiasm and affection for the books, which were first published in Japan by its oldest and largest publishing house, the Toppan Printing Company, in the early 1950s.[16] In 2002–03, "The Picture Book World of Garth Williams," a retrospective exhibition of Williams' work featuring a large selection of his Golden Books illustrations, toured Japan.[17]

As an upstart company during the 1920s, Random House had made its first foray into the democratization of book ownership as publisher of the Modern Library budget editions of literary classics. Nearly a century later, as a division of the German-based Bertelsmann publishing empire, Random at last acquired the juveniles list that it had, in part because of that list's populist flavor, attempted for decades to copy, compete against, and raid for talent. For those who knew a bit of publishing history, the Random House acquisition provided a striking illustration of the extent of Golden's impact on the industry as a whole. The seller, Richard Snyder, had received his introduction to publishing at Simon and Schuster, from Albert Leventhal. And within months of the acquisition, heading the Random House division to which the Golden list now belonged was the son of a longtime member of Western's sales department.[18]

Sir Arthur Conan Doyle, author of the Sherlock Holmes stories, once wrote: "It is a great thing to start life with a small number of really good books which are your very own."[19] Perhaps Golden Books' greatest legacy lies in the simple but extraordinary fact that, poised at the crossroad of commerce and culture, the people who created them did more than anyone to forge that life-enhancing connection for generations of children.

Bob Staake Remembers Aurelius Battaglia

Little Boy with a Big Horn, *1950, by Jack Bechdolt,
illustrated by Aurelius Battaglia.*

Q: Did you have Golden Books as a child?

A: Growing up in Redondo Beach, near L.A., during the 1960s, I was a big Dr. Seuss fan and a big Golden Books fan. At home, I had Golden Books everywhere.

Q: What did you like about them?

A: Looking now at the books, I see that the art in so many of them is lush and evocative and ambient and lyrical and decorative, all at the same time. As a kid, I wasn't aware that the illustrations worked on all those levels. But even then, as one who was already interested in art, I could almost feel the artists applying the thick, milky textural paint to their illustration board to create what seemed like magical illustrations. I think I could also tell that the people who created the artwork had had a good time doing so. That good feeling became completely infectious.

Q: Do you have a favorite Golden artist now?

A: I especially admire the work of Aurelius Battaglia, a designer with a wonderful less-is-more approach to illustration. He had the ability to build a character from general shapes and forms and to add decorative elements that would give it dimension without being overbearing to the point of detracting from the character. I also love the way Battaglia would sometimes take a sponge dipped in paint and dab it on his board or use other such improvised techniques to create special effects. As a result, you see true texture in his art.

Q: Do you have a favorite among his books?

A: The one I've always liked best is *Little Boy with a Big Horn.* Look, for instance, at the page on which the kid is off to the left, playing his tuba, while to the right we see a pastoral scene with waving trees and a horse-drawn carriage, a barn, some cows, a windmill, and some flowers—all distilled to their bare elements. Even the music stand is completely abstracted. It all just sings and captivates. It evokes Grant Wood. You want to be in that world. There's a spontaneous quality to his work, and a quality of layering.

The right page, top half, for "the preacher couldn't write a sermon," illustrates another one of Battaglia's special qualities: the strength of his silhouettes. Look closely at the preacher plaintively sitting at his table with that pained look painted onto his face and with a crow quill pen in hand, as he tries to write his sermon. If you were to take the core illustration and turn up the contrast to where it was a solid black silhouette, the illustration would still work.

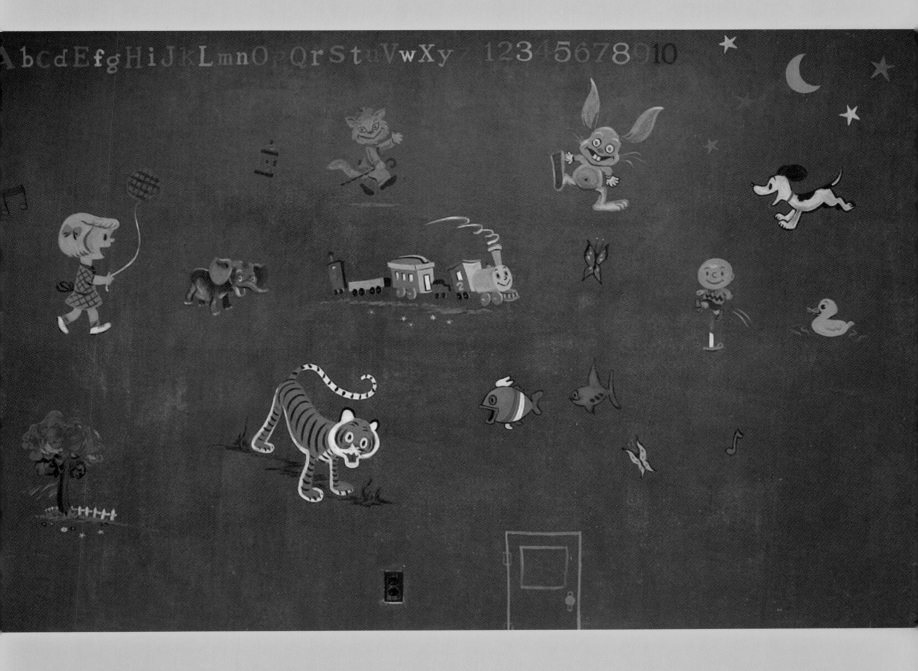

Reflections on a Golden Egg

By Abigail Weisgard

I think that Margaret Wise Brown and my father, Leonard, made *The Golden Egg Book* together when they stayed up at her house on a beautiful little island in Maine—the place called the Only House. From the stories Leonard told us, it seems Margaret and he were very good friends, very compatible, and they confided in each other about just about everything. They had an almost magical way of being creative together. They both worked incredibly hard for long stretches at a time, but they both thrived on it. Margaret would go out and pick flowers for him to paint, and she would just fill the room with those flowers—so many that he often ended up getting hay fever. But

The Golden Egg Book, *current edition.*

he loved how extravagant Margaret was, how playful on a grand scale. An Easter picnic would become a treasure hunt for grown-ups; she'd hide bottles of wine in the bucket down the well.

Those treasure hunts became a part of our childhood as well, for Leonard was the same way. He was just as fond of the grand gesture and always ready to see the magical and extraordinary side of life. Once, my mother, Phyllis, asked him to come back with flowers for our living room, and Leonard came back with a whole truckload of them. And you do get that sense from *The Golden Egg Book;* his pictures are in praise of the abundance of the world and the sheer beauty of life. When we'd read the book together, every flower and every berry was identified and celebrated. But Leonard was also mischievous; when he read that story to us, he would continue it in his own peculiar way. There weren't just a Bunny and a Duckie. There was also a Bad Bunny with a life of his own, and if we went by a dilapidated old house, Leonard would remark that this must be the house where the Bad Bunny lived, and a falling-down factory would be the Bad Bunny Factory. Leonard and Phyllis would create very elaborate Easter baskets with cutouts and decorations and candy, but Leonard would also stick a few odd surprises in there, and you'd take a bite of a chocolate that you thought would be delicious and it would have slimy green liquor in it instead. "That must come from the Bad Bunny," Leonard would say as we spat the stuff into our little napkins.

A Few Words About Richard Scarry's Working Technique

By Huck Scarry, Richard Scarry's Son

People often asked Richard where he got the ideas for his books. "Outside, in the street!" was invariably his reply. Richard Scarry was a very funny man, and so funny things were always happening around him. He would jot down little thumbnail sketches of incidents he saw on his many trips all over the world, and his frequent stays in Venice and on the French Riviera. Places abundant with mayhem and the absurd were regular sources for his whimsical details.

But although full of fun, Richard took his work very seriously. He was always at work right after breakfast, and put in a full day until five or six.

Many of Richard's books demanded a great deal of research, and before beginning to draw, he would spend weeks, sometimes months, poring over reference books, sorting and organizing information. Richard also kept filing cabinets filled with clippings of photos and illustrations of anything he thought he might need to draw one day.

Being first and foremost an artist, Richard would sketch out the complete new book project with little more than stick figures on tracing paper. Texts, written on the typewriter, were cut out and taped in place, for presentation to his editors.

People often ask if Richard ever tested his book sketches with children. But having happily remained very childlike himself, he didn't need to. He simply drew in the books what he wanted to see there, and that was that.

Richard also knew that parents, who would read the same pages over and over again, needed to find fun in his books. Many of the amusing details found in his busy pictures were put there not just for the children, but for parents to have fun discovering them as well.

Once the general layout for a new book was approved, Richard moved forward to do rough sketches, again on tracing paper, but now with

From Richard Scarry's I Am a Bunny.

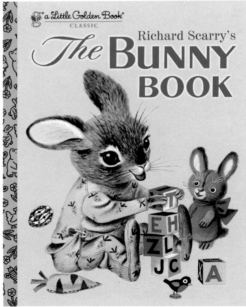

I Am a Bunny, *current edition.*
Bottom: The Bunny Book, *current edition.*

Facing page: From The Bunny Book.

all his characters and details clearly in place. Here, Richard's genius and skill came into full play. He had a masterful sense of design and composition, and an amazing talent for explaining through drawings often very complicated information in a deceptively simple and always lighthearted way. Anyone who has ever attempted a cutaway drawing of a windmill or a steamship can only marvel at Richard's renditions!

Next came "final line," the black line drawings done with a soft pencil on translucent acetate (more robust than tracing paper), which would go off to the photoengraver. There an offset film of the drawings was made, and a print of this was done on illustration paper or board in very pale blue ink.

This was the "blueboard" technique; using the black-line offset film overlay as a guide, Richard could then paint his colors onto the separate illustration paper, following the pale-blue outlines, much as a child colors a coloring book.

The "coloring-up" stage was always a rather lengthy affair, especially because his drawings were so busy and detailed. I remember helping my father to color for a couple of weeks at a time, painting in first everything to be in red—then the yellows, the oranges, blues, greens, ochres, and so on, until at last no blank spots remained—or so we thought. If you have a sharp eye, you might discover an unpainted paw or ear in one of his books!

Whenever asked by a parent to autograph a book, Richard usually added a little drawing of one of his characters along with his signature. If the parent apologized for the tattered look of the book, my father would laugh and reply that the greatest compliment he could receive was the sight of one of his books, bumped and torn, and now held together with tape, after hundreds of readings!

Before developing his pencil-drawn illustration style through the blueboard technique, Richard painted his book illustrations. In other words, there were no visible drawing lines—everything was applied in gouache paint, with subtle modeling, shadows, and textures—a tremendous amount of work!

Perhaps the most beautiful of these "painted" books is *I Am a Bunny* (1963), written by Ole Risom, my father's art director and best friend. For *I Am a Bunny,* Ole's young son Nicolas served as the central character.

The virtuosity of Richard's handling of gouache paint in layers—first "wet-on-wet," then on to full-bodied opaque, testifies to an incredible mastery.

The researched varieties of trees, flowers, birds, and frogs are all there, as well as intelligently and poetically composed design. It is truly one of Richard's finest works.

Another "painted" book, published in 1955 and written by my mother, Patsy Scarry, also has a little bunny as its central character. I was then two when *The Bunny Book* came out, and barely a year old when my parents were working on it. So, along with the dedication "For Huck" at the opening, there can be little doubt about what this baby bunny is.

At the time, our "little yellow-slicker family," as my father dubbed us, lived in a small red cottage on the Conklin Farm in Ridgefield, Connecticut. The pine floors, the cord rugs, and the Colonial furniture found in the book could also be found in Patsy and Richard's house.

My mother, a very gifted children's author, cleverly used this baby bunny and all his relatives to present an array of professions in this "what-will-I-be-when-I-grow-up" book. What is funny, and what my mother never knew (or did she?), is that she was a prophet. For Little Bunny never did become a lion tamer, nor a nice little mailman, nor a doctor, nor a brave fireman. Little Bunny really *did* become a nice daddy bunny, with no fewer than four little bunnies of his own to play with, to read stories to, and to put to bed. And when he's finished being Daddy Bunny, he writes and illustrates children's books, just as his parents did.

Amy Schwartz Remembers
The Golden Book Encyclopedia

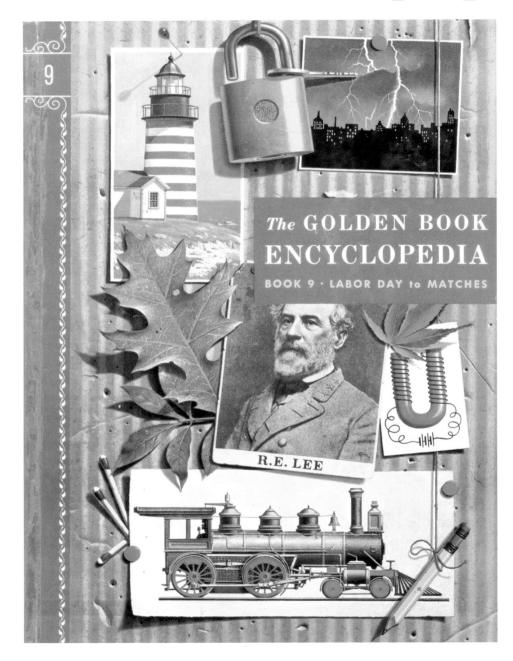

My strongest memory from my childhood of Little Golden Books is of the golden spines of the books, and especially the patterned inside back covers, where one could go through both the list of published books and the drawings of characters from various Little Golden Books, to see how many books one had read, as well as how many yet-unread treasures remained. As a children's book illustrator, it reminds me how important such design elements can be to a child.

I also have strong memories of *The Golden Book Encyclopedia.* Encyclopedias were, to me, mystical entities. It was almost unbelievable to me that some child would be lucky enough to own an entire *Encyclopaedia Britannica,* perhaps bought from the equally mystical door-to-door salesman. Encyclopedias represented All Knowledge. Anything, anything at all you wanted to know, would be in the encyclopedia.

My mother's solution was *The Golden Book Encyclopedia.* It was on sale in San Diego at the checkout stand of our local Food Basket—volume by volume at an affordable price. Letter by letter, my mother bought us the entire set.

Looking over these volumes today, I am impressed by both the clarity and the wit of the writing. But what I remember from my childhood, besides the thrill of *owning* an encyclopedia, are the visual elements. The cover of each volume was a collage, pictures of objects covered in that volume against a textured background, reflecting an artistic style of the time. I found them sophisticated, fascinating, and a little bit nausea-inducing. Somehow those backgrounds of cork or wood or stonework, with the occasional pinned bug specimen, didn't quite agree with me.

Then there was the interior. State maps with little symbols telling you where paper and pulp were milled, or where sugar beets or peanuts were grown. The national maps were even more lavish, with actual paintings of the pleasures and treasures of each country. Artwork by many illustrators, in many different styles, was used in the encyclopedia.

To my young eyes this mélange seemed god-given. I never questioned the juxtaposition of clean line drawings next to realistic renderings next to quite stylized artwork. I loved the look of those pages. I don't know how much I actually read the encyclopedia, but I loved looking at it.

Who *Was* Mary Reed, PhD?

Mary Maud Reed was born in 1880 in Lock Haven, Pennsylvania, a small town "nestled," as she recalled in an unpublished memoir, "among mountains and hills on the Susquehanna River." As a lively, mischievous child, she enjoyed swimming, rowing, ice-skating, and, in flood season (her favorite), simply getting covered in river mud. Young Mary had been born into a family of teachers, and she herself grew up to embrace "progressive" ideas about education aimed at replacing the traditional emphasis on discipline and rote learning with more relaxed, child-centered approaches to learning.

Mary Reed, probably 1950s. Courtesy of Special Collections and University Archives, University of Oregon Libraries.

After graduating from Teachers College, Columbia University, Reed held a succession of teaching and supervisory positions throughout the Northeast and the Midwest, ending the practice of corporal punishment at more than one school where she worked and attempting always to replace overly formal styles of teaching with a heightened alertness to children's real interests and developmental needs.

On joining the faculty of Teachers College as head of the recently organized Kindergarten and Elementary Education Department, Reed immersed herself in efforts to devise new ways to allow children greater personal independence within the classroom. As she recalled in her memoir, "a library table" where children, after finishing their assigned work, would be free to go "seemed to be the first step in this direction. [But] a library table called for books—many books. We gathered all the books available but there were few"—comparatively few books, that is, designed expressly for children of the youngest ages. "I appealed to Scribners but they did not have [a spirit of] adventure. One of my students during a summer session told me about Artists and Writers Guild. 'They are the people who have adventure,' she told me. 'Why don't you contact them?'"

Reed tells what happened next:

"On my return to college after a brief vacation in Europe I had contacts with George [sic] Duplaix and Lucille Ogle. They had worked out a pattern which seemed delightful to me. My memory is a little vague here but I remember having meetings with Lucille Ogle and George Duplaix and other members of the staff of Artists and Writers. The Little Golden Books went over with a bang. . . . To Lucille, George and Albert [Leventhal] belong the glory of opening a new epoch of children's books. I will always feel honored that they made me a partner of this great enterprise." [September 3, 1958]

Reed's consulting work consisted of reviewing and commenting on all Golden projects from a developmental standpoint. She herself also co-authored two Little Golden Books: *My Little Golden Dictionary* (with Edith Osswald, illustrated by Richard Scarry, 1949) and *Numbers: What They Look Like and What They Do* (with Edith Osswald, illustrated by Violet LeMont, 1955). Mary Reed died in 1960 at the age of eighty.

Acknowledgments

I wish to express my heartfelt thanks to Mary Janaky, the dedicated Golden Books archivist (now retired), who welcomed me so graciously to her inner sanctum of original Golden Books artwork, first editions, realia, and company records in Racine, Wisconsin, and helped me make the most of my time at the archive.

My special thanks, too, to Steve Santi, Golden Books collector extraordinary, for all the information he shared, the many rare items he made available for reproduction, and his painstaking and pioneering work as the compiler of *Collecting Little Golden Books*.

The following curators and staff were of great help to me by making accessible a variety of artwork, manuscripts, and other materials of special interest for this project: Linda Greengrass, librarian, and Kate Kearns, project archivist, Bank Street College of Education Archive; Ruth Janson, coordinator, rights and reproductions, Brooklyn Museum; Jane O'Cain, exhibits curator, Charles M. Schulz Museum and Research Center; Mimi Kayden, HarperCollins Children's Books; Patrick Lemelle, library programs coordinator, Institute of Texan Cultures at the University of Texas at San Antonio; Dr. Karen Nelson Hoyle, professor curator, Kerlan Collection, University of Minnesota Libraries; Linda J. Long, manuscripts librarian, Knight Library Special Collections and University Archives, University of Oregon; Terri J. Goldich, curator, Northeast Children's Literature Collections, University of Connecticut; Richard Ammann, archivist, Racine Heritage Museum; William J. Maher, university archivist, University of Illinois at Urbana-Champaign Library; and Mariana S. Oller, Wellesley College Library.

My thanks also go to the following individuals, who generously shared their knowledge, memories, artwork, and archival material: Charles Antin; Avi; Bud Baker; Robert T. Bakker; Bette Bardeen; Dorothy A. Bennett; Kevin Blair; Harry Bliss; Dik Broekman; Marc Brown; Suzy Capozzi; Ann Carlson; Ana Cervantes; Janet Chenery; Grace Clarke; Mel and Ginni Crawford; Edith Kunhardt Davis; Melanie S. Donovan; Michel S. Duplaix; Richard W. Eiger; Connie Epstein; Thea Feldman; Vergilio Fernandez; Aimee Garn; Chip Gibson; Steven Guarnaccia; Barbara Shook Hazen; Susan Hirschman; the late Clement Hurd; the late Edith Thacher Hurd; Thacher Hurd; Motoko Inoue; Alice Jonaitis; William Joyce; Tatiana Koly; J. P. Leventhal; Jane Leventhal; the late Greta Schreyer Loebl; Elisabeth Lortic; Alice Low; Richard Lowe; Samuel E. Lowe, Jr.; Ann M. Martin; Becky McDonald; Holly M. McGhee; George E. Miller; Rich Moore; Patricia Mould; Naomi Shihab Nye; Lilian Obligado; the late Lucille Ogle; Alice Provensen; Susan Raab; Victor Ramirez; Elizabeth W. Retan; the late Ole C. Risom; Frank D. Rosengren; Ellin Rothstein; Lois Sarkisian; Huck Scarry; the late Miriam Schlein; Linda Schreyer; Janet Schulman; Deborah Wilkin Springett; Bob Staake; Joyce Stein; Eric Suben; Marge Ternes; Robin Warner; Abigail Weisgard; Christina Weisgard; Ethan Weisgard; the late Leonard Weisgard; Alicia Williams; the late Garth Williams; the late George Wolfson; Betty Ren Wright; Jerome Wyckoff; and Dan Yaccarino.

I am grateful to Kate Klimo, vice president and publisher of Random House Children's Books, for giving me the chance to write this book and for leading a department whose staff members routinely bring such a high level of professionalism and enthusiasm to their work.

It would be hard to adequately thank my editor, Diane Muldrow, for her deep and unwavering commitment to this project and for her astute judgment and warm friendship at every stage. Her devotion to the legacy of Golden Books has contributed much to making this a better book.

I wish also to thank my copy editors, Jennifer Black and Barbara Perris, for their probing, insightful reading of my manuscript, and art director Roberta Ludlow, for her elegant design work.

To Eric Carle, my thanks for his thoughtful comments.

To my agent, George M. Nicholson, my abiding gratitude and friendship.

To my wife, Amy, and son, Jacob, love always.

Part One: "The Boys Have Done a Pretty Good Job. . . ."

1. John Buenker and Richard Ammann, *Invention City: The Sesquicentennial History of Racine, Wisconsin* (Racine: Racine Heritage Museum, 1998), iv.

2. Don H. Black, *EH: The Life of E. H. Wadewitz* (Racine: privately printed, ca. 1955), 11–24.

3. Roy Spencer quickly became a one-third partner in Western, along with E.H. and Al. After enjoying a stint in the U.S. Navy and finding that he did not like the printing business, Al, however, chose early on to sell his one-third share of the business to the other partners and return to sea as a member of the Merchant Marines. Bill—or W.R.—who was fourteen years younger than E.H., remained with Western for the rest of his working life, succeeding E.H. as president in 1952 when E.H. was elevated to the position of chairman of the board. The fourth Wadewitz brother, Otto, joined the company a few years after Bill and worked for Western for many years while also becoming a local figure of note as Commodore of the Racine Yacht Club. Black, 43–49.

4. For the early history of Western, see "The Story of Western, 1907–1962, Part I," *The Westerner* (April 1962), 11–13, which chronicles the company's development through the early 1920s. This material is summarized in Steve Santi, *Collecting Little Golden Books: A Collector's Identification & Price Guide*, 5th ed. (Iola, WI: Krause Publications, 2003), 5–12.

5. Samuel E. Lowe, Jr., interview by author, by telephone, 4 March 2005.

6. Richard Lowe, interview by author, by telephone, 12 March 2005.

7. Black, 68.

8. Ibid., 83.

9. Buenker and Ammann, 118.

10. Ibid., 70–76; *The Westerner: Commemorative Issue* (Winter 1982), 7.

11. Information about the origins of Big Little Books may be found at www.biglittlebooks.com.

12. Michael Barrier and Martin Williams, eds., *A Smithsonian Book of Comic-Book Comics* (New York: Smithsonian Institution Press and Harry N. Abrams, 1981), 9–16.

13. Samuel E. Lowe to Walt Disney, Racine, WI, 19 April 1933, Random House Archive.

14. Michael Barrier, *Hollywood Cartoons: American Animation in Its Golden Age* (New York: Oxford University Press, 1999), 49.

15. Roy O. Disney to Samuel E. Lowe, Hollywood, CA, 16 May 1933, Random House Archive.

16. Roy O. Disney to Samuel E. Lowe, Hollywood, CA, 9 June 1933, Random House Archive.

17. Samuel E. Lowe to Kay Kamen, Racine, WI, 13 July 1933, Random House Archive.

18. Kay Kamen to Samuel E. Lowe, New York, NY, 10 November 1933, Random House Archive.

19. Kay Kamen to Samuel E. Lowe, New York, NY, 10 November 1933, Random House Archive. Kamen wrote Lowe at least two letters that day.

20. During Michael D. Eisner's tenure as Disney's chairman of the board, Disney opened its book licenses to other publishers on a competitive basis. The resulting loss to Western, not just of revenue but also of a trusted and prestigious long-time partner, doubtless contributed significantly to the company's financial woes in the years that followed.

21. "The Story of Western, 1907–1962, Part II," *The Westerner* (May 1962), 3.

22. Nancy Williams, "Artists and Writers Guild, Inc.," *The Westerner* (February 1950), 3.

23. Ibid., 3–7.

24. Ibid., 3; Mary Janaky to author, by e-mail, 15 April 2004.

25. Kenneth C. Davis, *Two-Bit Culture: The Paperbacking of America* (Boston: Houghton Mifflin, 1984), 94–95. See also "Ding Dong Dell," *The Westerner* (May 1949), 11–14.

26. Michel Duplaix, interview by author, tape recording, New York, NY, 7 November 1994.

27. Jerome Wyckoff, interview by author, by e-mail, 12 November 2004.

28. Duplaix, interview by author.

29. Lucille Ogle's papers may be found in the Special Collections division of the Knight Library, University of Oregon, Eugene, OR. Ogle's papers include biographical material, editorial correspondence, photographs, artwork, and memorabilia.

30. Connie Epstein, interview by author, by telephone, 5 January 1995.

31. E. B. White, "Here Is New York," in *Essays of E. B. White* (New York: Harper & Row, 1977), 121.

32. Lucille Ogle, interview by author, New York, NY, 8 September 1982.

33. George Wolfson, interview by author, tape recording by telephone, 6 October 2004.

34. George M. Nicholson, interview by author, tape recording, New York, NY, 14 December 2004.

35. Ogle, interview by author.

36. Jane Werner Watson, "The Golden Years of Golden Books" (estate of Jane Werner Watson, photocopy), 17 February 1988, 3–4.

37. Richard W. Eiger, interview by author, tape recording, New York, NY, 27 September 2004.

38. Ibid.

39. Ogle to Ruth Adler, New York, NY, 18 December 1967, Lucille Ogle Papers (Coll. 201, Box 5, Folder 1), University of Oregon.

Part Two: Entrepreneurs and Émigré Artists

1. William W. Parish, "The Story of Little Golden Books," *The Westerner* (March 1951), 10–14. For more on the history of Simon and Schuster, see Peter Schwed, *Turning the Pages: An Insider's Story of Simon & Schuster, 1924–1984* (New York: Macmillan, 1984); and John Tebbel, *Between Covers: The Rise and Transformation of American Book Publishing* (New York: Oxford University Press, 1987).

2. Schwed, 1–8, 75–77.

3. J. P. Leventhal and Jane Leventhal, interview by author, tape recording, New York, NY, 20 April 2004.

4. Lucille Ogle, interview by Greta Schreyer Loebl, Greta Schreyer Loebl photocopy of tape recording transcript, New York, NY, n.d.

5. Albert R. Leventhal, "Children's Books in the Mass Market," *Publishers' Weekly* (21 November 1953), 2106–08.

6. "Leventhal Joins A and W," *The Westerner* (December 1957), 7.

7. J. P. Leventhal and Jane Leventhal, interview by author.

8. "Albert Rice Leventhal," *Publishers Weekly* (19 January 1976), 30–31. Leventhal's obituary made note of the long roster of publishing luminaries Leventhal had mentored and championed. The "sampling" listed in the piece included Robert Bernstein, president, and Anthony M. Schulte, executive vice-president, of Random House; Robert Gottlieb, president and editor-in-chief, and Nina Bourne, vice-president,

advertising, of Knopf; Harold Roth, president of Grosset & Dunlap; Jerry Mason, president of Ridge Press; Bruno A. Quinson, president of Larousse; George M. Nicholson, editorial director of Viking Junior Books; James R. Louttit, president and editor-in-chief of McKay; and DeWitt C. Baker, president of Baker & Taylor.

9. Eiger, interview by author.

10. Parish, 12.

11. Schwed, 19.

12. Davis, 36–55. Davis deals with paperback publishing primarily as a twentieth-century phenomenon. However, important experiments with the paperback format can be traced at least as far back as the early nineteenth century, when America's western expansion and advances in the manufacture of paper created the mail-order market and the means of producing inexpensive paperbacks ranging from novels to self-improvement manuals. On more than one occasion, the U.S. government acted to protect traditional publishers by requiring that paperbacks be shipped at the same rate as clothbound books. When one enterprising upstart, Park Benjamin, attempted to circumvent government protectionism by formatting paperbacks as newspaper supplements, Congress in 1843 acted decisively at the behest of mainstream publishers to make such supplements subject to the same high shipping rates as books.

A second wave of paperback experimentation accompanied the growth of the nation's railroads. Train stations, and passenger trains themselves, became points of purchase for "cheap" paperbound recreational reading matter published by the Beadle Brothers, Rand McNally, and others. Paperback publishers experienced tremendous growth as they began to offer low-priced editions of novels by foreign authors to whom it was unnecessary, under then-current law, to pay a royalty. In 1891, Congress's enactment of the International Copyright Law, which mandated royalties for foreign authors, once again restored the advantage to the traditional houses, which could better afford to pay.

In the late nineteenth century, the invention of pulp paper improved the economics of paperback publishing. During the 1920s, George Delacorte was among the first publishers to exploit pulp paper in a variety of print formats that eventually included the comic book. Another fascinating venture begun at this time was "Little Blue Books"—one wonders of course if the name played any part in inspiring the name later chosen by Western and Simon and Schuster—an entire "university in print" of low-cost paperbacks, which the publisher, a proud Communist living in Kansas, sold primarily by mail order. In addition to these and other American attempts during the 1920s and 1930s to satisfy a rising demand for inexpensive books, the venture that was most instrumental in setting the stage for the creation of Pocket Books was the launch in England of Penguin Books, a paperback series of high-quality literature whose publisher apparently copied the success of Whitman and other American firms by selling its books primarily through the British five-and-dime stores.

For additional information about paperback publishing history, see the series of articles on this subject posted by the Hyde Park Book Store, Boise, Idaho: http://paperbarn.www1.50megs.com/paperbacks.html.

13. Bud Baker, interview by author, tape recording, New York, NY, 10 March 2005.

14. Barbara Bader, American Picturebooks from Noah's Ark to the Beast Within (New York: Macmillan, 1976), 278.

15. Parish, 12.

16. Edward J. Jennerich, "Ludwig Bemelmans," in Dictionary of Literary Biography, Vol. 22: American Writers for Children, 1900–1960, ed. John Cech (Detroit: Gale Research, 1883), 37.

17. For an account of the making of Pat the Bunny, see Philip B. Kunhardt, Jr., The

Dreaming Game: A Portrait of a Passionate Life (New York: Riverhead Books, 2004), 214–27.

18. Ibid., 223. See also "Campaign for 'Pat the Bunny,'" Publishers' Weekly (8 February 1941), 734–35.

19. "Samuel Lowe Books Found World Over," Kenosha Evening News, 6 April 1956.

20. Richard Lowe, interview by author.

21. Robert van Gelder, "How to Sell Sixty Million Books Yearly," New York Times (2 March 1941), 2.

22. According to the publisher's son Richard Lowe, the name "Bonnie Books" was suggested by his father's finding a supply of colorful Scottish-style plaid decorative tapes in a Milwaukee bindery to place along the spines of the new twenty-five-cent books.

23. Nancy Williams, 3.

24. Ogle, interview by author. For a detailed account of the early years of the Bank Street Writers Laboratory, see Leonard S. Marcus, Margaret Wise Brown: Awakened by the Moon (Boston: Beacon Press, 1992; New York: Harper Perennial, 1999), 79–80.

25. Judith Marcus, "Tibor Gergely, 1900–1978: An Appreciation," Tibor Gergely: Catalogue of an Exhibition of Paintings and Drawings (Madison, NJ: Library, Fairleigh Dickinson University, May 11–September 1, 1986), 9.

26. Ogle, interview by Greta Schreyer Loebl, 5.

27. Judith Marcus, 17.

28. Greta Schreyer Loebl, interview by author, tape recording, New York, NY, 10 May 1999. In 1955, Gergely received a Caldecott Honor from the American Library Association for his illustrations for Wheel on the Chimney, by Margaret Wise Brown (Lippincott). In addition to his paintings, Gergely arrived in New York with hundreds of the drawings, sketches, and caricatures he had created in Europe. According to Greta Schreyer Loebl's daughter, Linda Shreyer, Gergely incorporated faces and other elements from this earlier phase of his work in the illustrations he produced for Golden Books. Linda Shreyer, interview by author, New York, NY, 4 January 2006.

29. Bader, 124.

30. "Feodor (Stepanovich) Rojankovsky, 1891–1970," Something About the Author, vol. 21 (Detroit: Gale Research, 1980), 127.

31. Elisabeth Lortic, Tatiana R. Koly, et al., La Maison des Trois Ours: Hommage à Rojankovsky (Paris: Édition Les Trois Ourses, 1998). Also, Tatiana R. Koly, interview by author, tape recording by telephone, 14 January 2005.

32. For information about Paul Faucher, see http//members.lycos.fr/amisperecastor; also see Bader, 123.

33. Quoted in Bader, 124.

34. Duplaix, interview by author.

35. Michel Duplaix, "Rojan, un Robinson russe en Amérique: une arrivée remarquée," La Maison des Trois Ours, 24–25.

36. The Navemar let off about three hundred passengers in Bermuda and Cuba en route to its final port of debarkation, Brooklyn, New York. "Ship, Packed Like a Cattle Boat With 769 Exiles, Here From Spain," New York Times (13 September 1941), 19, 27.

37. Rojankovsky had come to America not a moment too soon. Following the United States' entry into World War II in December 1941, German U-boat activity in the Atlantic intensified; in late January 1942, a U-boat sank the Navemar on its return voyage from Cuba to Spain. "The Navemar Is Sunk Off Portuguese Coast," New York Times (27 January 1942), 6.

38. "The 'West' in Western," *The Westerner* (August 1949), 4.

39. *The Westerner: Commemorative Issue* (Winter 1982), 20.

40. Parish, 12.

41. Ibid.

42. "A Statement About the How's, Why's and Wherefores of Little Golden Books," *Publishers' Weekly* (19 September 1942).

43. Ibid.

44. See *Publishers' Weekly* (31 July 1943), 330–31; and (21 November 1953), 2106–08.

45. *Publishers' Weekly* (31 July 1943), 330–31.

46. Photocopy of Simon and Schuster advertisement, Random House Archive.

Part Three: "Books and Bread"

1. Leonard S. Marcus, *Margaret Wise Brown*, 57–58.

2. Schwed, 167. A few of the first illustrators did, however, secure the right to discreetly sign their cover art.

3. Santi, 7.

4. The person responsible for adding the gold tape as a design element of Little Golden Books was Robert D. Bezucha of Western's production department. Wolfson, interview by author.

5. Leah Carter Johnson, "A Texas Author: Janette Sebring Lowrey," *The Horn Book Magazine* (January 1947), 56–61. For further insight into Lowrey's personality and professional life, see Ursula Nordstrom's letters to her in Leonard S. Marcus, *Dear Genius: The Letters of Ursula Nordstrom* (New York: HarperCollins, 1998 and 2000).

6. It is not known why Lowrey was not given author credit for the book or, for that matter, why the illustrations for *Baby's Book* were credited to "Bob Smith," but the cover art was signed "Louise Altson."

7. Frank D. Rosengren, interview by author, by telephone, 22 December 2004.

8. Jane Werner Watson recalled the flat fee paid to Lowrey in an unpublished article, "Has Anyone Here Ever Had a Little Golden Book?", 8 pages, estate of Jane Werner Watson. In later years, Lowrey described herself to a reporter for the *North San Antonio Times* (27 March 1986) as "possessing a small talent but a terrific urge to write." In another of her rare press interviews, Lowrey noted that "to hear and see words which are put together well is very good training for the senses." To illustrate her point, she quoted from the best known of her sixteen published books: *"And down they went to see, roly-poly, pell-mell, tumble-bumble, till they came to the green grass. . . . Children,"* the author concluded, admiring her own handiwork, "just love that sentence. It's the one they always memorize." Quoted in the *San Antonio Light* (17 April 1963).

9. From a Simon and Schuster advertisement published in the *New York Times* (9 December 1942).

10. John Canemaker, *Before the Animation Begins: The Art and Lives of Disney Inspirational Sketch Artists* (New York: Hyperion, 1996), 39–48.

11. Mary Anderson, Tenggren's niece, quoted in Ibid., 40–41.

12. Barrier, 250.

13. Canemaker, 44.

14. Employee dissatisfaction at the studio culminated in a two-month strike that ended on July 28, 1941, when Disney and the Screen Cartoonists Guild agreed to submit their dispute to arbitration. The strikers succeeded in establishing the studio as a closed, or all-union, shop. Barrier, 306–309.

15. For information about this artist, see "Corinne Malvern, 1905–1956," *Something About the Author,* vol. 34 (Detroit: Gale Research, 1984), 148–49; Stanley J. Kunitz and Howard Haycroft, eds., "Gladys Malvern," *The Junior Book of Authors*, 2nd ed. (New York: H. W. Wilson, 1951), 211–12; and her obituary, *New York Times* (10 November 1956), 19.

16. "Meet the artist . . . Masha," *Story Parade* (April 1946), 52. Stern was born to Russian-Jewish parents in Brooklyn, in 1909, and studied at Pratt Institute and the Art Students League. She wrote of her early professional years: "After leaving Pratt Institute in 1930, I spent nine years with a novelty firm as a designer, developing my understanding of technique, style, public taste and my own talent. For the past five years I have been concentrating on Book illustration." Quoted in Bertha E. Mahony, Louise Payson Latimer, and Beulah Folmsbee, comps., *Illustrators of Children's Books, 1744–1945* (Boston: The Horn Book, 1947), 362.

17. "Meet the Artist: Miss Elliott," *Story Parade* (January 1946), 53.

18. Bader, 282.

19. Bertha E. Mahony et al., *Illustrators* (1947), 309.

20. "First Lady Urges Normal Child Life," *New York Times* (5 January 1942), 22.

21. Santi, 7.

22. Mary Janaky, nine-page Western historical time line, 1999, Random House Archive.

23. Watson, "The Golden Years," 21.

24. Georges Duplaix to Lucy Sprague Mitchell and Raymond Abrashkin, 17 December 1943, New York, NY, Bank Street Archive. During the early months of 1943, sales of the first twelve books had been further spurred by a guardedly favorable omnibus review of the line by Anne T. Eaton, writing in the *New York Times Book Review* (14 February 1943), 25. Eaton wrote in part: "Parents and teachers of pre-school children will be grateful for these twelve attractive little books at a price within the reach of even the most limited pocketbook. . . . The editing and illustration of this series is uneven. The pictures in 'Prayers for Children' are over-sweet. Winifred Hoskins has illustrated 'The Golden Book of Fairy Tales' with more vigor than imagination and the books themselves are too lightly put together to be more than ephemeral. Nevertheless, the Little Golden Library will provide a pleasant book experience for the young child who later on, if his library grows as it should, will possess Mother Goose, the folktales and other classics of childhood in more durable form, to last him through his childish years."

25. Bader, 278.

26. According to Bud Baker, Georges Duplaix and Albert Leventhal were part of a small group of Sandpiper partners who received 7 percent of the gross annual income from Golden Books, to be divided among themselves according to a preestablished formula. Whatever else Sandpiper might have been created to accomplish, the generous partnership arrangement was clearly designed to keep Leventhal and the others from shopping their services elsewhere. Baker, 10 March 2005.

27. Watson, "The Golden Years of Golden Books," 23.

28. Miriam Schlein, interview by author, tape recording, New York, NY, 25 June 2004.

29. The "doorman" story was recounted in Leonard Weisgard, interview by author, handwritten notes, Traelløse, Denmark, 26 October–5 November 1982.

30. Dorothy A. Bennett, *Sold to the Ladies!, or The Incredible but True Adventures of Three Girls on a Barge* (New York: George W. Stewart, 1940).

31. Zim, who proved to be a popular science writer of extraordinary scope and intellect, had come to Bennett's attention through Albert Leventhal, whose daughter Jane had had Zim for a science teacher at the Manhattan Ethical Culture School.

32. Schlein, interview by author.

33. Dorothy A. Bennett, interview by author, handwritten notes, El Cerito, CA, 23 April 1984.

34. Edith McCormick, "Anatomy of a Paradox: 'Librarians Hate Us' but the Public Loves Golden Books," *American Libraries* (May 1981), 251.

35. For a detailed account of the Bank Street Writers Laboratory, see Leonard S. Marcus, *Margaret Wise Brown*, 85–88.

36. Bader, 283.

37. Georges Duplaix to Lucille Sprague Mitchell and Raymond Abrashkin, New York, NY, 17 December 1943, Bank Street Archive.

38. Minutes of Bank Street Trustees meeting, New York, NY, 5 June 1945, Series 2, Folder 23, Bank Street Archive.

39. Linda J. Long, interview by author, by telephone, 4 November 2004. Long recalled this anecdote from an interview she had recently conducted with Elizabeth Orton Jones.

40. Ogle to Eloise Wilkin, 11 February 1969, estate of Eloise Wilkin.

41. Watson, "The Golden Years," 8.

42. In Eloise Wilkin and Deborah Wilkin Springett, *The Golden Years of Eloise Wilkin* (privately printed, 2004), 47, the artist's daughter identifies the book that caught Ogle's attention as *Kitty Come Down,* by Frances A. Bacon, illustrated by Eloise Wilkin (New York: Oxford, 1944).

43. Wilkin and Springett, 47.

44. Ibid., 40.

45. Ibid., 12–13.

46. Ibid., 33.

47. Jane Werner [Watson] had been among the first Guild staffers to see Wilkin's portfolio, "almost as big as she was," as the editor recalled in her unpublished memoir. The two women soon became friends and on several occasions also proved to be ideal collaborators for books touching on their shared interests in religion and the natural world. Watson eulogized her friend in "Eloise Burns Wilkin, 1904–1987: The Soul of Little Golden Books," unpublished.

48. Wilkin and Springett, 40–42.

49. Ibid., 44.

50. Ibid., 59.

51. Ibid., 59.

Part Four: Books for Baby Boomers

1. Watson, "The Golden Years," 12.

2. William P. Gottlieb was a photographer and music critic best known for his photographic portraits of such jazz greats as Louis Armstrong and Billie Holiday.

3. David Riesman with Nathan Glazer and Reuel Denney, *The Lonely Crowd: A Study of the Changing of American Character* (1950; abridged edition, Garden City: Doubleday Anchor, 1953), 129–31, 144. Ellen Lewis Buell, in her foreword to *A Treasury of Little Golden Books,* gave a dissenting opinion. Recalling *Tootle* as a book that "nearly drove one father mad because he had to read it 150 times aloud," Buell went on to note: "This is the book singled out by that august sociologist, David Riesman, as an example of 'other-directed' conformity. Maybe so, but I can't help thinking that in this case Dr. Riesman has confused conformity with responsibility. I'll go along with the children

who laugh at the story, love it, and know (without thinking about it) that there is work to be done in the world."

4. Eric Suben, interview by author, tape recording by telephone, 8 November 2004; Baker, interview by author.

5. Bank Street "Studies and Publications" report, 5 November 1946, Series 9, Folder 69, Bank Street Archive. The practice of slotting books went in and out of favor at Western. Bud Baker recalls that during his eighteen-year career with the company, from 1951 to 1969, retailers were free to order individual titles, though only in multiples of six dozen.

6. *The Westerner: Commemorative Issue* (Winter 1982), 9.

7. Black, 84–86.

8. Watson, "Has Anyone Here," 6.

9. Watson, "The Golden Years," 9.

10. "A Note About This Catalogue," *Golden Books and Other Juveniles,* annual catalog (New York: Simon and Schuster, 1947).

11. Bruce Bliven, Jr., "Child's Best Seller," *Life* (2 December 1946), 59–66.

12. Weisgard, interview by author.

13. Leonard S. Marcus, *Margaret Wise Brown*, 183–206.

14. Ibid., 181.

15. Baker, interview by author.

16. "The Little Golden Books and How They Grew: A Supermarket Success Story," four-page, full-color Simon and Schuster advertising piece, n.d., Random House Archive.

17. Baker, interview by author.

18. Watson, quoted in Walter Retan and Ole Risom, *The Busy, Busy World of Richard Scarry* (New York: Harry N. Abrams, 1997), 26.

19. Ibid., 12.

20. Ibid., 26.

21. Santi, 405.

22. Retan and Risom, 33.

23. Garth Williams to author, Santa Fe, NM, (postmarked) 14 February 1983, collection of author.

24. Leonard S. Marcus, *Margaret Wise Brown,* 198–99.

25. Roy O. Disney to Lucille Ogle, Burbank, CA, 15 June 1948, Lucille Ogle Collection, Box 28, Folder 4.

26. Jerome Wyckoff, interview by author, by e-mail, 12 November 2004.

27. Louise Seaman Bechtel, "Margaret Wise Brown: 'Laureate of the Nursery,'" *Books in Search of Children: Speeches and Essays by Louise Seaman Bechtel,* ed. Virginia Haviland (New York: Macmillan, 1969), 123.

28. Leonard S. Marcus, *Margaret Wise Brown*, 263.

29. Ogle, interview by author.

30. Watson, "The Golden Years," 9–10.

31. Leonard S. Marcus, *Margaret Wise Brown*, 284–85.

32. J. P. Leventhal and Jane Leventhal, interview by author.

33. J. P. Leventhal and Jane Leventhal, interview by author.

34. *The Magic Bus,* by Maurice Dolbier, illustrated by Tibor Gergely (1948); *The Make-Believe Parade,* by Jan Margo, illustrated by Eloise Wilkin (1949); and *The Kittens*

Who Hid from Their Mother, by Louise P. Woodcock, illustrated by Adele Weber and Doris Laslo (1950).

35. Leonard S. Marcus, *Margaret Wise Brown,* 228.

36. Ibid., 267–69.

37. Parish, 14.

38. Baker, interview by author; Eiger, interview by author.

39. Parish, 14.

40. Ibid., 13.

41. Fritz Eichenberg, "Artist Through the Looking Glass," *The Horn Book Magazine* (May/June 1949), 187–94.

42. Fritz Eichenberg to Ogle, 10 February 1963, Lucille Ogle Collection, Box 14, Folder 10.

43. Schlein, interview by author. Schlein, who was working as a secretary at Sandpiper Press at the time, recalled these events vividly. For the best published account, see "The Story Behind Doctor Dan," *The Westerner* (March 1951), 18–19.

44. André Bernard, *Now All We Need Is a Title: Famous Book Titles and How They Got That Way* (New York, W. W. Norton, 1995), 126.

Part Five: Cold War and Magic Kingdom

1. Reinhardt illustrated Krauss' first picture book, *A Good Man and His Good Wife* (New York: Harper and Brothers, 1944); Johnson illustrated *The Carrot Seed,* published the following year by Harper.

2. Schlein, interview by author.

3. John Canemaker, *The Art and Flair of Mary Blair: An Appreciation* (New York: Hyperion, 2003), 36–63. Blair contributed color and styling guidance for *Cinderella* (1950) and *Alice in Wonderland* (1951), among other projects.

4. Ibid., 46.

5. Ibid., 46.

6. Ellen Lewis Buell, "Rabbits, Ducks and Trucks," review of *Baby's House,* by Gelolo McHugh, illustrated by Mary Blair, *New York Times Book Review,* 12 February 1950, 18.

7. Dolores B. Jones, *Bibliography of the Little Golden Books* (Westport, CT: Greenwood Press, 1987), xvii.

8. Blair designed the Pepsi Pavilion's "It's a Small World" ride at the fair and later helped to re-create it in expanded form for both Disneyland and Walt Disney World.

9. Ursula Nordstrom to Ruth Krauss, New York, NY, 5 February 1951, HarperCollins Archive.

10. Nancy Nolte, "This Is Rockefeller Center," *The Westerner* (June 1952), 2–4.

11. Susan Hirschman, interview by author, tape recording by telephone, 5 July 2004.

12. Ibid.

13. Ibid.

14. Santi, 9.

15. In the *Westerner's* obituary tribute to Walt Disney (February 1967, 3), reference is made to E. H. Wadewitz as having been the third Doscar recipient, in 1953. However, Robert Tieman, of the Disney Archive, was unable to confirm this or to supply additional pertinent information. According to Tieman, Disney lacks detailed records concerning the first Doscars, although a handwritten note in the archive suggests that the very first recipient might have been Walt's brother and business manager, Roy O. Disney. Robert Tieman to author, by e-mail, 11 February 2005.

16. "Plans for Disneyland," *The Westerner* (January 1955), 17. According to Robert Tieman of the Disney Archive, Western contributed to the financing of Disneyland by purchasing 13.79 percent of the shares of Disneyland, Inc., for the sum of $200,000. According to Richard Schickel, *The Disney Version* (New York: Simon and Schuster, 1968), 306–07, the other major shareholders were ABC-Paramount (34.48 percent); Walt Disney Productions (34.48 percent); and Walt Disney (16.55 percent). According to the Disney Archive, Walt Disney Productions retained the right to buy back the other investors' shares, and exercised its option with respect to Western's stake in the theme park on June 29, 1957. Robert Tieman to author, by e-mail, 11 February 2005.

17. W. R. Wadewitz, introductory letter, *The Westerner: The Disneyland Issue* (August 1955), 2.

18. "Davy Crockett: Western Writer Quoted by *The New Yorker,*" *The Westerner* (December 1955), 14.

19. Mel Crawford, interview by author, tape recording, Washington, CT, 14 July 2005.

20. Watson, "The Golden Years," 28.

21. Ibid., 29.

22. Jane Werner [Watson] to Lucille Ogle, Athens, Greece, 23 May 1954, Lucille Ogle Collection, Box 11, Folder 6.

23. Martin Provensen to Jane Werner Watson, n.d., Lucille Ogle Collection, Box 9, Folder 10.

24. Western did not publish either series. Rajkamal Prakashan of New Delhi published the Indian readers. The "Living" series was published in the United States by Garrard. For details, see "Jane Werner Watson," *Something About the Author,* vol. 54 (Detroit: Gale Research, 1989), 166 and 172.

25. Alice Low, interview by author, tape recording by telephone, 3 December 2004.

26. In 1957, Lucille Ogle hired a young woman named Barbara Shook Hazen for the Guild's editorial staff on the strength of her talent as a poet and her experience as an assistant to the poetry editor at the *Ladies' Home Journal.* Ogle interviewed the applicant over lunch at the Mayan Room. Joining them was a Western vice president for production, Cliff Junceau. As Hazen sat at her place watching the two executives wolf down their food, she heard Ogle tell her colleague, "I'm hiring her. I like her poetry. She writes like Margaret Wise Brown!" Junceau was less sanguine, pointing out that the young woman's experience had little to do with the kind of editing that the Guild required. "No, you're not going to hire her," Junceau replied. "Yes, I am," said Ogle. The conversation continued in front of several colleagues during the elevator ride up to the twenty-eighth floor, where it was finally decided that Ogle should have her way. Hazen went on to write a great many Golden Books during her three-year stint at the Guild before launching a distinguished freelance writing career.

27. "Celebrate 25th Anniversary of Dell Comics," *The Westerner* (August 1954), 24.

28. Fredric Wertham, *Seduction of the Innocent* (New York: Rinehart, 1954).

29. "Four Billion Comic Books," *The Westerner* (February 1958), 16.

30. "Plans for Disneyland," *The Westerner* (January 1955), 18.

31. "Westerners at Opening," *The Westerner: Disneyland Issue* (August 1955), 20.

32. Lowrey had not written for Golden since 1943 but instead, spurred on by a voluminous correspondence with Ursula Nordstrom, had concentrated her efforts on writing serious fiction for teen girls. Lowrey eventually attempted to reprise her early Golden triumph with *Where Is the Poky Little Puppy?* (illustrated by Gustaf Tenggren, 1962), a book that, like many another sequel, failed to live up to its publisher's expectations.

33. Retan and Risom, 38.

34. Ibid.

35. Ibid., 38.

36. Ibid., 38.

37. "Western Joins the '500,'" *The Westerner* (September 1957), 6.

38. "Western Printing," *Racine Sunday Bulletin* (7 August 1955), 5.

39. Bader, 400.

40. Isaac Asimov, review of *The World of Science: Scientists at Work Today in Many Challenging Fields,* by Jane Werner Watson, *The Horn Book Magazine,* February 1959, 52–53.

41. Schwed, 177–78.

42. Davis, 272.

43. J. P. Leventhal and Jane Leventhal, interview by author, 20 April 2004.

44. Simon and Schuster press release, 10 November 1958, Lucille Ogle Collection, Box 14, Folder 2.

45. Baker, interview by author.

46. Lilian Obligado, interview by author, tape recording by telephone, 28 November 2004.

47. Baker, interview by author.

48. To minimize production costs for the *Golden Book Encyclopedia,* Western decided early on to recycle as many images as possible from earlier Golden publications. Because most Golden Books had been illustrated as works for hire, project editor Bertha Morris Parker and her colleagues had the pick of a vast archive of illustration art to which Western controlled all rights.

49. Joyce Antler, *Lucy Sprague Mitchell: The Making of a Modern Woman* (New Haven: Yale, 1987), 29–33.

50. "The Golden Book Encyclopedia," *The Westerner* (February 1959), 6.

51. Ted Okuda and Jack Mulqueen, *The Golden Age of Chicago Children's Television* (Chicago: Lake Claremont Press, 2004), 201–02. See also "Ding Dong School Rings the Bell," *The Westerner* (December 1953), cover, 3–4.

52. Okuda and Mulqueen, 202.

53. Quoted in Okuda and Mulqueen, 202.

54. Mary Janaky, "History of Golden Books Family Entertainment," two pages, n.d., Random House Archive.

55. Quoted in Schwed, 169.

56. Robert T. Bakker, interview by author, tape recording by telephone, 22 November 2004.

57. Lincoln Barnett, "The World We Live In: Part V, The Pageant of Life," *Life* (7 September 1953), 54–74.

58. Jane Werner Watson, *Dinosaurs and Other Prehistoric Reptiles,* illustrated by Rudolph F. Zallinger (New York and Racine: Golden Press, 1960), 51.

59. Lucille Ogle, introduction to *Rojankovsky's Wonderful Picture Book: An Anthology,* by Feodor Rojankovsky (New York and Racine: Golden Press, 1972), 7.

60. Michel Duplaix, "Rojan, un Robinson russe," 24–25.

61. Raphaël Dupouy, Alexis Obolensky, Michel Guillemain, and François Faucher, *Les Russes de La Favière* (Le Lavandou: Réseau Lalan, 2004).

62. Zim to Ogle, 1 December 1960, Lucille Ogle Collection, Box 40, Folder 1. Zim kept a pond stocked with piranhas at his Florida compound and had a parrot that he trained to say, "Tell the truth! Tell the truth!" On one occasion, as a sort of half-joking negotiating ploy, Zim left the parrot in the guest room where Western executive Richard Eiger was to spend the night in advance of a round of meetings. Eiger, interview by author.

63. Wilkin and Springett, 77–82.

64. Ellen Lewis Buell, foreword to *A Treasury of Little Golden Books* (New York and Racine: Golden, 1960).

65. Ogle to Jane Werner Watson, interoffice memo, 3 May 1961, Jane Werner Watson Collection, "Incoming Correspondence/Western," Knight Library, University of Oregon.

Part Six: "We *Are* Publishers. . . ."

1. Lucille Ogle to Jane Werner Watson, 10 June 1960, Jane Werner Watson Collection, "Incoming Correspondence/Western."

2. *53rd Annual Report: 1960 . . . A Record Year for Western Publishing Company, Inc.,* Random House Archive.

3. Wyckoff, interview by author.

4. Ruth Krauss to Ogle, 11 April 1961, Lucille Ogle Collection, Box 8, Folder 13.

5. Eager to solidify the public's emotional connection with the First Family, the media-savvy Kennedy White House had just released a series of such photographs for publication in the press.

6. Barbara Shook Hazen, interview by author, tape recording by telephone, 16 July 2004.

7. Hazel Jacobson to Jane Werner Watson, New York, NY, 6 July 1961, Jane Werner Watson Collection, Incoming Correspondence/Western.

8. "The Story of Western, 1907–1962, Part III," *The Westerner* (June 1962), 6. Also, Baker, interview by author, 10 March 2005.

9. Retan and Risom, 50.

10. Grace Clarke, interview by author, tape recording by telephone, 30 November 2004.

11. Eiger, interview by author. Scarry's most popular book was eventually published in twenty-eight languages.

12. Mary Janaky, "History," Random House Archive.

13. Young started his syndicated column, "To Be Equal," in 1963. At the time the piece in question ran, the column appeared in over 100 major newspapers and was heard on 40 radio stations across the United States. New Yorkers would have read Young's critique of children's literature in the *New York World-Telegram,* a liberal evening daily.

14. Clarke, interview by author.

15. The interoffice memo, dated August 10, 1964, was written by Lloyd E. Smith of Western's Racine headquarters. Ogle's reply to Smith is dated August 13. Lucille Ogle Collection, Box 29, Folder 13.

16. Ogle to Feodor Rojankovsky, New York, NY, 8 June 1965, Lucille Ogle Collection, Box 15, Folder 13.

17. Wilkin and Springett, 93–95.

18. Box 29, Folder 7 of the Lucille Ogle Collection contains several letters, interoffice memos, and related documents concerning this matter, dating from January to August 1968.

19. Ogle to Irving Adler, New York, NY, 1 February 1966, Lucille Ogle Collection, Box 5, Folder 1.

20. Ogle to Dr. and Mrs. R. Will Burnett, New York, NY, Lucille Ogle Collection, Box 5, Folder 14.

21. Ogle to Cornelius De Witt, New York, NY, 30 August 1966, Lucille Ogle Collection, Box 6, Folder 9.

22. Stuart A. Courtis to Ogle, Cupertino, CA, 22 February 1967, Lucille Ogle Collection, Box 39, Folder 13. With this letter, Courtis continued the correspondence initiated by him the previous summer.

23. Ogle to Stuart A. Courtis, New York, NY, 26 July 1966, Lucille Ogle Collection, Box 39, Folder 13.

24. Retan and Risom, 69–80.

25. Ibid., 74.

26. *The Westerner: Commemorative Issue* (Winter 1982), 24. For the best summary of Golden's achievements through 1967, see "Golden Books Celebrates 25th Birthday," *The Westerner* (December 1967), 2–9.

27. Mollie Tenggren to Ogle, 7 October 1967, Lucille Ogle Collection, Box 11, Folder 1.

28. Watson to Jack B. Long, 23 September 1968, Jane Werner Watson Collection, Outgoing Correspondence.

29. Baker, interview by author.

30. Watson to Robert E. Switzer and J. Cotter Hirschberg, 5 January 1970, Jane Werner Watson Collection, Box 1, Outgoing Correspondence.

31. Watson to Robert E. Switzer and J. Cotter Hirschberg, 17 January 1970, Jane Werner Watson Collection, Box 1, Outgoing Correspondence.

32. *The Westerner: Commemorative Issue* (Winter 1982), 24.

33. Ray Butman, "The History of Richard Scarry and His Works Published by Western Publishing Company, Inc., 1949 to 1989," unpublished manuscript, Random House Archive.

34. "Two Annual Writing Awards Will Honor Lucille Ogle," *The Westerner* (24 January 1969), 1 and 3.

35. Jane Werner Watson to H. M. Benstead, Santa Barbara, CA, 27 March 1971, Lucille Ogle Papers, Box 11, Folder 7.

36. Jane Werner Watson to G. J. Slade, 12 November 1971, Lucille Ogle Papers, Box 18, Folder 3.

37. Crown later took over the series, publishing two additional titles and reissuing the first eight titles with new illustrations.

38. McCormick, 256.

39. Clarke, interview by author.

40. Eden Ross Lipson, "Ole C. Risom, 80, Publisher of Children's Books," *New York Times* (24 August 2000), C23; Ole Risom, interview by author, tape recording, Syosset, NY, 3 November 1994.

41. Eiger, interview by author.

42. Selma G. Lanes, "All That's Golden Is Not Glitter," in *Down the Rabbit Hole: Adventures and Misadventures in the Realm of Children's Literature* (New York: Atheneum, 1971), 112–127.

43. Bader, 295.

44. Although aimed at older readers, Dell Yearling Books played a crucial role in legitimizing the paperback format. Strikingly—and ironically—Albert Leventhal was instrumental in setting the stage for the historic venture. In 1959, Leventhal hired a recent college graduate (and friend of his daughter's) named George M. Nicholson to oversee a line of children's books, called Guild Press Books, intended for the Catholic market. Impressed with Nicholson's work, Leventhal recommended him six years later to Dell president Helen Meyer when Meyer decided that Dell should launch a paperback juveniles imprint. Dell Yearling launched in 1967 with an impressive list led by E. B. White's *Charlotte's Web*.

45. Karen Raugust, "Happy Birthday, Big Bird," *Publishers Weekly* (8 November 2004), 24.

46. Eiger, interview by author.

47. "Major Pacts Are Inked," *The Westerner* (19 July 1974), 1 and 4. The new Dell printing contract took effect on January 1, 1976.

48. Janaky, two-page chronology, Random House Archive.

49. McCormick, 253.

50. Eric Suben, interview by author, tape recording by telephone, 8 November 2004.

51. Clarke, interview by author.

52. Eric Suben to author, by e-mail, 9 November 2004.

53. Melanie S. Donovan, interview by author, tape recording, New York, NY, 10 September 2004.

54. Tamar Lewin, "Children's Books: A Poky Puppy Is Still Golden," *New York Times Book Review* (17 April 1988), 37.

55. Suben, interview by author.

56. Randall Smith, "Western Publishing Gets Renewed Attention, but Some Who Recall Its '86 Drop Are Wary," *Wall Street Journal* (27 July 1987), 1.

57. Lewin, 37.

58. Suben, interview by author.

Part Seven: Circles

1. "Western Makes Publishing History, Produces One Billionth Little Golden Book," *Westernews* (26 November 1986), 1–3.

2. Baker, interview by author.

3. Christopher Byron, "A Tale of Two Dicks: How Bernstein, Snyder Wrecked Golden Books," *New York Observer* (28 September 1998), 1 and 23.

4. Geraldine A. Fabrikant, "Western Publishing and G. & W. in Merger Talks," *New York Times* (6 May 1988), D20.

5. Robin Warner, interview by author, by telephone, 17 February 2006.

6. Eben Shapiro, "Now It's Books 'R' Us As Toy Giant Expands," *New York Times* (28 September 1992), D6. The experiment worked well enough for the partners to add thirty stores by the end of 1992 and to announce plans, the following August, for a total of nearly two hundred stores by the end of the year. Continuing complaints from within the industry—both from independent booksellers, who argued that the new arrangement subjected them to unfair competition, and from publishers, who felt uncomfortable selling their books through a competitor—combined with Western's worsening losses to result in the abandonment of the scheme as of January 1, 1994. For details, see Bridget Kinsella, "Toys R Us Expands to 191 Outlets," *Publishers Weekly* (30 August 1993), 25; and "Toys R Us Assuming Management of Its Book Departments," *Publishers Weekly* (20 September 1993), 10.

7. Connie Goddard, "Fifty Years of Books 'For the Masses,'" *Publishers Weekly* (22 June 1992), 28–30.

8. Byron, 23.

9. Jim Milliot, "No Press for Western's Annual Meeting," *Publishers Weekly* (1 January 1996), 23. Amid widespread investor dissatisfaction, declining employee morale, and growing uncertainty about the company's future, Western took the unusual step of barring the press from its annual shareholders' meeting, held in December 1995.

10. Roger Rosenblatt, "See Dick Run, Again," *New York Times Magazine* (1 October 1995), 48–51.

11. Ibid., 48.

12. Christopher Byron, "Richard Snyder Tries to Help Golden Books, but It's Not Working," *New York Observer* (18 May 1998), 1 and 25; Geraldine Fabrikant and Doreen Carvajal, "Troubled Story at Golden Books," *New York Times* (10 August 1998), D1 and D6. For details of the inaugural list of Golden's adult trade imprint, see the *Write News* (11 November 1997), www.writenews.com. For information about the sell-off of the Golden Books Adult Publishing Group to St. Martin's Press, see "St. Martin's Press Acquires Golden Books Adult Publishing Division," *Write News* (26 April 1999), www.writenews.com.

13. Steven Zeitchik, "Random House Lands Golden Books Assets," *Publishers Weekly* (20 August 2001), 13 and 23.

14. "Golden Moments: Celebrating the Art and Artists of Golden Books, 1942–2004," exhibition of original illustration art, was on view at the National Arts Club, New York, NY, September 21–25, 2004, before moving to the Donnell Central Children's Room of the New York Public Library, where it remained on display through November 9, 2004. The exhibitions focused primarily on original art from the 1940s to the 1960s but also included examples from recent books published by Random House under the Golden Books imprint.

15. Dik Broekman, interview by author, tape recording, New York, NY, 9 June 2004.

16. "Japanese Publishers Reproduce Racine Firm's Child Books," *Racine Journal-Times* (27 March 1950), 4.

17. Leonard S. Marcus, "Garth Williams," introduction to *The Picture Book World of Garth Williams* (Tokyo: Book Globe, 2002), 4–9.

18. Carleton B. Gibson III spent most of his thirty-year career in Western's sales department. But the high point of his professional life came during the period of the early to mid-1960s, when he worked directly under Albert Leventhal. Gibson's son Chip—Carleton B. Gibson IV—rose through the publishing industry ranks to become president and publisher of Random House Children's Books in March 2002.

19. Arthur Conan Doyle, *Through the Magic Door* (1907; Gutenberg Project EBook #5317), chapter 2.

From The Train to Timbuctoo, *1951, by Margaret Wise Brown, illustrated by Art Seiden.*

GOOD NIGHT
AND
SWEET DREAMS.